MillenniuM

Circulus articus

Occanus occidentalis

Terra del Rey de portugall

Has antilhas del Rey de castella

Este he o mar do antre castella e portugall

Toda esta terra he descoberta p mādado del Rey de castella

Minha equinocialis.

Tropicus capricorii.

Mar oceanus

Pollus antarticus.

The Cantino World Chart, produced in Portugal c.1500.

PREVIOUS PAGE *God the Architect of the Universe,*
from a French bible of the thirteenth century.

MillenniuM

Edited by Anthony Coleman

INTRODUCTION BY JEREMY ISAACS

BANTAM
PRESS

London New York Toronto Sydney Auckland

The editor is grateful to the following people for their creative work
on the television series *Millennium*, without which this book would not exist:

Xiaosong Atiyah, Neal Ascherson, Rosalind Bentley, Helena Braun, Neil Cameron, Henry Chancellor, Richard Curson
Smith, Emma De'Ath, Mike Dibb, John Edwards, Felipe Fernández-Armesto, Henrietta Foster, Fiona Garlick,
Murray Grigor, Cate Haste, Rebekah Hay, Bernard Heyes, Jeremy Isaacs, Mark Kidel, Chloe Lederman, Alison McAllan,
Pat Mitchell, Sarah Newman, Caroline Ross Pirie, Peter Sommer, Catherine Stedman, Ben Steele, Samantha Todd,
David Wallace, Nicola Wicks, Gillian Widdicombe.

TRANSWORLD PUBLISHERS
61-63 Uxbridge Road, London W5 5SA
a division of The Random House Group Ltd

RANDOM HOUSE AUSTRALIA (PTY) LTD
20 Alfred Street, Milsons Point, Sydney,
New South Wales 2061, Australia

RANDOM HOUSE NEW ZEALAND
18 Poland Road, Glenfield, Auckland 10, New Zealand

RANDOM HOUSE SOUTH AFRICA (PTY) LTD
Endulini, 5a Jubilee Road, Parktown 2193,
South Africa

Based on the television series *Millennium*.
Copyright © 1999 and TM by CNN Productions Inc.

Published 1999 by Bantam Press a division of Transworld Publishers

Copyright © Transworld Publishers 1999

The right of Anthony Coleman to be identified as the editor of this
work has been asserted in accordance with sections 77 and 78 of the
Copyright Designs and Patents Act 1988.

A catalogue record for this book is available from the British Library.
ISBN 0593 044789

Designed by Robert Updegraff
Printed in Great Britain by Butler & Tanner Ltd

1 3 5 7 9 10 8 6 4 2

The television series *Millennium* is based on the book of the same title by Felipe Fernández-
Armesto. This book contains some passages by the original author, edited by Anthony Coleman,
who is grateful to Felipe Fernández-Armesto for his help in writing the present book.

Picture Acknowledgements

AKG, London: 1 (Oesterreichische Nationalbibliothek, Vienna), 8/9 (Bayerische Staatsbibliothek, Munich), 37 (Bibliothèque Nationale, Paris), 88 (Biblioteca Apostolica Vaticana); Scala, Florence: 2/3, 44, 54, 89, 90/91, 96, 114, 125, 128/29, 154/55, 198, 209; © CNN Productions: 10, 12 (Blue Sunflower Animation, London), 20, 22 (FrameStore Design, London), 24, 26, 30, 40, 41 (FrameStore Design, London), 42, 50, 51, 52, 60, 61, 69, 74, 98, 103, 110, 122 (FrameStore Design, London), 131 (FrameStore Design, London), 138, 148, 163 (FrameStore Design, London), 166 (inset), 171, 187, 206, 280, 281; British Museum, London: 13, 29, 192; Palace Museum, Beijing: 16; Bridgeman Art Library, London: 18, 36 (Bibliothèque Nationale, Paris), 65 (National Palace Museum, Taipei), 67 (Bibliothèque Nationale, Paris), 81 (British Library, London), 112 (National Gallery, London), 113 (Louvre, Paris), 116 (British Library, London), 118/19 (Bibliothèque Nationale, Paris), 130 (Private Collection), 145 (Bibliothèque Nationale, Paris), 146/47 (Private Collection), 152 (British Library, London), 157 (Private Collection), 168 (Victoria and Albert Museum, London), 172/73 (Château de Versailles), 174 (Royal Society, London), 175 (Trinity College, Cambridge), 176 (Stapleton Collection), 178 (British Library, London), 179 (Private Collection), 182 (Kunsthistorisches Museum, Vienna), 194 (Private Collection), 208 (Private Collection), 211 (Musée Franco-Americaine, Blerancourt, Chauny), 213 (Bibliothèque Nationale, Paris), 216 (Powis Castle), 224/25 (Guildhall Library, Corporation of London), 227 (Stapleton Collection), 228 (Science Museum, London), 229 (Science Museum, London), 230 (National Gallery, London), 236 (Bibliothèque Nationale, Paris), 247 (Private Collection), 248 (Kelham Island Industrial Museum, Sheffield), 250 (Central St Martin's College of Art and Design, London), 256 (Nasjonalgalleriet, Oslo); Werner Foreman Archive, London: 31 (Freer Gallery, Washington), 102 (Courtesy Entwhistle Gallery, London), 130 (British Museum, London); Magnum/Fred Mayer: 33; Sonia Halliday Pictures: 35 (both), 45, 46, 136, 137, 141; Cambridge University Library: 38/9; British Library, Department of Oriental Manuscripts: 49 (Or 718 f127v), 78 (MS Or 2780 f49v), 83 (MSS Add. 18866 f140); © National Geographic Society/O. Louis Mazzatenta: 56 (NGM 1988/06 747-); Bryan & Cherry Alexander Photography: 63; © Royal Geographical Society, London/ Paul Harris: 64/5; © Hulton Getty: 70 (Musée Guimet, Paris), 218/19 (Musée Guimet, Paris); Topkapi Saray Museum, Istanbul: 73; Bibliothèque Nationale, Paris: 75, 76, 100/101; Berlin, Staatsbibliothek, Berlin – Preussischer Kulturbesitz – Orientabteilung: 79; © Giancarlo Costa: 80; Hutchison Library: 84 (Liba Taylor), 135 (P. Edward Parker), 269 (Melanie Friend), 270 (Liba Taylor), 278; Biblioteca Ambrosiana, Milan: 93; British Library, Department of Manuscripts: 94 (MS Roy. 8 E VI f301), 124 (MSS Add. 27695 f8); Christine Osborne Pictures: 104; Robert Harding: 106; Philadelphia Museum of Art. Given by John T. Dorrance: 120; e.t. archive: 127, 214; Bodleian Library, Oxford: 132 (MS Arch. Seld. A. 1. F2); Tozzer Library, Harvard University: 151; Osaka Castle Museum: 158; Tokyo National Museum: 160; Victoria and Albert Museum, London: 165, 166; © LSH, Skokloster, Slott/photo Samuel Uhrdin: 169; The J. Paul Getty Museum, Los Angeles: 170; Science and Society Picture Library: 177, 200/201; Rijksmuseum, Amsterdam: 188; B & U International Picture Service: 190/91; Bayerische Verwaltung der Schlösser, Gärten und Seen, Munich: 195; Ann Ronan at Image Select: 204, 234; Peter Newark's American Pictures: 212; Christie's Images, London: 221; Courtesy Martyn Gregory, London: 222, 223, 242; Thomas Cook Archives, London: 231; Museum of the City of New York. Gift of Mrs. Robert M. Littlejohn: 238/9; Roger-Viollet, Paris: 240; Southwest Museum, Los Angeles: 241; © National Maritime Museum Picture Library, London: 246; Science Photo Library, London: 252/53; Mary Evans Picture Library, London: 255; © Hulton Getty: 256, 260, 264, 275; David King Collection: 262, 263; Camera Press, London: 266 (Sven Simon), 271 (Phil Coburn); Associated Press, London/Jeff Widener: 267; Superstock, London: 273; BFI Stills, Posters and Designs: 274; Telegraph Colour Library: 276. **Back jacket** Bridgeman Art Library, London: 11th, 12th, 13th, 17th and 18th centuries; Scala, Florence: 14th and 15th centuries; Hutchison Library (Liba Taylor): 16th century; © CNN Productions: 19th century; BFI Still, Posters and Designs: 20th century.

Maps by Hardlines, Charlbury, Oxfordshire: 11, 20, 34, 53, 67, 95, 105, 108, 121, 140, 156, 167, 184, 189, 203, 215, 232.
Extract on page 32 reprinted from *The Pillow Book* of Sei Shonagon, © Introduction and translation Ivan Morris 1967, by permission of Oxford University Press.

CONTENTS

In Mongolia Genghis Khan is revered as the culture-hero of modern nationalism and the symbol of Mongolian identity. In his own day, he was cast as a universal conqueror in the tradition of Alexander. (From Chapter 3.)

Introduction

The past has shaped our lives; a knowledge of that past informs and enriches us. Standing stones on moorland, a Roman road beneath our feet, a medieval cathedral in a city centre, the village church – all speak of those who came this way before us. Looking and listening, we learn more about ourselves. History caters to a deep need in us all; a growing appetite for history, and a widening enjoyment of it, has marked the century that ends this millennium. This book, *Millennium*, will be your and your family's guide to the last thousand years. *Our* history, the past we see and feel around us, is not everyone's history. Encountering the past of others can be one of the great pleasures of life. It has always been so for me. I still remember my first sight of Chartres, of Venice, of the Parthenon. I have always wanted to share that pleasure, not only the pleasure of delving into European history and culture, in which I was brought up, but the excitement of discovering the varied cultures of a wider world. It should not always be a surprise to find how impressive have been human achievements in Africa, in India and the east, in the Americas. But it often is. The wide world is richer than we know, until we open our eyes and, travelling in time, look for ourselves. Books and museums can guide us in these travels, and make the journey easier for us. So can television.

When Ted Turner in Atlanta called for a 'millennium project' for CNN I did not at first know what he meant, and could not respond. Then I gathered he wanted a television history of the last thousand years. This was as difficult a challenge as I have ever faced. Television histories of this century, like *The World at War* or *Cold War*, call on two priceless sources of information: news images on film and video, and the eye-witness testimony of those who were party to great deeds, or who witnessed and suffered their effects. Compiling a history of previous centuries is far trickier. I had faced the task once before, attempting a television history of Ireland. There are no moving images, and no eye-witnesses. You shoot what remains of the past: buildings, paintings, manuscripts. And you film the present for the past, showing people – on pilgrimage – for example, still doing today what their ancestors did centuries ago.

We can reconstruct the past, by dramatic re-enactment, or the re-invention and reconstruction of buildings and objects that 3D computer graphics now make possible. Add voices and music to colourful images, and the past comes to life. I said I would try to do what Ted Turner wanted; the television series *Millennium* is the result. In it we present elements of a thousand years of human endeavour in just ten hours of television.

The series owes a very great deal to Felipe Fernández-Armesto, author of a major book of the same title, *Millennium*. From that bulky and highly readable volume, however, I took in the main not information, but two principal ideas. The first is the idea of history not as one simple, linear sweep – just possible, perhaps, as the history of a dynasty; wholly impracticable in a history of the world – but instead as an aggregate of particulars; flashes of revelation, rather than an unbroken stare. Following his example, we would see cities at one moment only in their lives; meet people, individual men and women, just when they made their impact; capture culture on the cusp of growth and influence; describe the effects of new technologies; encounter ideas as they changed the world. We would leave out far, far more than we kept in of Fernández-Armesto's *Millennium*, mining it for choice nuggets. Our television series – we do the Renaissance in nine minutes! – would revel in brevity rather than attempt the impossible task of trying to squeeze everything in.

Secondly, Fernández-Armesto's book suggested to me that we should make sure we saw the world as a whole, looked at in the round, from space, not just from the perspective of our own culture. *Millennium*'s concern would be not Europe's history or America's history, but that of very many peoples of the world. If we look at the world from that perspective, we learn how inventive China has been, how influential Islam, how rich India; we should report, particularly for the first half of the millennium, its first five centuries, what the peoples of Africa and central Asia and the Americas achieved, before Europe by conquest and colonisation reached for world-wide hegemony.

Millennium therefore filmed in thirty countries, and divided its subject matter into fifty segments, each long enough to say one thing that we hope will stick with viewers, and whet your appetite for more. This book, richly illustrated, faithfully reflects the structure and content of the series. It reminds the reader what the viewer saw, and pins down in print and fixed image what flashed by briefly on the screen. But its fuller text adds information that the series could not carry.

It has been my good fortune to educate myself by making television programmes, in the hope that what I could grasp I could also, keeping them watching, explain to others. This book has the same aim. Echoing the brief vignettes of the series, it will tell you of many things you probably never knew: that twelfth-century Ethiopian Christians carved churches from solid rock at Lalibela; that the great African civilisation of Mali, in the fourteenth century, traded gold for salt; that in the eleventh-century court of Heian

Japan, two of the world's greatest books – *The Tale of Genji* and *The Pillow Book* – were written by women.

On another level, *Millennium* works differently. In the series, we tried to find some thematic unity in each century that would lend coherence to an hour of viewing without smothering the diversity within. So we attached labels – Century of the Stirrup, of the Scythe, of Sail – which reflected broad trends, and still allowed exceptions. The labels are suggestive, rather than definitive. Looking back on what we have done, I find that, from successive particular instances, three principal themes appear.

First, over the span of a thousand years, we see European, western culture, at first overshadowed by the east, begin to assert itself, so that it appears dominant today, with the United States pre-eminent as the world's only superpower. How long that will last – will China challenge for supremacy? – remains to be seen.

Second, as this millennium has progressed, a scientific explanation of how the world works, evident in scientific processes that have transformed our lives, has come to equal and arguably to displace religion in our understanding of the universe. People still believe, worship still flourishes, in some societies fundamentally. But science now offers answers to questions for which our ancestors a thousand years ago had none.

Third, perhaps most strikingly brought out in the television series, this world is now one world. At the start of the millennium one individual could not circumnavigate the globe; now we can do so in an hour, and send word round in a split second. From space, we can see our whole world.

The journey we take, in our television series and in this book, tracks human achievement over the millennium. It reports progress that has enhanced our life, and cruelties that still disfigure it. I am grateful to all those who have contributed, in two different modes, to this attempt to capture and reflect the past. I hope this book will, as one millennium ends and another begins, both serve as a record and stimulate interest in the world we share.

JEREMY ISAACS

CHAPTER 1

Century of the
SWORD

THE ELEVENTH CENTURY

A WORLD TRAVELLER at the dawn of the second millennium of our era would have had little reason to doubt that China was the largest, the oldest and in material terms the most advanced, the most productive civilisation on earth – or that it would remain so for ever. He could not have failed to notice, however, the indifference, if not contempt, with which it regarded the world outside it.

Islam, on the other hand, still expanding by conquest and trade across Asia, Europe and Africa, eagerly absorbed whatever was of value in the culture of the countries in which it found itself, building cities that were treasurehouses of art and learning as well as of commerce. In Baghdad, in Cairo, in Cordoba, this movement, whose first adherents had come out of the Arabian desert, had created urban societies outshining anything beyond the borders of China.

In India our traveller would have found a rich, complex civilisation from which, in the past, even China had been willing to learn, but which now seemed to be turning in upon itself; losing the influence it had once had on other countries and societies, it was ripe for conquest by Muslim invaders from the north.

Japan, which in earlier centuries had borrowed so much from Chinese models, had by now, in isolation from the rest of the world, developed a distinctive civilisation of its own, its ruling class cultivating an aesthetic sensibility the like of which would not be seen in the western world for almost another thousand years.

One of the less promising civilisations of the Eurasian landmass – at least to a superficial observer – would have been the one that occupied its western promontory. In western Christendom, churchmen struggled to recover the art and learning of the old Roman empire and to persuade or terrorise the descendants of the violent men who had conquered it into more gentle ways. But it was the rough vigour of western Europe's rulers, combined with the authority of the church, that presented Islam with its first major setback.

The Holy Roman Emperor Otto III as depicted in his gospel-book, flanked on his right by representatives of the church, on his left by the armed nobility.

THE MANDATE OF HEAVEN

One thousand years ago, the caravan routes from the west to China had to skirt the terrible Takla Makan desert. Its name meant: 'He who enters will never return.' Along the great highway known as the Silk Road, merchants made the same arduous but rewarding journeys their predecessors had been making for more than a thousand years already. They travelled east carrying gold and silver coin and the few other things that China wanted from them; on the return journey their saddlebags were stuffed with luxury goods that might have come from as far away as Mongolia and might well find their way into the hands of European potentates who had never seen a Chinese face and scarcely knew where China was.

After months of travel through bleak and inhospitable terrain, traders from the west arrived at the remote oasis of Tun-huang, the gateway of China. Here, hollowed into cliffs rising out of the desert, was a Buddhist monastery, endowed by the gifts of passing merchants who sheltered there gratefully from the extremes of heat and cold. The honeycomb of rock-cut chambers hid fabulous treasures, for this was the largest Buddhist temple site in the world, a centre for the diffusion of Buddhism across central Asia and into China. Its 450 shrines were tended by monks who spent their lives decorating the remarkable interiors. The paintings on the walls and ceilings depicted not only the Buddha in his various aspects, but also the life of the caravan routes and the piety of the merchants – even, in some cases, the faces of the families they had left at home.

A camel train crosses the Takla Makan desert today.

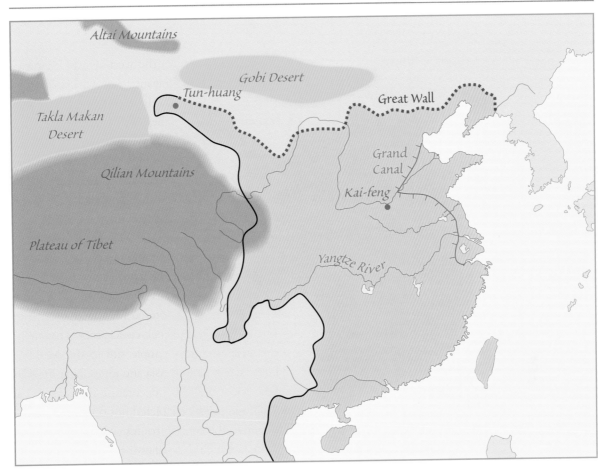

Religion and commerce met at Tun-huang. In its chambers were libraries of documents, precious Buddhist scriptures, but also commercial contracts left in the safe keeping of the monks. This was more than a monastery-cum-caravanserai. It was a great crossroads of the world in the millennium before ours, where the cultures of Europe and Asia met. The travellers who rested there were familiar with routes that stretched across thousands of miles, linking China, India, central Asia and what we call the near east, feeding into other routes that reached Japan and Europe and crossed the Indian Ocean to south-east Asia, maritime Arabia and east Africa. The cave complex, with its libraries and decorated chambers, reflected the metropolitan life of the most widely influential civilisation of the day.

A thousand years ago China was, and had long been, the biggest, the richest and the most advanced empire on earth. Chinese superiority had been around for a long time. It radiated along trade routes; it acted like a magnet on the cultures around its own edge, attracting and seducing them. Its ascendancy was based on three advantages: an economy, based on a diverse environment, that could supply concentrated manpower; a political philosophy, based on the age-old teachings of Confucius, that provided efficient government; and a scientific tradition, based on observation and practical utility, that guaranteed technological prowess.

Eleventh-century China, with the Great Wall, the Grand Canal linking the five principal rivers, and the Northern Sung capital of Kai-feng.

11

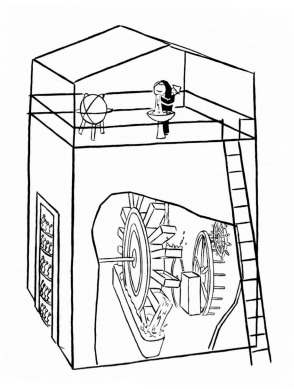

A water-clock. Mechanical devices such as this were already familiar in eleventh-century China.

Most world-shaping inventions available in the millennium before ours were invented in China, between one and thirteen centuries before they appeared in the west. These innovations included paper, printing, the magnetic compass, the seismograph, waterproofed material, the efficient harness, the suspension bridge, the crossbow, metalworking machinery, the stern-post rudder, canal lock gates, cast iron, porcelain and gunpowder – although the last was never used in warfare. Kites were used to pioneer dreams of flight, as well as to make music and to measure distances. Even the emperor designed kites. The world's first mechanical clock was made at the T'ang court in AD 725. The oldest known segmental arch bridge was built at Chao-hsien in Hopeh in the early seventh century AD. Nothing comparable appeared in Europe until the sixteenth century.

Paper money was invented in China in AD 812 and was in general use by the eleventh century. Printing with moveable type allowed letters to be reproduced and sent around the country. It was used to produce cheap editions of the Confucian classics for students preparing for the civil service examinations. In the year 1006 it was used to print and publish a thousand-volume encyclopaedia under the emperor's patronage.

China had existed as a unified country for 2,000 years. It regarded itself as positioned at the centre of the earth, and its culture had never been conquered. The more than 60 million people who lived in it in the eleventh century gave their allegiance to one man, a quasi-divine ruler who they believed had a mandate from heaven to rule all the peoples of the earth. Under the emperor the country was divided into administrative areas governed by a professional civil service selected by an examination system and divided into separate departments or ministries – for Administration, Finance, Rites, Defence, Punishment and Works. It administered justice, collected revenues, organised public education, and planned and supervised the construction of fortifications, roads, bridges and canals.

This vast empire was held together by the secular philosophy of K'ung-fu-tzu, known in the west as Confucius, who had been born in the mid-sixth century BC and was therefore a near-contemporary of the Lord Buddha. He sought the revival of a utopian state which had supposedly existed in the remote past. The essence of his teaching was support for those institutions that were likely to promote order and harmony – above all, the family and the social hierarchy with the emperor at its head – and observation of the obligations of man to man in all their subtle gradations within the social order: 'Let the ruler rule as he should, and the minister be minister as he should. Let the father act as a father should and the son as a son should.' His precepts advocated reverence for custom, good manners and correct behaviour; obedience and loyalty to superiors, whether in the family or in the state; absolute integrity; scrupulousness in the discharge of duties.

Confucianism was not a religion, but the writings attributed to Confucius, gradually codified over the centuries following his death, were treated as something very much like religious texts. The examinations for entry to the civil service were based on them. At times they were treated with great rigidity: the candidate had merely to memorise the Four Books and then write an essay in the traditional form, in which the number of paragraphs and even the number of words in each paragraph were strictly prescribed; if he could do this in decent calligraphy he passed the examination and became at a stroke a government official, a scholar and a gentleman. At other times the emperor would require the essay to be written in verse. In the eleventh century a reform party introduced a new examination system to test the intellectual quality of the candidates, whose essays, to be written in prose, had to respond to questions about ethical standards. In this they could quote the authority of Confucius himself, for had he not said: 'If a person can recite the

A Chinese merchant and his family united in prayer, depicted in a wall painting at Tun-huang.

300 Odes, yet does not know how to act when given an official mission, what is the practical use of all that study?'

The Confucian teachings were used to select and train generations of Chinese officials who, at their best, were trustworthy, incorruptible and humane. Essentially conservative in nature, designed to preserve tradition and continuity and to resist change, they explain why the Chinese civil service system survived changes of dynasty and barbarian invasions. They may also explain why, despite its extraordinary inventiveness, China did not become the dynamic industrialising and expanding society that would emerge in Europe in the centuries that followed. For good or ill they had shaped Chinese society and ways of thinking for more than a thousand years, and would continue to do so until China's Marxist government officially denounced them in the middle of our century. They may yet survive Marxism.

The centralised Chinese state both needed communications to control its vast territory and had the organisational powers and the control of human resources necessary to provide them. The technologies of papermaking and printing enabled it to store information; route-finding enabled the bureaucracy to send and receive it. Instructions and reports as well as goods and revenues travelled by road, but also by water. The Grand Canal, begun in the sixth century with the press-ganged labour of 3 million men and women, connected the five great rivers of China into one navigable waterway, capable of carrying vessels of 500 tons. It was 2,500 kilometres long and at times ran 42 metres above sea level. A thousand years on, this waterway still carries goods from the north to the south.

Chinese civilisation was remarkable not only for its dominance but for its endurance. Dynasty replaced dynasty, sometimes violently, but the mandate of heaven simply passed from one to another; the first Sung emperor had usurped power as recently as 960. At intervals, barbarians from north of the Great Wall invaded; but, remarkably quickly, the invaders adopted Chinese ways and often became, quite simply, another kind of Chinese. This had happened several times in China's past and would happen again in the next thousand years.

The Chinese liked to argue that their mandate from heaven was as indivisible as the sky itself. The very identity of the country depended on that idea. Their relationships with the rest of the world were normally governed by the principle that only China counted and that other peoples were simply barbarians clinging to the rim. But in the eleventh century the mandate of heaven was split in two. Formerly despised barbarians from the wastes of northern Asia, the Khitans, had set up their own rival 'empire'. In the last years of the tenth century, in a period of Chinese weakness, they had absorbed enough Chinese political culture, and retained enough traditional barbarian toughness, to challenge the empire on its own moral ground. The Khitan state of Liao had its own civil service which, selected by examination on Confucian principles, defended the legitimacy of Khitan emperors. In 1004, having failed to defeat the Khitan militarily, the Sung emperor made a peace treaty with them. To preserve the myth of indivisibility the relationship between the two emperors was henceforth expressed in the language of a fictional blood relationship. The Khitan gave up their claim to disputed territory south of the Great Wall; the Sung agreed to pay tribute in silver and silk. The two empires were to live in a state of peaceful coexistence until the Khitans and the northern Sung were defeated by a common enemy.

The Sung lacked the military prowess of their predecessors, the T'ang, and there was something Confucian about this diplomatic settlement. Ou-yang Hsiu, a reforming official of the time, advocated a resigned attitude to the problem of the division of the heavenly mandate. In the long run, he maintained, civilisation would always win its encounters with savagery. The barbarian would be shamed into submission where he could not be coerced; influenced by example when he could not be controlled by might; deflected by fingertips when he could not be pummelled by fists; 'subjected by kind-ness' when he could not be won by war. Or, as a fellow-reformer put it:

> Put away . . . armour and bows, use humble words and . . . generous
> gifts . . . send a princess to obtain friendship . . . transport goods to
> establish firm bonds. Although this will diminish the emperor's dignity,
> it could for a while end fighting along the three borders . . . Who would
> exhaust China's resources . . . to quarrel with serpents and swine?
> Barbarian attacks in earlier times were compared merely with the sting of
> gadflies and mosquitoes . . . Now is the moment for binding friendship
> and resisting popular clamour. If indeed Heaven . . . causes the rogues to
> accept our humaneness and they . . . extinguish the beacons on the
> frontiers, that will be a great fortune to our ancestral altars.

The northern Sung had made their capital at Kai-feng, located on China's northern plain at an important junction of the canal and river system. It was at that time almost certainly the greatest city in the world, enclosing within its triple ring of defensive walls both a court and a thriving centre of commerce and industry, with an enormous export trade in iron manufactures; China in the eleventh century was producing almost as much iron as the whole of Europe in the seventeenth. Kai-feng's population of perhaps 600,000–700,000 people was cosmopolitan enough to include the only documented Jewish community in China at that time, which survived until the beginning of our own century. It was a city of enormous vitality; the markets were open twenty-four hours a day, the streets filled with merchants, crafts-men, hawkers, food sellers, entertainers, fortune tellers, shoppers and gawk-ing crowds of visitors. Its taverns sold rice wine in silver cups; its restaurants offered their own specialist delicacies, including ices, for the citizens of Kai-feng enjoyed a more varied diet than anywhere else in China. Fish was a par-ticular delicacy, caught by cormorants:

The Rainbow Bridge at Kai-feng in a scroll-painting of the Sung period. The building in the right foreground may be the world's first restaurant.

They tie a cord around the bird's neck, so that a small fish just passes through his throat. But he cannot swallow a big fish.

The birds are very tame, and attend to everything as if they had a human heart.

The Kai-feng palace cooks invented dumplings made from fish mixed with duck and ginger: a variety of dim sum, and a dish still enjoyed across the world today.

In its shops, paper money could buy silks and brocades and delicate porcelain, antiques and works of art, and a multitude of products unheard of in the West: printed books, mechanical toys, painted fans, lavatory paper, medicines from the huge Chinese pharmacopoeia.

The threat to the Sung dynasty came not from the Khitans but from another wild race from beyond the Great Wall. The Juchen had none of the Khitans' sophisticated veneer. They were, envoys reported, 'sheer barbarians, worse than wolves or tigers'. This time Ou-yang Hsiu's optimism seemed ill-founded. In the next century the Juchen swept down and devastated Kaifeng after bribery had failed to buy them off. China was split by the sword. The Sung moved their capital south. The empire had lost territory to the barbarians, but it survived; Confucian scholars remained confident that their culture would last for ever. For China always captivated its conquerors, and turned them into Chinese.

The Garden of Islam

There was only one culture in the eleventh century that spanned oceans and crossed deserts. During the 400 years since its foundation by the prophet Muhammad in western Arabia, Islam had become the biggest – that is, the most widely dispersed – civilisation the western world had ever seen.

The teachings of Muhammad had equipped the Arabs to inherit empire. Islam was not only a religion but a way of life and a blueprint for society, complete with a demanding but unusually practical moral code, a set of precepts of personal discipline, and the outline of a code of civil law. In secular terms, Muhammad seems to have been fired by moral indignation with the waste, inequality and chaos of the society which surrounded him. He inspired his followers with a sense of their own unique access to the truth of God, and a conviction that war against non-believers was not only justified but sanctified. Within 100 years of his death, his designated successors as 'commanders of the faithful' had built up an empire that stretched from the Indus to the Atlantic.

In about 1000, Muslims occupied villas in the Algarve and oases in the Sahara. Where they had not conquered they congregated in merchant communities, thousands strong – in Daylub and Malabar, in Canton and the Malay archipelago – for Muslim warriors had become Muslim traders, exchanging goods around half the world. A merchant might send Persian saffron to China, where it fetched a high price, then ship Chinese porcelain to Greece, Greek brocade to India, Indian iron to Aleppo, Aleppo glass to the Yemen, and Yemeni striped cloth to Persia. In the eleventh century the growth of trade in the Red Sea alone so enriched Cairo that a Persian visitor confessed: 'I could see no limit to its wealth and nowhere have I seen such prosperity as I saw there.' It was the capital of an empire whose frontier rested on the Atlantic.

Where trade went, religion followed. From the steppes of central Asia to the bustling towns of north Africa, mosques appeared. Over distances of up to 4,000 miles, Muslims could travel within a single world, united by the call to prayer. The Syrian geographer Al-Muqaadadasi, who died at the turn of the millennium, surveyed this world in detail, from Syria to Khourasan, with an easy conviction of its cultural unity and a courtier's consciousness of its essential urbanity. Its cities were like princes, he thought, attended by chamberlains, lords and foot-soldiers, who were its provincial capitals, towns and villages. Travellers could feel at home anywhere in the garden of Islam, cultivated, walled against the world, yielding, for its privileged occupants, shades and tastes of paradise.

But every paradise has its serpents. The political unity of Islam bequeathed by Muhammad had long since been shattered. In theory the caliph, the deputy or representative of the Prophet, had authority over one undivided Islamic nation; but in the eleventh century there were rival caliphates in Egypt and Spain, and the Islamic world was divided into separate, and sometimes mutually hostile, principalities.

OPPOSITE The Great Mosque at Cordoba. Mosques like this appeared all over the Islamic world, their distinctive architectural style reflecting both Persian and Byzantine influences.

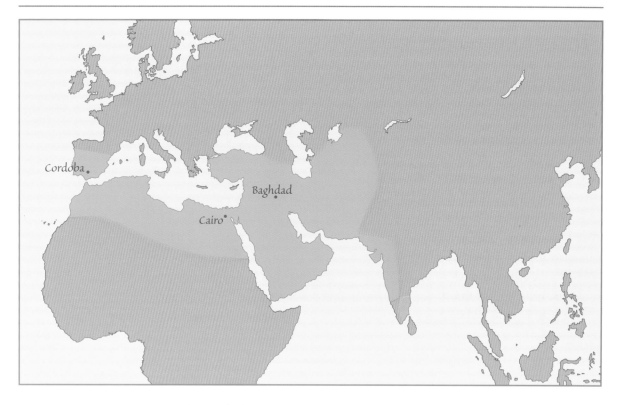

ABOVE *The Islamic world in the eleventh century, stretching from the Atlantic in the west to the Indus in the east.*

One of the easternmost was that of Mahmud of Ghazni, ruler of Afghanistan, warrior and patron of art and learning. Today Afghanistan is a wasteland ruined by war. One thousand years ago it was one of the most splendid places in the world. In the early eleventh century the orchards around Herat stretched for a day's march. Four hundred poets thronged the court of Mahmud of Ghazni, hoping to have their mouths stuffed with pearls in reward for immortalising the monarch in verse. Mahmud tried to gather into his palace all the learning of the world – the science which Arabic writers transmitted from the fragments of Greek and Latin libraries. His war elephants guarded the trade routes between the Oxus and the Indus and carried armed men to loot the temples of India.

BELOW *Tanners at work in modern Morocco, using methods that would have been familiar in eleventh-century Cordoba.*

At the western extremity of Islam was Cordoba, in the region of Spain the Arabs called Al Andalus. At the dawn of our millennium it was the biggest and richest city in the western world. One writer counted 85,000 shops, 900 baths and 1,000 mosques: 'It has no equal in North Africa, and hardly in Egypt, Syria or Mesopotamia, for the size of its population, its markets, the cleanliness of its streets, its mosques, the number of its caravanserais.' Like most Islamic cities of the period, Cordoba was cosmopolitan. Its market, the souk, was a warren of traders; the coffee shops hummed with tales of profit and loss, of shipments and caravans. Leather workers, dyers, tanners, jewellers and silversmiths thronged its streets. Thirteen thousand weavers produced the silks and brocades for which the city was famous. Its tannery was the largest in Europe, making leather for saddles and shoes, buckets and belts.

Cordoba was also a centre of learning, where the great legacy of knowledge from Greece and Rome was saved and copied (its most admired copyists were women). Its greatest library – there were seventy-one in the city – was the envy of the Christian world, claiming to hold 400,000 volumes at a time when the largest in Christian Europe contained only 600. Arab scholars produced encyclopaedias and treatises on medicine and astronomy which Christian monks would acquire, translate and copy in their turn, recovering via Islam the heritage of classical learning.

At the heart of this throbbing city was the Great Mosque, built on the site of a Roman temple dedicated to Janus. The design ingeniously incorporated

NEW WARRIORS FOR ISLAM

The divisions of Islam encouraged enemies outside its boundaries and lit flashpoints of resistance at the frontiers.

The most numerous and powerful assailants invaded, in the course of the tenth and eleventh centuries, from the steppes of Asia. Yet, trampled by Turkish hooves, the Garden of Islam would also be fertilised by the passage of nomad cavalry. Today almost all Turkic peoples are Muslim. The Turks of that era were ferocious barbarians who inspired Muslims with fear. Boys were not named until they had lopped off heads in battle. A hero was judged by the number of times he could plait his moustache behind his head. Even the women were war-trained. Seljuk, the founder of the most successful dynasty of Turkish conquerors of that time, dreamed of conquering the world.

The best way to fulfil that destiny, he found, was to adopt Islam and accept a role as a warrior for the faith. The Turks were assimilated and turned into an accession of strength – a new 'army of God'. Islam's ability to domesticate its barbarian enemies without sapping their strength gave it an enormous advantage over other, rival civilisations.

The destiny of the Turks was echoed, at the western edge of Islam, by that of the Almoravids, ascetic warriors from the recesses of the Sahara. They became champions of strict orthodoxy, heroes of holy war. But their version of Islam was adapted to life in the desert, carrying traces of the pagan culture from which they had emerged. Like the Tuareg of today, their men veiled their faces; their women wielded enormous power.

The outstandingly powerful woman of the Almoravid world was the formidable Zaynab al-Nafzawiya, renowned in the mid-eleventh century for beauty, wealth and influence. According to legend, she rejected all the men who sought her hand in marriage until, by divine inspiration, she chose Abu Bakr bin Umar al-Lamtumi, the peerless cameleer, as her consort.

Abu Bakr is credited with a civilising mission as the founder of Marrakesh. But he was a frontiersman at heart. Departing for the south to conquer pagans and blacks, he divorced Zaynab and left her to his cousin, Yusuf ibn Tashfin. 'I cannot live out of the desert,' he told the couple on his return. 'I came only to hand over authority to you.' Returning to his campaigns, he died in battle, reputedly somewhere among the Mountains of the Moon.

It was Zaynab's new husband Yusuf who restored Muslim Spain when it was hard pressed by Christian conquerors from the north. And it was the Almoravids who defeated the great pagan kingdom of Ghana to the south of them and brought Islam to west Africa.

The Medinat az-Zahrat as it would have appeared in the eleventh century, in a computerised reconstruction.

columns from a Roman temple, a bath-house and a church into one of the largest mosques on earth.

But Cordoba's greatest attraction lay outside the city walls. It was the Medinat az-Zahrat, the royal palace of 'Abd-ar-Rahman III, who claimed to be caliph of the west. Beginning in 936, 10,000 workmen are said to have built the palace with 4,000 columns under roofs of silver and gold.

> The city of Az-Zahrat was one of the most splendid, most renowned, and most magnificent structures ever raised by man . . . In the raising of this sumptuous building the caliph lavished countless treasures.
>
> Six thousand blocks of stone, great and small, cut into various shapes and either polished or smoothed, were used every day . . . The number of beasts of burden daily employed was 1,400, some say more, besides 400 camels belonging to the Sultan, and 1,000 mules hired for the occasion.
>
> (Ibn Khallekan)

This vast palace-city was home to soldiers, courtiers and diplomats; also to some 3,000 slaves and a harem of 6,300 women. The ponds and lakes in its gardens were reputed to be so extensive that 1,200 loaves of bread a day were needed just to feed the fish. But chief among its marvels was the diwan or audience chamber of the caliphs, with its roof of gold and its fountains of quicksilver:

> The roof was in gold tile and translucent blocks of alabaster. Whenever the sun entered this room and the caliph wished to astonish his courtiers he had only to make a sign . . . and mercury in the centre of the room would move. The room itself seemed to turn while the rays of light pierced the room, frightening the assembly. It was the abundance of mercury in Spain which gave [the caliph] the idea for this mechanism.   (Ibn Bashkuwal)

The garden, in the world of Islam, was a mirror of paradise. Gardening was an esteemed art supported by princely patronage, and inspired a body of practical literature. For his gardens at Cordoba the caliph sent agents to Syria and Egypt to bring him back rare specimens to intoxicate the senses, as recounted by the great scholar Ibn Said:

> The caliph planted a most beautiful garden to which he brought all kinds of rare and exotic plants and fine trees from every country. His passion for flowers and plants went even so far as to induce him to send agents to Syria and other countries, with a commission to procure him all sorts of seeds and plants.

Gardeners in Muslim Spain were employed on every project that might enhance luxury, from concocting compost to inventing recipes for *foie gras*. They were learned men, steeped in Aristotle and the occult. Some were also keen practical gardeners. It was the Arabs' skill in using the precious resource of water that created an agricultural revolution in Al Andalus. Some 5,000 water wheels and water mills were said to line the banks of Cordoba's river, the Guadalquivir, creating two harvests every year. Applying the same irrigation techniques to the royal grounds, the Arab horticulturalists created gardens out of hillsides.

For the small Christian states to the north, the power and opulence of Cordoba suggested the image of biblical Babylon. They imagined it burning at the Day of Judgement: 'Mourn, mourn for this great city; for all the linen and purple and scarlet that you wore, all your finery of gold and jewels and pearls. Your huge riches are destroyed in a single hour.'

The paradise that was Al Andalus was defended by thousands of Berber mercenaries from the desert of north Africa – until these fanatical horsemen, seduced by the sybaritic splendours of the land they had come to protect, fell to squabbling over it. Muslim Spain was reduced to a collection of city-states. Cordoba itself was sacked by Berber mutineers and then by Christian crusaders, and though it later recovered it never again reached the heights of culture and luxury it had achieved at the beginning of the eleventh century. To the Christians, this Babylon had received its just deserts.

INDIA: THE CINDERELLA CIVILISATION

Hindu temple at Khajuraho. Its erotic sculptures would have been profoundly shocking to an Islamic visitor.

Of the civilisations contemplated at the T'ang and Sung courts of China, the best known and the least despised was that of India. This immense country, fertile and full of riches, enclosed in the north by the highest mountains in the world and surrounded in the south by ocean, had developed its own distinctive culture. It was the birthplace of two great religions, Hinduism and Buddhism, the former of which had spread into south-east Asia, the latter finding a home in China and Japan. It had long been regarded as a source of great wisdom. Indian astronomy, mathematics and philosophy were admired by neighbours on every side. For centuries scholars had been going there in search of enlightenment: Buddhists to obtain pure versions of their scriptures, others for instruction in the sciences.

Gradually, for reasons not perfectly understood, this pre-eminence was surrendered, and by the end of the first millennium India seemed disappointingly backward to a Muslim visitor. Abu-Rahman Muhammed Al-Biruni was a philosopher, astrologer and mathematician and one of the most learned and independent-minded men of his day, steeped in the works of Plato and Aristotle. He came to the country in the service of Mahmud of Ghazni, ruler of Afghanistan, whose forces had just begun their pillage of the north of India, and spent fifteen years travelling, studying and writing about it. Its culture was so foreign to him that he could scarcely begin to understand it, and his disenchantment was profound.

> The Hindus believe that there is no country but theirs, no nation like theirs, no kings like theirs, no religion like theirs, no science like theirs. They are haughty, foolishly vain, self-conceited and stolid. They are by nature niggardly in communication of that which they know, and they take the greatest possible care to withhold it from men of another caste among their own people, still much more, of course, from any foreigner. According to their belief . . . no created beings besides them have any knowledge or science whatsoever . . . At first I stood to their astronomers in the relation of a pupil to his master, being a stranger among them. On having made some progress, I began to show them the elements on which this science rests, to point out to them some rules of logical deduction, and the scientific methods of all mathematics, and then they flocked together round me from all parts, wondering, and most eager to learn from me, asking me at the same time from what Hindu master I had learnt those things, whilst in reality I showed them what they were worth, and thought myself a great deal superior to them, disdaining to be put on a level with them. They almost thought me to be a sorcerer . . . You mostly find that even the so-called scientific theorems of the Hindus are in a state of utter confusion, devoid of any logical order, and in the last instance always mixed up with the silly notions of the crowd, e.g. immense numbers, enormous spaces of time, and all kinds of religious dogmas, which the vulgar belief does not admit of calling into question . . . I can only compare their mathematical and astronomical literature, as far as I know it, to a mixture of pearl shells and sour dates or of pearls and dung, or of costly crystals and common pebbles . . . If those dreamers had more assiduously studied arithmetic, they would not have invented such outrageous numbers.

Some of these complaints no longer seem well informed. Al-Biruni's quarrel with 'immense numbers' was aroused by traditional Indian calculations of the age of the universe; yet orders of magnitude which made its origins timeless or endowed it with thousands of millions of years of life are affirmed by what we think of as modern science. In part, as he himself acknowledged, his efforts to understand the Indians, and vice versa, were impeded by cultural distance. 'The Hindus', he said, 'entirely differ from us in every respect, many a subject appearing intricate and obscure which would be perfectly clear if there were more connexion between us.'

To Al-Biruni the religion of the Hindus was even more of an enigma. They had no one sacred book like the Koran of the Muslims or the Bible of the Christians, no one prophet or body of doctrine, and a seemingly infinite number of gods. Within the bounds of one religion he encountered an incredible diversity, hundreds of different sects unified, it seemed, only by the basic rituals of Hinduism – purification and the making of sacrifices. 'Every day the Brahmin washes himself thrice; at the time of rising . . . at the time of setting and between them in the middle of the day.'

Where there was no river to provide the sacred water great tanks were built:

In every place to which some particular holiness is ascribed, the Hindus construct ponds intended for the ablutions. In this they have attained to a very high degree of art, so that our people, when they see them, wonder at them, and are unable to describe them, much less construct anything like them.

The river Ganges at the city of Varanasi (Benares), sacred to Hindus.

Most sacred of all was the water of the river Ganges. Al-Biruni watched the pilgrims flock to the holy city of Varanasi (Benares), many of them intending to spend their last days there. 'Their anchorites wander to it and stay there for ever, as the dwellers of the Kaaba stay forever at Mecca. They want to live there to the end of their lives, that their reward after death should be the better for it.'

Al-Biruni failed to understand that, for the Hindu, the divine was one all-powerful, all-pervasive force. What he saw was the hundred different ways, human or animal, in which the divine manifested itself – as Shiva, Krishna, Rama, Hanuman the monkey god, Ganesha with his elephant head, the goddess Kali – all of them shockingly, to a pious Muslim, represented in paint and carved stone. The essential oneness of Hinduism was split into myriad different cults, each focusing on a different deity; and each deity had its own following, its own temples, shrines and rituals dedicated to its worship.

All over India, marvellous structures were built by the Hindus as residences for their gods. The most spectacular that survive are to be found at Khajuraho in central India, where twenty-five of what was once a city of ninety temples remain. Built by the Candella Rajput kings of the tenth and eleventh centuries and dedicated to Shiva and Vishnu, these are sublime examples of Hindu architecture and sculpture. The structure of the temples is symbolic of the Hindu world-view, each up-reaching layer representing the Hindu aspiration to a higher plane of existence. But it is the explicitly erotic sculptures that have given Khajuraho its fame. Although the carvings have been interpreted as a three-dimensional illustration of the *Kama Sutra*, the ancient text on the science of love-making, it is much more likely that they celebrate the marriage of Shiva and the goddess Parvati, whose divine coupling perpetuates the universe. Nothing more clearly exemplifies the way in which Hinduism pervaded every aspect of life.

The Hindus had their sacred texts in the ancient hymns of the vedas and the legends incorporated in the *Mahabharata* and the *Ramayana*. Al-Biruni learned Sanskrit to enable himself to read these epics, describing the *Mahabharata* as 'a book which they hold in such veneration that they firmly assert that everything which occurs in other books is also in this book'. These ancient works, each of them much longer than Homer's *Iliad* and *Odyssey* combined, were often learned by heart; they are still the most popular entertainment for mass audiences in India today, but they are far more than colourful tales of gods and heroes. Part of the *Mahabharata*, the *Bhagavad Gita* (the Lord's Song), ostensibly a battlefield dialogue between Krishna and the hero Arjuna, is virtually the Indian gospel, recognised in our century as a profound meditation on the relationship between humankind and the divine.

Al-Biruni decried the beliefs of the Hindus as witness to their insularity and arrogance, thereby displaying his own arrogant insularity, but his account is nevertheless a reliable guide to what was happening. The subcontinent was ceasing to be what it had been in the past: a source of intellectual initiatives that could reshape the rest of the world. The political and cultural expansion of the previous millennium was over. India became the Cinderella civilisation of the next thousand years, overshadowed by her three more powerful sisters, China, Islam and Christendom.

Al-Biruni had his own explanation for India's time of decline, which he ascribed to the sword of his master, Mahmud of Ghazni:

> Mahmud utterly ruined the prosperity of the country, and performed there wonderful exploits, by which the Hindus became like atoms of dust scattered in all directions, and like a tale of old in the mouth of the people . . . This is the reason, too, why Hindu sciences have retired far away from those parts of the country conquered by us, and have fled to places which we cannot yet reach, to Kashmir, Benares and other places.

Mahmud was indeed an effective conqueror and raider, who extorted fortunes from Indian temples on the pretext of waging holy war: 'India is full of riches, entirely beautiful and delightful, and as its people are mainly infidels and idolaters, it is right by order of God for us to conquer them.' Mahmud's raids must have been culturally impoverishing. In 1019 he gathered so many captives that the slave markets of Afghanistan were glutted; and his famous library was presumably enriched at India's expense. But the failure of Indian initiative happened over a longer term and in a wider context than Al-Biruni was able to observe.

THE WORLD OF THE PILLOW BOOK

In the early centuries of the first millennium Japan had taken much of its culture from China, whose civilisation it strove to resemble. By the eleventh century it was confident enough to have developed original and quite distinctive features of its own. Embassies to China, which had once kept the Japanese elite in touch with their parent culture, were discontinued. Thanks to the nature of the surviving sources, Japanese society was more meticulously documented, more intricately described by diarists and novelists than any other in the world at the time. But by comparison with the vast and teeming world of China as described by writers of the day, the society of Heian-period Japan seems shuttered and blinkered, introspective and self-absorbed. Inside the imperial palace, time ran on a different clock from that of the real world: many official engagements happened in the middle of the night. Ladies rarely ventured beyond the palace and would spend all day confined to their rooms, the only men they saw being their fathers, husbands and lovers.

The authentic voices of aristocratic Japan at this time are women's, because one aspect of the newly asserted 'Japaneseness' was the use of the vernacular as a literary medium in place of – or alongside – Chinese, a practice in which male writers were not yet fully free to indulge. The two outstanding witnesses of the time were the favourite writer of the imperial court of Heian, Lady Murasaki Shikibu, author of the forty-volume novel *The Tale of Genji*, and the deliciously louche female diarist, Sei Shonagon, whose collection of notes, anecdotes and observations of everyday life at court is known as *The Pillow Book*. Both were imperial ladies-in-waiting. Both dedicated themselves with unremitting commitment to the snobberies and sensibilities of court life, with its contempt for the business of the empire which produced and paid for its luxuries. These two matchless observers, with eyes equally beady for intrigue, were accomplished manipulators of gossip in the dimly lamp-lit world of the court, shaded by screens, where alliances, sexual and political, were made in the hours before dawn.

Naturally, they hated each other. 'Sei Shonagon', her rival wrote,

has the most extraordinary air of self-satisfaction. Yet, if we stop to examine those Chinese writings of hers that she so pretentiously scatters about the place, we find that they are full of imperfections. Someone who makes such an effort to be different from others is bound to fall in people's esteem, and I can only think that her future will be a hard one. She is a gifted woman, to be sure. Yet if one gives free rein to one's emotions even under the most inappropriate circumstances, if one has to sample each interesting thing that comes along, people are bound to regard one as frivolous. And how can things turn out well for such a woman?

OPPOSITE *A screen painting of the seventeenth century illustrates an incident from* The Tale of Genji.

Nature clipped and controlled in a Heian garden, an ideal landscape created to match the delicate sensibilities of aristocrats such as Sei Shonagon.

These forebodings turned out to be prophetic. Of the two women, Sei had the more brilliant and brittle reputation. She sniped at too many rivals, sneered at too many enemies, rejected too many lovers, was perhaps too much a prisoner of the society of the court.

When I make myself imagine what it is like to be one of those women who live at home, faithfully serving their husbands – women who have not a single exciting prospect in life yet who believe they are perfectly happy – I am filled with scorn. I wish they could live for a while in our society, so that they might come to know what delights it has to offer.

She outlived the empress on whom she depended for patronage and died unprotected, in a shabby, lonely hovel.

Murasaki, too, had her misfortunes – her husband died prematurely in a plague – but she remained a darling of the court and saw her vast novel of court life become the most sought-after book of its day.

Between them the two women chronicle the life of their world, with its cult of sensibility, its ceremonies and rituals, its strict hierarchy. Their values elevate poetry over prowess, aesthetics above ethics. They esteem a sensitive failure more highly than a coarse success. They are at their most admirable when saddened by fragile beauty or touched by the mutability of things.

Sei Shonagon's writings provide a revealing self-portrait. 'I am the sort of person who approves of what others abhor and detests the things they like. I set about filling the notebooks with odd facts, stories from the past, all sorts of other things, often including the most trivial material.' She delighted in lists of her favourite things and her pet dislikes: the latter included everything boorish, vulgar, inelegant and provincial. The sight of carpenters eating – in a rare glimpse of the world of work – inspired mock bewilderment at the carnality of marginal human specimens, doubtfully supposed to belong to the same species as herself.

Apart from literature and the rituals of the court, Sei's strongest vocation was for sex. In the world of Heian it was quite usual for a man of rank to be polygamous, and promiscuity seems to have been accepted. Each night men would visit different women, and they were expected to leave before dawn. Within the walls of the wood-built palace, its rooms divided only by screens, there was little privacy for these assignations, and even the smallest sounds were heard by all:

Even during the day we cannot be off our guard, and at night we have to be especially careful. But I rather enjoy all this. Throughout the night one hears the sound of footsteps in the corridor outside.

Every now and then the sound will stop, and someone will tap on the door . . . It is pleasant to think that the woman inside can instantly recognise her visitor. Sometimes the tapping continues for quite a while without the woman's responding in any way.

The man finally gives up, thinking that she must be asleep . . . But this does not please the woman, who makes a few cautious movements so that her visitor will know she is really there.

Then she hears him fanning himself as he remains standing outside the door.

Sei Shonagon listed a lover's tiff as one of her '116 Annoying Things':

Woman and man quarrel. She fidgets then gets up. He asks her to come back to bed. She refuses. He goes back to sleep, taking the bedclothes. She gets back into bed. It is cold. Eventually she tries to come under the bedclothes with him. He pretends to be asleep.

She judges love and sex, like everything else, by aesthetic criteria: 'One's attachment to a man depends largely on the elegance of his leave-taking. A good lover will behave as elegantly at dawn as at any other time.'

Before his departure the lover would be expected to write a poem to his conquest. Every aspect of this billet-doux would be examined for signs of the lover's

Saigu no Nyogu, a poetess of Heian-period Japan, depicted in a modest posture of obeisance behind the screen in the foreground. Her poem is inscribed on the scroll.

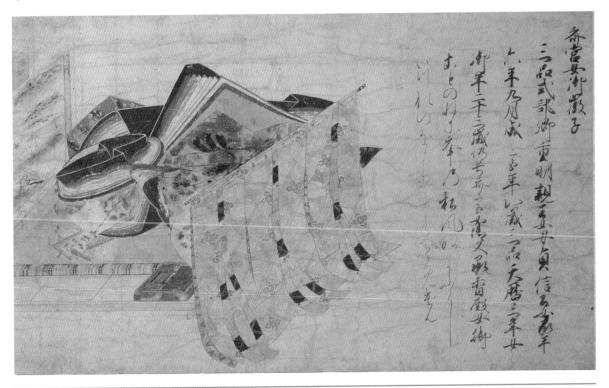

quality: the poem itself, the curve of the calligraphy, the colour of the ink, the smell of the paper, the 'elegant dexterity' with which it was folded and tied.

It is hard to say how oppressively this empire of sensibility ruled its subjects. The writings of Lady Murasaki and Sei Shonagon display a world of porcelain in which few traces of earthenware appear. The lower orders rarely intrude; the provinces are hardly mentioned except as places of exile ruled by boors, whose badly powdered faces reminded Sei Shonagon of 'dark earth over which the snow has melted in patches'. The revenues which sustained the court aristocracy were extorted from a peasantry who remain invisible in the court literature. In the feudal world of Heian there was no equivalent of the meritocratic civil service of China.

The obsessive and inward-looking world that Sei Shonagon recorded would not last long. In the next century the provincial administrators – men of the warrior or samurai class – would build up the private armies that were to challenge and eventually overthrow the central power. But the pure aestheticism that shines out of *Genji* and *The Pillow Book* was to remain a powerful strain in Japanese society until the present day.

Sei Shonagan's Likes and Dislikes

Sei Shonagon was much given to making numbered lists: 14 Hateful Things, 16 Things That Make One's Heart Beat Faster, 63 Embarrassing Things, and so on:

Hateful Things
❀ One has gone to bed and is about to doze off when a mosquito appears, announcing himself in a reedy voice. One can actually feel the wind made by his wings and slight though it is, one finds it hateful in the extreme.
❀ I cannot stand people who leave without closing the panel behind them.
❀ A man with whom one is having an affair keeps singing the praises of a woman he used to know. Even if it is a thing of the past this can be very annoying. How much more so if he is still seeing the woman! (Yet sometimes I find that it is not as unpleasant as all that.)

Things That Make One's Heart Beat Faster
❀ To sleep in a room where some fine incense has been burnt.
❀ To notice one's elegant Chinese mirror has become a little cloudy.

Embarrassing Things
❀ A man who gets drunk and keeps repeating himself.
❀ I cannot bear men to eat when they come to visit ladies-in-waiting. Men should not be allowed to eat!
❀ Lying awake at night one says something to one's companion, who simply goes on sleeping.

Adorable Things
❀ The face of a child drawn on a melon.
❀ Things that give a clean feeling.
❀ A new metal bowl.
❀ The play of light on water as one pours it into a vessel.

Elegant Things
❀ A white coat worn over a violet waistcoat.
❀ Anything indigo.
❀ Duck eggs.
❀ Shaved ice mixed with liana syrup and put in a new silver bowl.

Squalid Things
❀ The back of a piece of embroidery.
❀ The inside of a cat's ear.
❀ A swarm of mice, who still have no fur when they come wriggling out of the nest.

DIVIDED CHRISTENDOM

Perilous times were at hand for men's souls . . . when the millennium approached almost the whole world suffered the loss of great men, noble laymen and clerics.

And when the thousand years are expired, Satan shall be loosed out of his prison.

There were thunderbolts, drenching showers without number, winds of the most astonishing violence, and whirlwinds that shook the towers of churches and levelled them with the ground . . . The devil himself was seen bodily.

The year 1000 was a significant one only within Christendom – the rest of the world worked to different reckonings of historical time – but for many Christians it was momentous.

At this time an innumerable multitude of people from the whole world, greater than any man before could have hoped to see, began to travel to the Sepulchre of the Saviour at Jerusalem. Many wished to die there.

When some consulted the more watchful of the age as to what was meant by so many people, in numbers unheard of in earlier ages, going to Jerusalem, some replied cautiously enough that it could portend nothing other than the advent of the accursed Antichrist who, according to divine testimony, is expected to appear at the end of the world.

The church of the Holy Sepulchre in Jerusalem today. The Christians who crowd to it are still divided among themselves, as they were at the start of our millennium.

The Jerusalem towards which Christian pilgrims flocked at the first millennium was at the time in the hands of Muslims, as it had been for three centuries. Since 969 it had been controlled by the caliphs of Egypt, still tolerant of Christians and Jews but less so than their Arab predecessors. In 1010 the caliph Al-Hakim ordered the destruction of the Christian shrines. In 1071 the Seljuk Turks displaced the Egyptians and cut off the pilgrim routes entirely. The fact that the holy places of Christianity were in the hands of pagans 1,000 years after the death of Christ was a source of shame to the princes of the west, a challenge to their manliness – and a temptation to their cupidity, for it was well known that the riches of this world came from the east.

Then as now, it was a divided Christian church that worshipped in Jerusalem, its sects – Catholics, Orthodox, Armenians, Copts, Ethiopians – quarrelsome and mutually distrustful. Even today, when Catholics and Orthodox Christians share the Church of the Holy Sepulchre, neither trusts the other to hold the keys to the door: so they remain in the hands of a Muslim family, who over the generations for 800 years have locked it each evening and opened it the following day. In 1054 the breach between the Greek-speaking Orthodox church of Constantinople and the Latin church of Rome was made formal when the pope's representatives laid a bull of excommunication on the high altar of the cathedral of Constantinople, in effect denying the validity of its sacraments and thereby depriving Orthodox Christians of any prospect of salvation.

In terms of doctrine the difference between the two churches lay in a single word: *filioque* ('and from the Son'). This term had been inserted by the western

Divided Christendom. Christians were divided between the western church, centred on Rome, and the eastern or Orthodox, centred on Constantinople. Both claimed an imperial mandate. Neither could accept the authority of the other. Rome brought Christianity to the Norsemen; Constantinople converted the Russians, who still hold to the Orthodox faith today.

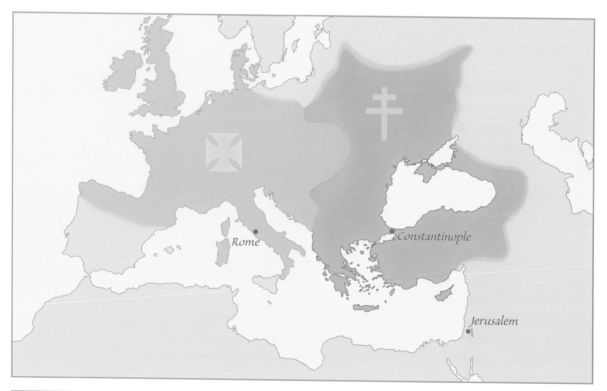

church into the Nicene creed, where it speaks of the Holy Spirit proceeding from the Father; the Orthodox church could not accept what it saw as a diminution of the unique divinity of God. This was the kind of question over which Christians had murdered and tortured each other centuries before, but it was not the sole or even the true cause of division between the churches in the eleventh century, which had much more to do with the fact that Constantinople, centre of the Orthodox church, could not accept the supremacy of Rome.

Two faces of Christ: (left) from an eleventh-century stained glass window in Strasbourg cathedral, and (right) from a mosaic of the same period in a church at Paphini in Greece.

Constantinople had lost much of the territory it had once held; its shrinking frontiers were threatened on all sides, by Arabs, by Turks, by Normans. It was an inward-looking civilisation, lacking the dynamism of the empire in its heyday, its court a byword for corruption, cruelty and intrigue. But it still regarded itself, with some justification, as the capital of the only 'true' Roman empire now that Rome itself was in the hands of crude barbarians. It had been the imperial seat of Constantine, the first Christian emperor. It was the home of a complex, sophisticated urban society, with an elaborate administrative structure, a money-based economy, and arts and amenities that baffled visitors from the west and left them gaping. It still had influence on the outside world; it had given the Slav peoples Christianity and literacy; the Arabs borrowed much from its architecture. It was a dying civilisation that did not know it was terminally ill.

The civilisation that was emerging in western Christendom after the disaster of invasion by Vikings, Danes and Magyars might be rough-hewn in external appearance but it was vigorous in comparison with the decadent east, which it despised: 'These soft, effeminate men with large sleeves, who wear tiaras and turbans, are liars, eunuchs, lazybones. They go about clad in

Crusaders besiege Antioch in Syria in 1098, from a twelfth-century manuscript. In the following year they would take Jerusalem and massacre its Muslim and Jewish inhabitants.

purple.' The western church carried immense weight. It had the imperial authority of Rome, legally granted to it, it claimed, by Constantine himself, at a time when men still looked back on the achievements of the Roman empire with awe and reverence. It was backed by the authority given to it by kings and noblemen whom it held in fear of their immortal souls. Powerful men gave it vast wealth and treasure in hope of escaping eternal damnation for their bloody deeds in this life; and its wealth and power in turn drew the sons of noblemen to become its bishops and abbots. Simple men also joined it, but it was an aristocratic church that dealt on terms of equality with secular potentates and felt free to rebuke them when necessary; the story of the Holy Roman Emperor Henry IV kneeling in the snow at Canossa in Italy to receive the pope's pardon sounds like pious legend but is historical fact.

Information is power in all ages, not just in ours, and in eleventh-century western Christendom the church controlled the information technology of the day. It had a virtual monopoly on literacy and on the production and circulation of books; it provided the chanceries of kings, controlled their communications, and drafted their treaties, their edicts and their laws. The man who became pope in the last year of the old millennium was Gerbert of Aurillac, the first Frenchman to do so. He took the name Sylvester, perhaps conscious of its significance at that moment, for Sylvester I was the pope who had received the Donation of Constantine that created the imperial Roman church. Gerbert was a man of extraordinary and wide-ranging learning, who counted mathematics, astronomy and music among his interests; he had works of scholarship translated from Arabic and distributed among the monasteries. It was churchmen like Gerbert who were bringing about a renaissance – a revival of ancient glories – in western Europe in the eleventh century, a renaissance made visible in the harmonious proportions of Romanesque churches, themselves expressing a massive authority.

It was the supreme self-confidence backed by this kind of authority, along with the charisma of some individuals, that had enabled monks to travel unarmed into the territory of pagans and bring their kings to Christ. Western churchmen had converted the recently savage Magyars of Hungary to Christianity; they had shared with Constantinople in the conversion of the Poles.

Although confident in its power, the church was not complacent. As Pope Urban VI put it, summoning the first crusaders in 1095: 'The world is not evenly divided . . . Our foes hold Asia and Africa too. Of Europe, the last region of the world, we Christians inhabit only a small part, for who will give the name of Christians to barbarians who live on the icy ocean like whales?' Christian cartographers in the eleventh century placed Jerusalem in the centre of the world; their maps were symbolic representations, not practical guides. When the crusaders finally set out in the last decade of the century they scarcely knew where they were going, or what they would find when they got there. When, with material aid from their Orthodox co-religionists in Constantinople, they came at last to the Holy Land, they were confronted by an enemy who was, by most standards, more civilised than themselves; but, by what might fairly be called a combination of brute force and ignorance, they at last prevailed. In the summer of 1099 they laid siege to Jerusalem. When they had taken it, they massacred its Muslim and Jewish inhabitants, man, woman and child. Then, still reeking with blood, they went to give thanks to God in the Church of the Holy Sepulchre. The Christian conquests in Syria and Palestine were the first major setback to Islam.

An eleventh-century map of the world produced in the abbey of St Sever. It shows Jerusalem in the centre.

While the church was urging a crusade in the Holy Land it was prosecuting another within its own frontiers: against the Moors in Spain, where the reconquest had begun. It was also turning its attention to those barbarians who lived 'on the icy ocean like whales' or in the clearings of the deep and uncharted forests that covered most of northern Europe, which Christianity had scarcely penetrated. What is known about European paganism suggests a variety of beliefs and practices: shamanism, totemism, animism, possibly human sacrifice. Whatever it was that the pagan peoples of the northern forests believed in, the men of the church saw it in much the same way as missionaries closer to our time saw the religion of black Africa: as a thing of darkness and demons. They saw themselves as bringing men out of terror and darkness into redemption and light – if also into the terror of eternal damnation. One by one, the warrior kings of the Norsemen converted to Christianity, banishing their old gods and demons to the forest beyond the clearing. In the next century the forests themselves would be tamed, the trees turned into cathedrals.

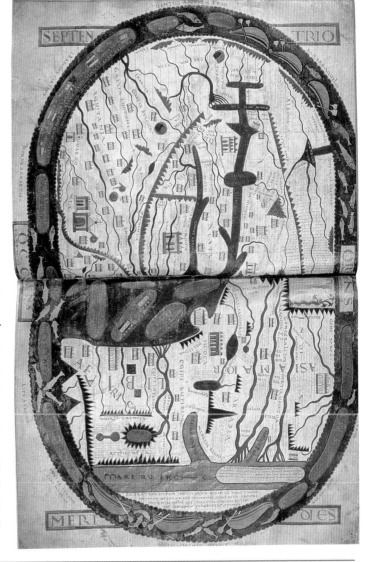

... mulunudmes paucum ... ...

ut cu hec omnia feceris uentu sup̄bie studea
missis omnib; que p eum dn̄s est sepe mirabili
libet huic interserere tractatiu. p quod potest
timitas inter cetera que fecit opa. comprobari
cuidam puerulo muto quem tamen ipse mutuir
uerba ad patrem deferenda commisit. recep̄a
⁊ honeste tractauerit. ⁊ inde grates ei p̄soluit. q
officio lingue accepto. patri de uerbo ad uerbum
letat. discretis ⁊ expressis articulis indicauit.

hic missus est in claram uallem. alius in ...fi
in martimundensem locum. quartus in ponti
tuor ramus cysterciensi radice productis. totu
dn̄s tam monasterior multitudine quã uirtu
p omnes mundi cardines ampliauit. ⁊ ad tu
nenti sup̄addidit grām. ut idem scilicet ordo

CHAPTER 2

Century of the
AXE

THE TWELFTH CENTURY

CIVILISATIONS CHALLENGE NATURE and adapt the environment to suit their ways of life. In the twelfth century, the assault on the wilderness was exceptionally intense: forests felled, landscapes transformed, stones shaped into cities. Civilisations remained separated by vast distances, rarely or never traversed. Yet they began – probably by chance – a more-or-less simultaneous experience of expansion, tackling the wild places with the cutting edges of their tools, clearing ground for settlement, planting and pasture.

Behind the expanding frontier, modest technical revolutions extended the range of business and the flow of wealth. More land under pasture or cultivation meant more productive agriculture, more food and clothing and therefore more people. The population of western Europe may have doubled while these changes took effect, between the early eleventh and mid-thirteenth centuries. In China a high point of population growth was recorded in the census of 1124, when 20 million households were claimed. No other states left comparably reliable statistics but the proofs of their expansion are the woodlands they cut down, the wastelands they civilised, the 'primitives' they tamed, the rocks they moved or carved or hollowed, the horizons they refashioned or smothered with buildings.

In extreme cases, wilderness became cities. Where cities already existed they tended to get bigger and develop more intensely felt civic consciousness. But beyond the reach of the hewers and builders, the domain of nature still covered most of the planet, almost unchallenged by peoples who lived in submission to their environment.

Cistercian monks fell the forest trees that will become the timbers of a new monastery.

THE CANYON BUILDERS

The Great Kiva, the largest and most splendid of the underground chambers at Pueblo Bonito, Chaco Canyon.

Las Vegas today is as glittering a desert town as you could hope to find: a big gamble, a high-risk experiment in changing nature, a city stirred out of the Nevada dust to dazzle the desert glare with neon architecture. It looks like an act of defiance of the environment by modern technology. But in the North American south-west, the ambition to build in the wilderness is at least a thousand years old.

The twelfth century was the time of these earlier builders' greatest achievements. They knew nothing of what most other civilisations were up to, yet they attacked the environment with an ambition typical of their time: a resolve to conjure culture out of nature. They felled forests, farmed the dust, imposed their own geometry on the wilderness and rearranged the landscape to suit human needs and tastes. The structures they perfected now lie in ruins; but they can be convincingly pictured over archaeologists' digs. The sites were big and costly, demanding an unstinting supply of human effort and precious resources. Raw materials had to be wrested from nature and carried over great distances by human teams – the only available source of power in a land without beasts of burden, where the wheel was unknown. At the site now called Pueblo Bonito in Chaco Canyon, the great gorge near the source of the Chaco river, the built environment took shape over a period of two hundred years, culminating in the twelfth century.

The labour started with a survey, the ground marked out in a semicircle. Transmitted by word of mouth and preserved in memory, or perhaps inscribed in the dust, the original plan for the site was sustained with tenacious fidelity, even though, as far as we know, the builders kept no permanent records. Typically, the buildings were planned with geometrical regularity: spacious plazas were surrounded by hundreds of round rooms and a honeycomb of rectangular spaces, all enclosed by massive outer walls. The outer chambers reached five storeys high in places, layered with floors of pine trunks, willow matting and baked clay. The main buildings were faced with dressed stone, smothered in adobe, which dries to the hardness of brick in the sun. Above ground, inside the outer circuit of walls, rose low, turret-like structures and hive-like chimneys. This was the realm of the sun, and the level of the sole, sacred pine – laboriously transplanted and strenuously cultivated in the dust of the plaza. From here ladders led down into underground chambers or kivas – thirty-two of them at Pueblo Bonito – of which the biggest and most splendid was the centremost, the Great Kiva. The chambers were adorned with the canyon people's finest building materials. To supply the gleaming roof beams, a conspicuous display of wealth in a treeless desert, thousands of tall Ponderosa pines were felled in forests on the hills, a hundred miles away across the dry flatlands, hewn to smoothness and hauled to the sites on pole frames.

The chambers had, perhaps, a dual function: they were sacred storehouses for the grain – a commodity so precious that work in the fields was seen as 'serving the grain' and the fruits of the harvest were venerated in the granaries. Corn, the seeds which stored the sun, was the god people ate; and corn fed the manpower explosion.

'Pueblo Bonito' rises from its foundations in a computerised reconstruction.

The results were hallowed by their makers and are revered today by the tribes who live nearby and who recall or re-imagine the rites of the past. The Pueblo consider themselves the heirs of the Chaco Canyon people and perpetuators of their culture. Zuni come to the sites to celebrate their sense of identity in ritual dance and storytelling. The underground stores and chambers are interpreted as architecture sacred to the spirits of their own ancestors.

In the great age of the canyon culture, its creators could gaze imperiously out over the surrounding land from temples, garrisons and administrative complexes, elaborate citadels that were centres of power. Political unity was enforced or celebrated in mass executions which have left frightening piles of victims' bones, crushed, split and picked clean as if at a cannibal feast. The sites were linked by unmistakable signs of statehood, over an area of impressive extent: more than 150,000 square kilometres, from high in the drainage area of the San Juan river in the north to beyond the Little Colorado in the south, and from the Colorado to the Rio Grande. The evidence for this is the extraordinary system of roadways, almost perfectly straight and up to 9 metres wide, which radiated from a cluster of sites around the Chaco Canyon as if in imitation of the sun. Only two needs can account for such an elaborate network: either some unknown ritual was being enacted, demanding and reinforcing close ties between the places linked; or the roads were there for the movement of armies. These roads branded the land with the human ambition to dominate, that same controlling passion which made so many twelfth-century peoples around the world score the earth with roads and smother it with cities.

From inside the road system came captives, sacrificial victims, tribute. From beyond it came exotic luxuries. Shells from the Gulf of California, copper bells and scarlet macaws' skins from Mexico were traded for the turquoise stones of the canyon people's own mountains: reflections of the sky, wrested from the earth – blue drops prized almost as dearly as water, the most precious commodity of all. Cisterns, dams and ditches to irrigate the corn-beds were cut with the same purposeful, organising, re-ordering geometry that shaped the layout of the buildings and decorated the canyon people's clay pots.

Like many overambitious builders in deserts, the people of Chaco Canyon overreached themselves. Their building era came to an abrupt end in the second half of the twelfth century, when protracted droughts made life insupportable. The political world collapsed. The citizens withdrew to fastness in the rocks of the high mesa, protected by vertiginous paths and narrow entrances, where they lived by cropping the tops of the tablelands. The canyon people's was a typical twelfth-century story. Like similar experiments elsewhere in defiance of the environment, they have left behind them spectacular monuments abandoned in improbable places, the doomed cities of over-inspired imaginations.

OPPOSITE *A ladder leads into the interior of the Great Kiva, granary and sacred space.*

THE FELLERS OF FORESTS

Forests were the victims of the century of the axe wherever civilisations were at work in the world. In Europe, trees covered most of the land north of the Alps. When the frontiersmen of the church set out to raze them and build monasteries it was not just to exploit the land or to obtain timber for building; they were inspired by passion: a hatred of the wilderness as the devil's abode, a bias towards light, a desire to reconsecrate ground profaned by paganism.

The pilgrim guide-writer of the time known as 'Aimery Picaud' saw himself as carrying civilisation with him from the slick city surroundings of the great French abbeys and cathedrals which were his usual habitat. Users of his guide started from Vezelay, rebuilt in Burgundy to resemble a vast glade to accommodate the growing numbers of pilgrims on the way south to the shrine of St James at Compostela in Spain. He travelled where hermits and kings had combined to break paths across mountains which still bristled with savages, unspeakable bestiality and memories of old gods. In defiance of the surrounding darkness, inside some of the shrines along his route a new architecture mocked and challenged the forest: outstripping the trees, raising arbours of enduring stone, opening clearings.

The greatest patron of the arts in the Christendom of his day dreamed of light: Suger, Abbot of the Benedictine monastery of St Denis near Paris. Unable to sleep 'on a certain night' in 1136, Abbot Suger rose and set off to search the forest for twelve trees mighty enough to roof the new sanctuary he was planning for his abbey church, which was to be full of light and was to 'elevate dull minds to the truth'. Suger was a small man with a big ambition: to build the greatest, most beautiful church in the world and fill it with jewels and gold and a gleam to resemble that of heaven.

Abbot Suger, twelfth-century patron of the arts, depicted on one of the stained-glass windows of St Denis.

The work was nearly finished. We asked our carpenters and those of Paris where we could find beams. 'Not round here,' they said. 'Not enough forest left. You'll have to get them from Auxerre. It will take a long time. Cost quite a bit too.' When I got back to Matins, I began to think that I had better go round all the nearby forests myself. I got up early, set aside all my other work, took the measurements of the beams we needed and set off for the forest of Iveline. On the way we stopped at the Valley of Chevreuse to summon the keepers of our own forests and the locals well known for their woodcraft. We questioned them under oath. Could we find there – no matter how much trouble – any timbers of the size we needed? They smiled – and would have laughed if they dared. 'Nothing of that sort can be found in the entire region.' We scorned them and began, with the courage of our faith, to search through the woods; and towards the first hour we found one timber adequate to the measure. Through the thickets, the depths of the forest and the dense, thorny

OPPOSITE The nave of the great pilgrim church at Vezelay, France, begun in 1100.

tangles, by the ninth hour or sooner we had marked down twelve timbers (for so many were necessary) to the astonishment of all – especially the bystanders. When they had been carried to the sacred basilica we placed them with exultation over the new roof space to the praise and glory of our Lord Jesus. And we could not find one more timber than we needed.

Suger's St Denis was the beginning of the style of architecture that would much later come to be known as Gothic, a new look for the world. Erected by means which economised on wood and reduced the need for scaffolding, it was a style adapted to shrinking forests.

Suger's inspiration was mystical. St Denis, who gave his name and, it was presumed, his celestial favour to the abbey, was supposed to have become a Christian on hearing St Paul preach in Athens on the theme of the unknown God. The monks believed – falsely, but fervently – that the most valued item in their library was Denis's own account of his mystical ascent, through 'the cloud of unknowing', into the presence of God. His vision of heaven

GOTHIC ARCHITECTURE

The style of architecture we now know as Gothic had its beginnings in the twelfth century in the Abbey of St Denis, near Paris, and it continued to dominate in Europe up to the end of the fifteenth century. (The term 'Gothic' was coined as late as the sixteenth century by Italian art historian Giorgio Vasari, after the Goths, the Germanic barbarians often accused of destroying classicism.) It is an architecture of light, of upward aspiration. Stone ribs were made to curl inside the vaults of roofs like intertwined branches to support ever loftier and more elegant interiors. Enormous arched windows filtered the divine light through coloured glass. The effect was to draw the eye upwards in contemplation of heaven.

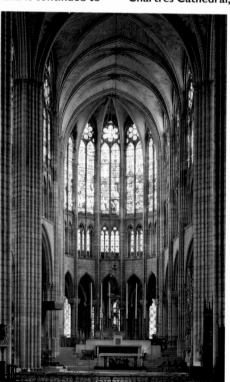

The nave of St Denis.

The most noted examples of the Gothic style can be seen at Notre Dame in Paris, begun in 1160, and Chartres Cathedral, with its tall and pointed arches, begun in 1194. The adoption of the Gothic style marked a new impetus in building on an unprecedented scale. Buildings became larger and higher, walls, securely buttressed, became thinner, window and doorway openings larger. The knowledge of structure in masonry was extended, and with this advance in technique came the means to erect buildings which were little more than shells of stone ribs and pillars, maximising the internal space. As the need for thick, solid walls decreased, so the architectural design could become more complex, with intricate tracery work and ornately carved balustrades and windows becoming a mark of the later Gothic style.

gleamed through the dark night of the soul with gem-like light and a glint intense as gold. The abbey was rich enough to supply the materials which could embody this vision: jewelled altar-vessels, gilding for Suger's twenty new altars, kaleidoscopes of stained glass.

Generations of royal patronage had enriched the foundation of St Denis, which was the burial place of the kings of France. Suger, as well as a monk, was a royal councillor, well connected in circles of wealth and power. At the height of his career he was co-regent of the realm – a great man in the secular politics of his day, in a state whose leaders sought the support of men of sanctity and education. Worldly involvement, indeed, was unavoidable for men of God – though they routinely professed preference for the cloister and the library. Worldly wealth, however, was another matter. The Cistercians, the most dynamic religious order of the century, asked what the God who favours poor Lazarus would think of monks as rich as Dives? Their idea of what heaven was like conflicted with Suger's. They favoured gaunt spaces empty of distracting ornaments and seductive treasures. One Cistercian monk, Idung of Prufening, imagined himself denouncing Suger's preference for

> beautiful paintings, beautiful bas-reliefs, carved in ivory usually and
> each embossed with gold, beautiful and costly cloaks, beautiful hanging
> tapestries in different colours, chasubles with golden orphreys, chalices
> of gold and precious stones, books illuminated with gold leaf: necessity
> and utility do not require all these things, only the lust of the eye does.

He was echoing Bernard of Clairvaux, the effective leader of the Cistercian movement and the most famous monk of the day, who openly denounced Suger's taste:

> Oh vanity of vanities, but more folly than vanity! Every part of the church
> shines, but the poor man is hungry! The church walls are clothed in gold,
> while the children of the church remain naked . . . Tell me then, poor
> monks – if indeed you are poor – what is gold doing in the holy place?

Nevertheless, while theological and aesthetic debate raged, monastic builders were at work on all frontiers in a common project: to civilise the pagan wilderness. The Cistercians razed woodlands and drove flocks and ox-teams into the areas they cleared, where now scores of their vast abbeys lie ruined. In this zeal to penetrate the forest, they were following the example of the founders of their order, who in

> 1099 set out eagerly for a wild region known as Cîteaux, a locality in
> the diocese of Chalon [in Burgundy], where men rarely penetrated
> and none but wild things lived, so densely covered was it then with
> woodland and thorn bush. When the men of God arrived there and

realised that the less attractive and accessible the site was to laymen the better it would suit themselves they began, after felling and clearing the close-grown thickets and bushes, to build a monastery.

The Cistercian Order alone would go on to build over three hundred monasteries all over Europe.

Idung of Prufening knew a thing or two about the domestication of the wilderness, since he came from the very edge of the frontier of deforestation in Pomerania, the land to the east of Germany, on the shore of the Baltic. 'What is grinding gold into dust,' he asked, 'and illuminating huge capital letters with that gold-dust if it isn't useless and idle work? . . . We put great effort into turning the land to cultivation, which God created and instituted . . . Many are the times when we eat our bread in the sweat of our brow upon returning from that work.'

It was at about the time that Suger was plucking the last great roof-timbers from central France that Bishop Otto of Bamberg set out with a few companions to bring Christianity to pagan Pomerania. The 'vast and bristling forest' was

> as hard to follow as to describe: we should have been more likely to perish in it. For this wood had never previously been crossed by mortal men, except by the ruler of Poland on a mission of plunder prior to the projected subjugation of the whole of Pomerania. He sliced a path for himself and his army, marking and lopping trees. We held fast to the marks, but with great difficulty owing to the serpents and wild beasts of many kinds . . .

A new sacred geography was laid out with the measuring-rod. Where the flaws and folds of woods and downs had once been worshipped, new settlements were centred on cathedrals or monasteries and stamped with the uniform plan of the colonial town. In some places the profusion of churches must have seemed crushing to sprites and demons displaced and exorcised: the island of Rugen in the Baltic, for example, which boasted one church every 30 square miles within five years of the people's conversion in 1168. By the end of the twelfth century – and for the next 150 years – a new cathedral was built somewhere in western Christendom every year.

Yet it would be a mistake to see forest-clearance and temple-building as uniquely Christian enterprises: they were part of a civilising mission in which pagans – at least, pagans in transition towards Christianity – could also take part. The people of Gutzkow in Pomerania paid 300 talents for the construction of a new shrine to their gods in 1120; a few years later Otto of Bamberg wanted to proclaim the arrival of Christianity by pulling it down. The builders were distraught: would it not be wiser, they asked, just to turn it into a church?

THE HEWERS OF ROCKS

If the piety which pushed back European frontiers was impressive, it was surpassed elsewhere. While in Europe churches rose into the sky, in the Horn of
Africa they were gouged out of the ground. In Ethiopia, a country with a
Christian tradition eight centuries old, a great building project was designed to
transform a wilderness into an image not just of civilisation, but of paradise. In
the twelfth century the country was emerging from a dark age which consigned
records to oblivion and obscured most individual personalities from view. Unity
was recovered and expansion resumed; a modest renaissance began, and
Ethiopia regained the fame it had enjoyed in its former periods of grandeur.

Towards the middle of the century, the country even became the focus of a
European fantasy. Crusaders from western, Latin Christendom, fighting to
keep a hold on the lands where Christ had lived, were threatened by the
strength of Islam. They were desperate for allies. To feed hopes and allay fears,
they invested belief in a legend: a great Christian emperor from beyond the
bounds of Islam would come to their aid, turn the enemy's flank, and rescue
Jerusalem. When the story of this mythical saviour, called 'Prester John', was

*An Ethiopian
manuscript illustration
shows how the Lalibela
churches were cut with
adzes out of the living
rock.*

St George's, one of the rock-hewn churches of Lalibela.

first heard in the west in 1145, he was identified with the ruler of Ethiopia. The world was innocent of racism in its virulent modern forms and western Christians were anxious to know their black sister-civilisation better. For most of the next three hundred years, Prester John would be sought ever further afield – in India and central Asia – but Ethiopia never lost its special place in the esteem of the west.

There was not much real chance, however, that Ethiopian armies would come to the crusaders' aid. For Ethiopians, surrounded by Islam and challenged by paganism within their own frontiers, this was a time of internal crusade, typified by the tireless pilgrimages. The most renowned saint of the day, Tekla Haymanot, made converts, dethroned idols, wasted 'the devil's wood' and appropriated 'devils' trees' to build churches. Another saint, King Yemrehane Krestos, earned this reproach from Satan when, following the same impulse as his brethren in Christian Europe, he began chopping wood for building:

Why do you make me leave my rocks, where I have dwelt while
So many men adored me and which was my delight? . . . Then
Yemrehane cut down all the trees and brush and had it all burned
With fire.

By the end of the twelfth century or early in the thirteenth, the Ethiopian kings were paying in gold for building materials purchased from Egypt and putting them to use to honour Christendom and defy heresy and paganism. At the city of Lalibela, eleven monastery-churches emerged with geometrical precision out of veins of rock. According to local tradition, it took twenty-four years to complete just one of them. Literally hewn out of the bedrock, they are housed in huge pits – sunk 40 feet or more, so deep that their towers hardly peer above ground level. It is as if the builders were trying to inject Christianity into the heart of the earth. The biggest is 110 feet long and 76 feet wide. The ambulatories around them – which, on holy days, fill with streams of colourful pilgrims – are the results of excavation. The lavish interiors were hollowed out by tunnellers equipped with adzes, to embody a dream of what heaven would be like. 'What tongue', asked the author of a work intended to promote pilgrimages, a couple of centuries later, 'is capable of giving a description to them? I cannot explain to you the construction of their walls, and do not expect me to describe the interiors of the churches, for I cannot. He who beholds them will never be able to gaze his fill, and his marvelling at them is so great that his heart is never tired in admiring them.'

OPPOSITE *Pilgrims process around a church 40 feet below ground level.*

King Lalibela, after whom the city is named, and who is credited with building ten of the sunken churches, is, like all the rulers of his dynasty, unknown

from sources of his own time. The records were lost in later wars or, as some scholars think, deliberately erased by the next dynasty. The traditions recorded later are of only limited, indirect use as guides to Lalibela's real life and conduct; but they reflect some of the enduring values of the society which preserved or invented them and the esteem which the architecture of his world inspired. The legend that Lalibela was uplifted in his work by a vision of heaven, which he then sought to realise on earth, aligns him with the universal civilising impulse: to remodel nature to match an ideal which arises in the mind:

> After showing him what churches are like in heaven, God said to Lalibela 'It is not for the passing glory of this world that I will make you King, but that you may construct churches like those you have seen . . . You are worthy of bringing them out of the bowels of the earth through my power, but not through the wisdom of men, for mine is very different to that of men.' And God sent his angels to help build the churches . . . of such art and craftsmanship that no man could have accomplished without the wisdom of God. He embellished the interior and he adorned it not with gold and silver but with sculptures carved from the rock. Thus he ended the construction of the churches reproducing everything he had seen from the seventh heaven all carved without wood for the windows, nor mortar for the stones – all made from a living rock.

King Lalibela, the soldier saint, as imagined by an Ethiopian painter in the fifteenth century.

The emphasis on the king's personal beauty, 'without defect from head to foot', is an inference from the aesthetic perfection of the masterpieces ascribed to his patronage. The legend of his selection for kingship in infancy by bees who clustered round his cradle suits an industrious builder who honeycombed the wilderness with churches. The stories of angels who worked on them as invisible masons and labourers reflect the superiority of the craftsmanship. The emphasis on the use of wage-labour to supplement the angels' work echoes a prejudice against slavery which often appears in the writings of Ethiopian monks.

For their admirers, the churches represented a noble extension of the art of the possible, a defiance of worldly practicalities, and a place of pilgrimage intended to rival Jerusalem: 'Any Ethiopian,' warned one version of Lalibela's life, 'who having heard of churches so worthy of renown, fails to go to the holy city to see them, is like a man who has no wish to see the face of our Lord Jesus Christ.' Early promotional literature, which perhaps reflects Lalibela's own programme, even put words into the mouth of Christ: 'I blessed this place, and from now onwards let it be a holy place, as Mount Tabor, or as Golgotha, the place of my crucifixion, or as Jerusalem. If a man undertakes pilgrimage to it, it is as if he went to my

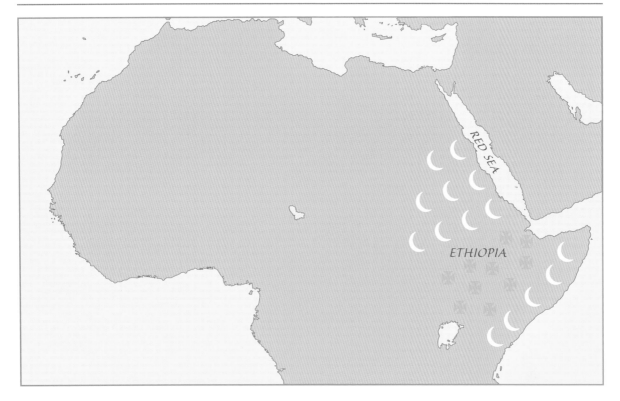

sepulchre in Jerusalem. And if he receives my flesh and blood in those churches he will be absolved of all his sins.'

With the sacred agenda came a political programme. Ethiopian rulers had long claimed descent from King Solomon, builder of the temple of Jerusalem; they were, moreover, traditionally proclaimed as custodians of the Ark of the Covenant – the chest containing the tablets on which the laws given by God to the ancient Israelites were inscribed – supposedly as trustees of Solomon, who sent it to Ethiopia for safe keeping. Lalibela's dynasty, however, may never quite have filled the Ethiopian throne with confidence and comfort. The Awga, the people from whom they sprang, were speakers of an alien language, who were probably always regarded as intruders by some, at least, of the metropolitan elite. Lalibela's New Jerusalem was therefore a demonstration of his legitimacy as the heir of Solomon – or even his rival: 'My tongue is confounded,' wrote one of his biographers, 'and is powerless to recount the virtues of Lalibela, the most famous of mortals for his wisdom and great justice, most like to Solomon, that sage among men. For Solomon built two monuments in twenty years – a temple for the Lord and a palace for himself. Lalibela built ten churches out of a single rock, with the help of God's Son.'

Lalibela's attempt to create a version of heaven in a former wilderness signified his determination to colonise new frontiers, to justify his conquests, to arouse patriotic and religious fervour, and to inspire war against the Muslims whose lands almost surrounded the Ethiopian empire. His churches may have been unique in their construction, but they embodied an ideal typical of the century.

In Ethiopia Lalibela set out to build a religious state, a spiritual centre that would rival Jerusalem. His Christian empire grew rich on trade with the Red Sea, raised churches on the highest hilltops – and kept the surrounding Muslims at bay.

THE MAKERS OF CITIES

Perhaps the best way to measure the expansion of twelfth-century frontiers is by the growth of cities – ways of organising life imposed on nature by man. Examples could be found at the time all over Europe and Asia, but for civic sensibility, assertively – sometimes bloodily – proclaimed, the best-documented and most concentrated examples are in western Europe, and especially in Italy.

The ways cities were built reflected the needs and nature of the societies they housed. They were walled around for defence, and sometimes had walled quarters within them to keep enemies in rival districts from each other's throats. They were often designed in imitation of ancient or ideal models. They were scattered with market-spaces, embellished for display and adorned with the self-advertisements of competing neighbourhoods, families and individuals. All the features we associate with cities today were present in those of the twelfth century: dense settlement, civic pride, economic specialisation, industrial workshops, administrative complexes, facilities for long-range as well as local trade, and clusters of what are now called service industries. As St Isidore once said, 'Walls make a city, but a civic community is built of people, not of stones.'

The ancient Roman idea of a city republic was revived in the twelfth century along with other aspects of antiquity. The 'boni homines' – the traditional bosses of Italian towns – were transformed into elected 'consuls', who held or claimed sovereign power. The popes fostered Roman memories by collecting antique art and making a public display of their pedigree as heirs of the ancient emperors. Pride in the same tradition animated the mob which converged on the Capitol, the seat of the city in 1143, to proclaim a republic. The rebels elected their own 'senators' and 'consuls'. The pope fled.

Civic politics were inspired by a Christian as well as a classical vision. In Italy, cities' self-awareness arose from pride in two kinds of possession: Roman antiquities and the relics of saints. Cities which had no ancient past invented one in spurious chronicles; those with no relics forged or stole them. The Veronese in the twelfth century had a particularly intense pride in their city because it boasted so many intact buildings from the Roman period: many of them, indeed, are still there. But where the commune of Verona is shown in the tympanum of the cathedral in its moment of creation, it is the patron saint, Zeno, who, 'with a serene heart, grants to the people a standard worthy of defence'; and on the façade of the church of Santa Anastasia, he presents the assembled citizens to the Holy Trinity. Whenever the people of the city gathered in sight of these images, civic identity was symbolised and reinforced.

It was worth fighting to obtain the prestige conferred by saintly bones. Among the seventeen churches in dispute between Arezzo and Siena was one near the river Arbia, burial place of St Ansanus, a martyr of the reign of Nero. A succession of conflicting judgements on the question of who owned the relics was handed down by royal courts until 1107, when the Sienese – in what they claimed was a pre-emptive strike – carried them to Siena by force, singing, 'Come, father Ansanus, return to us, Lord, delay no longer in returning to your city.' The city's knights, in the vanguard, dispersed a force sent out from Arezzo to intercept the raiders. All classes united to guard and venerate the saint. Many sick pilgrims, cured in Siena's hospital, spread the word. The five districts of the city stopped fighting each other and established a rota, 'So that the holy relics should never be without a numerous guard of clergy and people . . . To supply these vigils, the houses of monks and nuns, the common people and oratories with their people, flocked with wholehearted devotion, according as they belonged to one of the five divisions.' This was the kind of event which turned a court into a city and shifted people's allegiance from a ruler to the commune. The city collectively became the heir of the bishop, the saint the emblem and source of its authority. The prosperity lent to his place of repose was now transferred inside the city's walls. Siena began to increase mightily in size and wealth.

The city was a state of mind – as all these examples show – but it was also a creative, transforming space, which drew people in from the countryside and changed their lives. In the streets of Siena today, when the festival known as the Palio comes round, an observer can still capture a sense of what it was like for two types of twelfth-century denizen: when the rural aristocrats converted into citizens; and people who were obliged to live in the narrow spaces of the city came into conflict.

The Palio is a twice-annual bareback horse-race round the main piazza, disputed between the traditional districts of the city in a lavish costume-party: the teams don medieval motley and feudal flummery. The pageant is a dazzling assertion of the continuity of civic traditions and the tenacity of a sense of community rooted in medieval experience. It belongs to an abiding history of the ritualisation of conflicts within the city. The Palio evolved from games which channelled the rivalry of different quarters and jousts which trained the city's warriors: these were part of the life of the twelfth-century piazza. Candidates for knighthoods erected pavilions in the central square and feasted and jousted for a fortnight.

The horse allotted to the contrada of the Snail falls while racing in the Palio.

These tourneys were not just for show but serious training sessions for all too frequent wars. For the lure of the profits to be made from extending cities' jurisdiction drew their governments into campaigns of conquest beyond the walls. Their armies were led the same way by the need to force rural aristocrats out of banditry and into the service of the city. They had to be beaten or bought.

The Ardengeschi family, for instance, sold the strategically menacing hill of Orgia, just beyond the South Gate, to the city of Siena and had to renew their renunciation of the property with an annual oath before the whole population in front of the cathedral. The tenor of such oaths and the process by which rural warriors became responsible citizens is captured in words uttered at a ritual of submission of 1197.

> We . . . swear on the Holy Gospels that henceforth we shall be Sienese citizens, and shall preserve and protect every person of the city of Siena and of its suburbs and their goods . . . And we promise to reside within the walls for three continuous months in time of peace as well as in time of war . . . And we swear that we will give ear and attend to the commands of the Sienese consuls.

The more powerful citizens who now shared the restricted space of cities protected themselves, and threatened each other, by building fortified tower dwellings, which also served, like the skyscrapers of Manhattan or Chicago, as a way of maximising occupancy of precious real estate. Seventeen such towers survive today in the Tuscan city of San Gimignano; there were once seventy-three of them. In medieval times Siena and other Tuscan towns were similarly crowded with towers.

Gradually the city took over the countryside – absorbing the aristocracy, extending jurisdiction, planting dependencies, transforming landscape. Inside the walls, lives unfolded which, even at humble social levels, were dignified by the pride of citizenship and perpetuated in writing. They can be glimpsed in the oldest surviving documents of everyday urban life in Europe – more detailed than the archives of any city in the world since the great days of ancient Mesopotamia or Syria. We should pause to listen to some of the voices which can still speak to us through these sources – voices of startling ordinariness, uttering anxieties instantly recognisable to city-dwellers in the western world today. The examples which follow come from the year of the oldest surviving official archives in Europe, 1156.

There are stories of families breaking up and growing up. Among the cases memorialised by Giovanni the scribe in Genoa was that of Alberto di Nigrone, whose divorced wife had colluded with a Pisan merchant to cheat her former husband of the price of her Saracen slave-woman. On 25 August, Limberto di Lavorante ended a dispute with his father-in-law, a banker, by declaring himself content with 'fourteen pounds in coin, part of the dowry of my wife, Martina'. On 1 May, one of Giovanni's clients declared:

> I Baialardo, . . . set you, my son, Ansaldo, free, and I release you from
> paternal control and power. And you may possess all your businesses,
> purchases, proceeds of sales, exchanges, trades, rentals, transfers and
> other contracts, to operate freely and without paternal constraint, and
> so that you may be as much in your own right and your power as those
> who were responsible for themselves in the time of the Roman
> emperors, and so that you should have the right to receive and issue
> summons. And thereto the consuls of the republic add their
> confirmation and lend their authority.

And there are stories of neighbours: stories of bloody quarrels and precarious deals, sometimes disclosing the expensive glamour of the high-risk, long-range trades in exotic products which could make citizens rich or ruined. On 1 August,

> In the presence of witnesses, I Bono Vasallo di Castello, declare that I
> owe to you, Bono Giovanni Malfigliastro, fifty pounds, which Ogerio
> de Ripa formerly owed you, and which I promise to give you by

2 August next in the form of pepper and dyewood, as is stipulated in your contract with Ogerio himself. He commuted this debt for a house which I bought from him.

Where archives amassed by the official clerks or notaries have not survived, occasional intimate details of ordinary lives sometimes found their way into monastic records, amid the timeless lists of benefactions and the roll-call of relentlessly accumulating property empires. In Siena in 1164, for instance, the declaration of a member of the noble Berardenghi family found its way into the list of the family's donations to a monastery it had founded. This raw tale of the city discloses in heartfelt language, which keeps breaking through the legal niceties, a plot worthy of a great novelist: an aristocratic household, which uses a wet-nurse to suckle its young; a feudal habit of extorting service from social inferiors, yielding to an urban way of getting things done by paying for them; and a gallery of typical fears, ranging from the city's of loss of sovereignty to an emperor or marquis to the writer's of capture in battle.

> It pleases me, Rinaldo, son of Guido, to give . . . to you, Tezza, daughter of Azo, and nurse to a certain daughter of mine, Alteviduta by name, two pieces of land . . . in accordance with the title of purchase which is already held by your husband, Geradino, in exchange for a house [and certain sums of money] . . . These properties, which belonged to my father, and are situated between the upper and lower paved roads, I now give for the nursing of my daughter aforesaid, Alteviduta, and I therefore remit the dues attached to them which were paid hitherto, and the triennial payment in tribute and all unjustly demanded service which was formerly extorted from the property of your husband, Geradino, by me and my bailiffs. I renounce them in your favour, Tezza, and that of your heir, and I promise and bind myself and my heirs never more to exact or seek anything unjustly from you and your heirs, unless I or my heirs should buy back the land, or shall owe tribute by any chance to the emperor or marquis, or – God forbid – we should, by any profoundly remote chance, be captives for ransom.

Western Europeans like to think of civic identity as a peculiar property of their own civilisation. But, like most western self-congratulation, this claim to exclusivity is ill-founded. In much of twelfth-century India, the growing cities were stamped with all the hallmarks recognisable to Europeans: civic consciousness, guild life, assemblies of citizens, markets, a measure of autonomy and, in consequence, disputes with rural communities involving tension over jurisdiction and revenues. An inscription recording grants to a Jain shrine at Belgaum in north Karnataka in 1204 conveys a sense of the urban space. Houses are designated by blocks and streets; the shops of clothiers, goldsmiths, jewellers and oil merchants appear; gardens, reservoir tanks and paddy fields are identified. The range of consumer goods listed conjures up a world of wealth: horses and rice; betel and buffalo; spices and sugar; fruits and palm leaves; cotton and finished cloth. An inscription of 1123 at Terdal, in Sangali, captures the citizens' sense of pride and superiority as it celebrates the colourful, fragrant rice fields, gardens, reservoirs, fortifications, moat, temples, thousands of fine dwellings, gentry 'like the trees of Paradise', corn, milk, textiles, jewels, money-changers. And the city of Anahillapura was praised in terms framed to emphasise how civic solidarity brings wealth:

> eighteen miles of walls, within which there were many temples and colleges, eighty-four bazaars, . . . one for money-changers, one for perfumes and unguents, one for physicians, one for artisans, one for goldsmiths; there were distinct quarters for navigators, bards and genealogists. The eighteen castes inhabited the city. All were happy together.

The civic histories of eastern Christendom, too, contain recognisable echoes of those of western Europe. The city of Novgorod near the Russian Baltic coast contended against a hostile climate, beyond the limit of the grain lands on which the citizens relied for sustenance. But its control of trade routes to the river Volga made it rich. It never had more than a few thousand inhabitants, yet its progress is chronicled in grand monuments: the citadel walls and five-domed cathedral in the 1040s; in the early twelfth century a series of princely foundations; and in 1207 evidence of the rise of what would now be called a middle class: the merchants' church of St Paraskeva in the marketplace.

The revolt of Novgorod in 1136, in which the hereditary prince, Vsevolod, was deposed, marks the creation of a city-state on an antique model – a republican commune like those of Italy. The identity of the revolutionaries emerges dimly from annals and charters: the merchant-alderman Boleslav, the town crier Miroslav Gyuvyatinich, the councillor Vasyata. Bourgeois values, though not explicitly uttered, resound clearly in the list of Vsevolod's alleged faults: 'Why did he not care for the common people? Why did he want to . . . wage war? Why did he not fight bravely? And why did he prefer games and entertainments rather than state affairs? Why did he have so many gyrfalcons and dogs?' The bishop, Nifont, was on the side of the old order: he refused to solemnise the marriage of the new prince, who had campaigned against Pskov where the deposed Prince Vsevolod had entrenched himself. While ecclesiastical support eventually gave the ousted ruler the posthumous solace of canonisation, in Novgorod itself the spirit of communalism was dominant, and the citizens' principle was, 'If the prince is no good, throw him into the mud!'

THE DOMAIN OF NATURE

Beyond the swing of the axe, outside the well-documented worlds of felled forests and hewn stones, most of the planet was still the domain of nature – even where humans inhabited it. Around the civilisations of the city-builders, peoples despised by them as 'nomads', with their less aggressive attitude towards nature, were waiting to take their revenge on the usurpers. Beyond the realm of the canyon-builders of the North American south-west lived highly mobile peoples who followed the bison; around Ethiopia were hostile herdsmen, the Galla and the tribes of the Adel; on the edges of China and Russia, would-be invaders from the steppeland were in the saddle. European colonists were disputing unfavourable environments with reindeer-herders in Scandinavia, forest-dwellers south of the Baltic and Inuit in Greenland.

Australian Aborigines labour over an intricate painting made of small fragments of rock which they will later remove, leaving no trace behind.

A rock painting of a kangaroo, Nourlangie Kakadu National Park.

In certain cases – in Aboriginal Australia, in much of the world's rainforest belt, in some desert-dwelling communities and among Inuit peoples – today's way of life seems little changed since the twelfth century, and indeed for centuries or millennia before that.

Australia may seem like a strange case on which to focus: of Aboriginal history, virtually nothing is known which is specific to or distinctive about the twelfth century. Nor, at the time, did any peoples of Australia have to compete with cultures intent on major transformations of the environment. But the ways of life traditionally practised in Australia prior to the arrival of European colonists represent a clear instance of a world where people have conducted their relationship with the environment with extreme restraint and with conspicuous success.

Australian Aboriginals, for instance, do not build enduring monuments but, until white settlers transformed their country, they sustained enduring societies. They made shelters of bark, stripped from the living tree without felling, and constructed windbreaks scrabbled together out of brushwood. Their artistic and ritual lives were laborious and time-consuming, but took expression in evanescent forms of song and dance. Even their paintings were made to be overlaid by others in great galleries of natural rock, or dabbed into the sand to be blown away by the wind. Instead of refashioning the rocks into cathedrals or temples of their own imagining, they found their sacred spaces ready-made for them by nature. According to their view of the universe, landscapes were laid out in a remote 'dreamtime' – the legendary dawn of time, when supernatural beings sang the world into existence. Rainbow serpents, giant lizards and men of lightning shifted, piled and carved it. Valleys formed where they slept, billabongs where they drank and great canyons where they fought. Ginga, the giant crocodile, made the rocks. Marrawuti the sea-eagle brought water lilies and planted them on the floodplain.

These generalisations apply widely. Yet, in a land as big as Australia, which encompasses so many contrasting environments, cultural uniformity would be impossible. Although Aboriginal peoples are often mistakenly supposed to be mired in 'timelessness', their own cultures changed and diverged during the forty thousand years or so of their occupation of their lands. This is strikingly demonstrated by their languages: although trade – in ochre for body-paint, for instance – keeps neighbouring peoples in contact, their languages are often mutually unintelligible.

Their relationship to nature similarly encompasses a wide range of approaches. Some communities risked making selective changes in their environment. On estuarine coasts they farmed molluscs and heaped the shells in middens which survive – the nearest thing to permanent buildings any of these peoples have left. On the Murray–Darling river system they dug canals for eel-farming. Inland they used fire to manage the grazing grounds of kangaroos – with effects that did not always bear out the romantic conviction that Aborigines are 'at one' with nature: in some areas the consequence was burnt-out, over-exploited land on which nothing grows today. But every initiative was disciplined by a conviction that the best way to exploit nature was by cooperation, not mastery; and the usefulness of disciplined control by fire is recognised today, with traditional Aboriginal methods of management applied in national parks.

We tend to judge civilisations by the ambitions revealed in their surviving monuments; but most of them are in ruins. If one contemplates world history with a long-term view, it is apparent that sometimes the best strategy is restraint: not building for the future but investing in eternity. It is equally apparent that societies with an aggressive attitude to nature are also effective in conflict with human enemies; and that those who tend to submit to nature end by submitting to human conquerors. Such was the fate of Aboriginal Australia, virtually destroyed when compelled to compete. In some cases, however, when societies which deferred to nature competed directly with rivals of greater ambition, the more modest solutions proved more practical. In the twelfth century the result of encounters between, say, environmentally aggressive colonists and environmentally submissive natives (for example, the Thule Inuit of Greenland and European Norse settlers) could not be so easily predicted.

When cultures are isolated, technology gets simplified. The relative stability of the Aboriginal world was a result not of the people's uninventiveness, but of their isolation. In the remotest outpost of Aboriginal cultures, in Tasmania, isolation reversed what we think of as the normal model of progress: technologies were abandoned as time went on, until even the kindling of flame was forgotten and replaced by custodianship of fires that were never allowed to go out. In parts of Australia, Aboriginal cultures rejected an astonishing range of technologies which had once been available to them, including bows and arrows, hardwood swords, bone tools, fishing and perhaps stone tools. Similarly, Inuit technology peaked early in the people's history. Once their long-range migrations were over, their rivals outlived and their encounters with strangers interrupted, they developed few new techniques.

The human environment of Eurasia, by contrast, was crammed with juxtaposed cultures and opportunities for exchange, and here conditions stimulated the rapid turnover of ideas and the circulation of innovations. In the thirteenth century the civilisations of Europe and Asia would leap into close contact and dynamic development, bound together by new, horse-borne routes of communication, in the century of the stirrup.

CIVILISATION VS NATURE

Civilisations progress largely through the conquering of nature, the subjugation of the natural world to the will of man. But in some instances progress is achieved through cooperation with nature rather than mastery of it. The history of the Inuit of Greenland is a good example of this. Norse settlers arrived in sub-Arctic Greenland at about the same time as the migrating Thule people got there by canoe. The Norsemen's technology was, by present-day standards, much more advanced than that of the Thule. Their big wooden ships, held together with iron nails, must have seemed madly extravagant to the Inuit in their skin canoes. In the early years of settlement the environment had much to offer both sets of newcomers. There were no forests but there were some useful willow scrub and copses of dwarf birch and rowan. There was no grain, but there were lyme grass, flax and many edible herbs and berries. Fish, birds and caribou abounded. The Norse settlement of Brattahlid, with its seventeen convents and churches of stone, its tithe barn and large festal halls, stood in stark contrast to the Inuit's dwellings, which were temporary and made of turf or snow.

An Inuit hunter in his kayak waits for a seal to surface.

Yet it was the Inuit who survived in the long term in this hostile environment. The Norse Greenlanders are thought to have disappeared from the northern regions of their settlement by the early 1300s, and during the following century, in circumstances still imperfectly explained, they vanished from the rest of the island. They seem to have run out of ecological options as the climate became colder and life harder. By contrast, nothing has been able to destroy the Inuit way of life, which relies on hunting and gathering in the environment nature provided. Only through adapting to the demands of the environment, rather than trying to turn nature to their own ends, did the Inuit survive and prosper where their more technologically advanced competitors failed.

CHAPTER 3

Century of the
STIRRUP

THE THIRTEENTH CENTURY

UNTIL THE THIRTEENTH CENTURY, people who considered themselves civilised avoided the European steppe. This vast, flat grassland, which stretches from the river Danube to the Sea of Japan, was imagined as teeming with terrors. In this space mapmakers drew men with dogs' heads, headless monsters and the fabled Sciapod, who lay on his back under the shade of his one great foot. Here Alexander the Great was supposed to have locked the savage races of the earth behind iron gates. Occasionally, however, they broke out and smashed China or ravaged Europe. Only some of the dangers were imaginary.

Though the steppe was lush with grazing, it had long been as divisive as a desert, keeping the civilisations at either end apart. In the thirteenth century, all that changed. First, the peoples beyond the steppe, from Christendom to Japan, were united in horror of the most devastating conquerors this bleak land had yet bred; then they were linked together by a peace which those same conquerors imposed. For a hundred years the steppe became a highway of rapid communication, joining the great civilisations and helping transfers of culture across the breadth of two continents.

Mongolian herdsmen. Like their thirteenth-century ancestors, today's Mongols are still born to the saddle.

THE MONGOL ONSLAUGHT

Genghis Khan.

BELOW *The Mongols storming and capturing Baghdad. When it fell, the caliph, the last heir of Muhammad, was trampled to death.*

A people of unprecedented destructive and creative power made this opportunity, launched the conquests, opened up the road, forged the links. The Mongols' technological prowess made their horse-borne armies unbeatable for mobility and firepower. They lived on a diet of meat, milk and blood from their horse herds, and so had no need of cumbersome baggage trains or supply lines; their use of saddle, harness and stirrup left the mounted archers' hands free to use the lethal double-curved bow to full effect. They could outride any opponent, changing horses in the thick of the battle; a favourite tactic was a mock retreat, firing backwards on the enemy while leading them on into an ambush. The territory they won stretched from the Pacific in the east to the Danube in the west – the largest continuous land empire the world has ever known. This extraordinary achievement would have been unthinkable without a single strategic genius, a man who gave himself the name of 'World-Ruler': Genghis Khan.

Today, that name inspires extremes of odium and adulation. In the west, it evokes images of tyranny and ruin. In Mongolia, equally inappropriately, Genghis Khan is revered as the culture-hero of modern nationalism and the symbol of Mongolian identity. In his own day, he was cast as a universal conqueror in the tradition of Alexander; a divinely elected scourge of civilisations; a quasi-natural force, as withering as a steppeland wind; a great peacemaker and lawgiver.

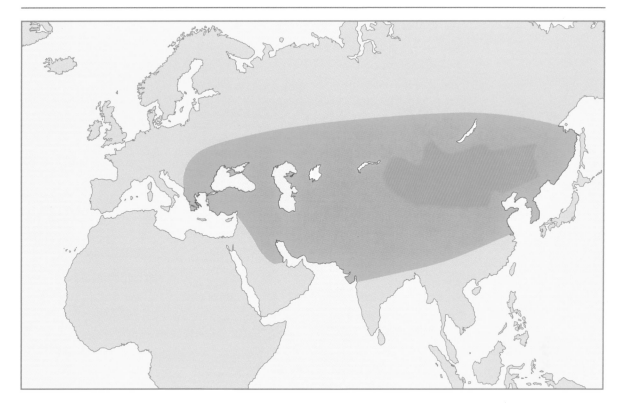

Born in 1162, by the time of his death sixty-five years later Genghis Khan had united the steppeland in a single empire twice the breadth of the modern United States. By 1241, Mongol armies had reached the Elbe and the Adriatic. In 1256, Mongols exterminated the previously unassailable mountain fastnesses of fanatical Islamic terrorists in Persia; in 1258, when Baghdad fell, the last heir of Muhammad was trampled to death. In 1276, Genghis's successors attained the most ambitious objective their illustrious forebear had set himself: the conquest of China.

Genghis Khan's charisma is illustrated by his effect on Ch'ang Chun, a Chinese wise man – a magician, some said – summoned to his presence in 1219. 'Long years in the caverns of the rocks' had brought the sage a reputation for holiness; yet at the age of seventy-one he declared himself 'ready at the first call of the Dragon Court' to undertake the three-year journey from China to an encounter with the khan in what is now Afghanistan, at the foot of the Hindu Kush mountains. With twenty Mongol guards and nineteen disciples, he travelled through some of the most inhospitable country in the world – across the Gobi desert, through 'mountains of huge cold' and into a wasteland believed to be haunted by demons.

The tone of the meeting at the journey's end, however, was highly amicable. While the peaceable, scholarly Ch'ang Chun might have felt some discomfort in the presence of a conqueror whose especial pleasures reputedly included 'to shed my enemies' blood and wring tears from their womenfolk', lines composed by one of the sage's disciples in honour of the khan suggest that the attractions of

The Mongol empire. In the thirteenth century it became the largest continuous land empire the world has ever known, twice the size of the United States and stretching from eastern Europe to the Pacific. The shaded area to the east represents Mongolia today.

the Mongol life were deeply felt: 'Heaven is weary of the inordinate luxury of China. I remain in the wild region of the north. I return to simplicity and seek moderation once more . . . I have the same rags and the same food as cowherds and grooms, and I treat the soldiers as my brothers.'

Discipline, loyalty, austerity, solidarity: as a propaganda image for the khan it was successful; as a formula for victory, it was invincible. Mongol conquests reached further and lasted longer than those of any earlier nomad empire because Genghis Khan brought a previously unknown political unity to the steppeland world. 'My supreme purpose', he proclaimed, 'is to unite all my people. My greatest joy – to put my enemy beneath my knee.' He called himself 'lord of all who live in felt tents', and this was more than self-glorification: the confederation of tribes he put together really did represent a combined effort of the steppe-dwellers against the civilisations that surrounded them. This communal enterprise was animated by a simple ideology, imposed in battle and enforced by terror: the God-given right of the Mongols to conquer the world: 'As there is one sole sun in the sky, so there shall be one sole sovereign on earth.'

Wherever Mongol armies went, their reputation preceded them. Armenian sources warned westerners of the approach of 'precursors of Antichrist . . . of hideous aspect and without pity in their bowels . . . who rush with joy to carnage as if to a wedding-feast or orgy'. They looked like monkeys, it was said, barked like dogs, ate raw flesh, drank their horses' urine, knew no laws and showed no mercy. Rumours piled up in Germany, France, Burgundy – even Spain, where Mongols had never been heard of before but now became the bogeys of haunted imaginations. According to Pope Alexander IV, their nature was inhuman and their origin demonic, 'erupting from the secret confines of hell'.

The psychology of terror continues to work only if threats are backed up by bloodshed, and the Mongols lived up to their billing. Mongol sieges routinely culminated in massacres: at the fall of Herat in Afghanistan the invaders wiped out the entire population of the city. When the Mongols captured Beijing, the streets were 'greasy with the fat of corpses'. Some part at least of the exaggeration in chroniclers' assessments of the consequences of these excesses can surely be put down to the effects of shock. One horrified commentator in Persia wrote: 'If from now to the Day of Judgement nothing hindered the natural increase of the population, it could never reach one tenth of its density before the Mongol conquest.'

Yet there was more to the Mongols than a talent to destroy. As his career progressed, Genghis Khan became a visionary lawgiver, a patron of letters, an architect of enduring empires – and an astute treasurer: when one of his generals proposed the extermination of 10 million Chinese subjects, the khan decided instead to let them live and have a plan drawn up to extract 500,000 ounces of silver, 80,000 pieces of silk and 400,000 sacks of grain from them in tax. And his summons to Ch'ang Chun declares his willingness to pick brains as well as bones and purses:

In the space of seven years I have succeeded in accomplishing a great work – uniting the whole world in one empire. I have not myself distinguished qualities. But my calling is high, the obligations incumbent on me are also heavy; and I fear that in my ruling there may be something wanting. To cross a river we make boats and rudders. Likewise we invite sage men and choose assistants for keeping the empire in good order.

His end, too, was not what one might expect from the popular account of his life: the bloodthirsty conqueror and subjugator of peoples died in a hunting accident.

Genghis Khan was not alone among his people in his eagerness to tap into the expertise of others. The Mongols may have won their empire through a superior style of battle and an indomitable will to conquer, but their success in consolidating it owed a great deal to their adaptability and inclusiveness, a readiness to learn by example and incorporate what their newly subject neighbours had to teach. At the same time they held proudly to the core of their unique way of life, which is still recognisable among the tents and herds of today's steppeland nomads. At court and at pasture, on the roads and at the way-stations, when the Mongol terror subsided the deeper secrets of Mongol success could be discovered.

The economy of the Mongol empire, as well as its military success, was based on the horse and the camel.

THE MONGOL PEACE

An empire so large and so rapidly acquired as that of Genghis Khan generated an urgent need for competent administrators. For bureaucrats the khan turned at first to Uighur men of letters, for of all the steppeland peoples of the region the Uighurs had the longest acquaintance with literacy. They supplied his secretaries, his propagandists, his court historians, the scribes of his laws and the transcribers of the Mongols' language. As the empire grew, they were supplemented with a cosmopolitan array of court literati: Chinese, Tibetans and a variety of Muslims and Christians from central Asia. Around this increasingly sophisticated imperial centre, the network of roads and communications established by the rapacious Mongol armies stabilised into a great system of travel and trade. To those who looked back in the next generation it seemed a golden age: 'Under the reign of Genghis Khan, all the country between Iran and the land of the Turks enjoyed such peace that a man might have journeyed from the land of sunrise to the land of sunset with a golden platter on his head without suffering the least violence from anyone.'

Once they had learned the benefits of civilisation which the roads could bring, the Mongols became highway police. They patrolled a system of communications which formed the axis of the Old World, around which its great states and centres of culture were arrayed. Independent travellers from Europe to China, such as missionaries, ambassadors and merchants' messengers, could travel under Mongol protection along a sparsely inhabited northern route – safely, and at impressive speed: on the straight steppeland highway, teams of Mongol horses took one Italian envoy 3,000 miles in 106 days in 1246.

Travel on this route was by stages between yambs – military way-stations at approximately two-day intervals. A European visitor in the 1250s was clearly impressed by the system:

> When one of the great Khan's messengers sets out along any of these roads, he has only to go 25 miles and there he finds a posting station which in their language is called a yamb. As they draw near they sound a horn so that horses may be got ready for them. They tighten their belts and swathe their heads and off they go with all the speed they can muster. Thus in extreme urgency they can carry messages of state 300 miles in a day. At each of these stations there is appointed a clerk who notes the arrival and departure of each courier . . . and in these large and handsome buildings travellers will find fine beds, and other necessary articles in rich silk . . . where they are provided with everything they can want.

Not all travel made use of the new 'express' routes. Merchant caravans continued to wend along their laborious traditional roads to the south of the

OPPOSITE *A messenger mounts his horse in a painting of the thirteenth century. The Mongol khans established a system of posting stations with relays of fresh horses by means of which urgent messages could be carried 300 miles in a day.*

steppes, where the inertia of vested interests kept them. Because the route was so long, traders had to concentrate on small quantities of high-value goods, keeping to routes between the mountain ranges to the north of the Tibetan plateau, where there were settlements and oases at which supplies could be renewed. The discomforts were daunting: extremes of temperature, long periods of hunger and thirst, and stretches where the only fuel, if any, was horse dung. The Mongol peace eased the passage; robbers, official extortion, bureaucratic delays, tough terrain and natural obstacles delayed it. A Venetian party setting out in 1271 was 'hard put to it to complete the journey in three and a half years, because of snow and rain and flooded rivers and violent storms in the countries through which they had to pass, and because they could not ride so well in winter as in summer'.

A guide for China-bound Italian merchants – written in the next century, but capturing the conditions which prevailed throughout the period – included some handy tips. 'You must let your beard grow long and not shave.' At Tana on the Sea of Azov, the traveller should furnish himself with a good guide, regardless of expense. 'And if the merchant likes to take a woman with him from Tana, he can do so.' On departure from Tana, only twenty-five days' supplies of flour and salt fish were needed: 'Other things you will find in sufficiency and especially meat.' It was important to be accompanied by a close relative; otherwise, in the unlikely event of the merchant dying on a road said to be 'safe by day and night', his property would be forfeit.

Silver was the currency of the road, but on arrival had to be exchanged with the Chinese authorities for paper money. 'This is of yellow paper and stamped with the seal of the lord . . . and with this [the merchant] may readily buy all that he desires.' Passage was cheap, carriage costly. The costs of the journey out could be reckoned at only one-eightieth of the value of silver cash carried; but the budget for the return trip, to include all expenses and the costs of servants, would be almost as much per pack animal as the entire outward trip together.

The Italian guide describes the route in detail in terms of days' journeys between towns, each stage taken under the protection of Mongol police. Rates of exchange are specified at each stop. Suitable conveyances are recommended for each phase of the expedition: ox-cart or horse-drawn wagon to Astrakhan on the Caspian Sea, depending on how fast you want to go and how much you want to pay; camel-train or pack-mule thereafter until you reach the river system of China. Though horses were favoured for personal travel, commercial transport relied on camels: they carried 400–500 pounds in weight each, could keep going with less regular feeds than horses, and had hooves which did not sink into the sand of the central Asian wilderness. Nor was desert the most daunting terrain to be faced: the greatest obstacle on the route was the Altai mountains. 'Before the days of the Mongols,' explained the Bishop of Beijing in 1341, 'nobody believed that the earth was habitable

beyond these . . . but the Mongols by God's permission, and with wonderful exertion, did cross them, and . . . so did I.'

On the edge of the Takla Makan desert, between the Tien Shan and Kinlun Shan ranges, caravans paused for a week's refreshment and stocked up with the necessary provisions for the next month, during which there would be no access to further supplies. The normal rule for caravans was the bigger, the safer; but not much more than fifty men at a time, with their beasts, could hope to be sustained by the modest water-sources they could expect to find over the next thirty days. The worst danger was getting lost – 'lured from the path by demon-spirits'; sandstorms were believed to be a demon's device to confuse men and lead them astray. The Mongols recommended that travellers ward them off by smearing their horses' necks with blood.

> Even by daylight men hear these spirit voices and often you fancy you
> are listening to the strains of many instruments, especially drums and
> the clash of arms. For this reason bands of travellers make a point of
> keeping very close together. Before they go to sleep they set up a sign
> pointing in the direction in which they have to travel. And round the
> necks of all their beasts they fasten little bells, so that by listening to
> the sound they may prevent them straying off the path.

In paintings of the Mongol period, among scenes of steppeland life, the desert described by travellers comes to life. The chatter and beat of demon drummers and dancers animate the pictures; practitioners of horse-sacrifice whirl the bloody limbs of dismembered steeds around in savage ecstasy, while demons steal living mounts or snatch the bones of sacrificial victims as weapons.

Demons of the kind reported by travellers in the Takla Makan desert. The Mongols recommended warding them off by smearing the horses' necks with blood.

The architecture of the Mongol capital reflected the nomadic origins of its rulers.

The Mongol roads, stretching across and around the steppe, bore people, culture, information and skills from one end of Eurasia to another. In 1253 they brought a visitor from the far west of Europe who was to describe in vivid detail life at the court of the khans: William of Rubruck, a friar seeking allies for Christendom, converts for God and military intelligence for the king of France. 'We found the Mongols,' he wrote, 'and I felt at once as if I were entering another world.' Setting out across the Mongol empire by wagon in May, by November he was already 'famished, thirsty, frozen and exhausted'. A month later, he was high in the dreaded Altai mountains, where he chanted the creed 'among awesome crags, to put the demons to flight'. At last, on Palm Sunday 1254, he entered the Mongol capital, Karakorum. He was 200 miles west of Ulan Bator, the modern capital of Mongolia. He recalled: 'It is written of the wise man in Ecclesiasticus: "He shall try good and evil in all things." This I have fulfilled, but would that it were as a wise man and not as a fool.'

William recognised in Karakorum a type of urban growth known to him, for example, from St Denis. Just as Abbot Suger's abbey (see above, p. 46) had become a magnet for settlement, so the Mongol court attracted people to its otherwise ill-favoured location.

Of the city of Karakorum you must know that exclusive of the palace of the khan it is not as big as the village of St Denis, and the monastery of St Denis is ten times larger than the palace. There are two districts there: the Muslim quarter where the markets are, and many merchants flock . . . The other district is of the Chinese who are all craftsmen. Apart from these districts there are the large palaces of the court scribes. There are twelve pagan temples belonging to the different nations, two mosques in which the law of Muhammad is proclaimed, and one church for the Christians at the far end of the town. The town is surrounded by a mud wall and has four gates. At the east gate are sold grains, at the west sheep and goats, at the south oxen and the north horses.

Then, the city still looked little more permanent than a camp, though the mud walls enclosed the glitter of booty looted from half a dozen empires. Today it is a ruin.

William always insisted that he was a simple missionary; but he was treated as an ambassador and had the powers of observation of a spy. He realised that the seasonal migrations of Mongol life had a scientific basis and were calculated for military efficiency. 'Every commander,' he noticed, 'according to whether he has a greater or smaller number of men under him, is familiar with the limits of his pasture lands and where he ought to graze in summer and winter, in spring and autumn.' Little useful intelligence escaped William. But he also had a characteristic friar's interest in the culture of his intended converts, and set down detailed descriptions of how the Mongols lived that

Genghis Khan in his tent, a stylised version of the Mongol ger, in a Persian miniature of the thirteenth century.

were unsurpassed for centuries. 'I should have drawn everything for you,' William assured his readers, 'had I known how to draw'; but he managed to wield an accurate pen despite this deficiency.

A Mongol ger, or tent-dwelling, was laid out then on much the same lines as it is now. The construction was based on a hoop of interlaced branches, 'and its supports are made of branches, converging at the top around a smaller hoop, from which projects a neck like a chimney'. The covering was of white felt, smeared with chalk and ground bones, or blackened, 'and they decorate the felt around the neck at the top with various fine designs'. Patchwork over the entrance was adorned with birds, animals, trees and vines.

These dwellings are constructed of such size as to be on occasions thirty feet across. I myself once measured a breadth of twenty feet between the wheel-tracks of a wagon, and when the dwelling was on the wagon it projected beyond the wheels by at least five feet on either side. I counted twenty-two oxen to one wagon, hauling along a dwelling . . . The wagon's axle was as large as a ship's mast, and one man stood at the entrance to the dwelling on top of the wagon, driving the oxen . . . When they unload their dwelling houses, they always turn the doorway towards the south and . . . draw up the wagons with the chests half a stone's throw away from the dwelling on either side, so that the dwelling stands between two rows of wagons as if they were two walls.

The domestic arrangements were as they are today. There was one tent for each of the wives who belonged to the master of the household. The master faced the entrance from his couch at the northern end. The women sat to the master's left, on the east side, the men to his right: the opposite way round to that dictated by Chinese rules of precedence. The *onghodd* – the felt images in which the ancestral spirits reside – were arrayed around the walls: one each over the heads of master and mistress with a guardian image between them; others, hung respectively with a cow's udder and a mare's, on the women's and men's sides. The household would gather for drinking, preceded by offerings to the spirits, in the tent of the chosen wife of the night.

Mongka Khan (seated top right) with his wives and sons.

The palace at Karakorum had the same routines but better decor. William described the fountain, where a trumpeting angel topped a silver tree, entwined by a gilded serpent and guarded by silver lions; mare's milk bubbled from the maws of these beasts, while from the branches of the tree poured several liquors – made from rice or milk or honey – that were served at the khan's drinking bouts. (The Parisian goldsmith who built this contraption was still living in the Mongol capital, witness to the trans-Eurasian transfer of styles and cultures.)

William related detailed conversations with a new ruler in Genghis Khan's line. Mongka Khan was frequently drunk and habitually self-righteous, but his eager talk disclosed some of the qualities that made the Mongols of his era great: tolerance and flexibility, combined with a profound reverence for tradition. An interview began with a choice of drinks – wine, rice wine, fermented mare's milk or mead – which tended to set the tone for what followed. At his first audience with Mongka – short, flat-nosed and clad in 'a speckled and shiny fur like a seal' – William begged permission to reside at court, although, he said, 'we have no gold or silver or precious stones we can offer you, only our own persons, which we are offering with a view to serving God and praying to God for you'. He understood part of the translation of the ruler's reply: 'We have no need of gold or silver from you'; but 'beyond this I was unable to grasp a single complete sentence, which brought it home to me that [my interpreter] was drunk. And Mongka Khan too struck me as tipsy.'

Even when sober, Mongka was the kind of interviewee journalists dread: determined always to be in the right, willing to exploit his claim to deference or to abuse the courtesy of his interlocutor in order to win every argument. Whatever William said in explanation or defence of Christianity the khan re-expressed to suit his own purposes; whatever could not be adapted he dismissed, substituting a formula of his own choosing. William was convinced that he could have made converts if only he had found a good interpreter or – what might have been easier – the grace to work miracles like Moses. Yet despite his frustration, he recorded with candour the khan's sophisticated philosophy of religion, expressed with the sort of simile which seems to have been characteristic of Mongka's rhetoric. The khan compared religions to the five fingers of his hand. 'We Mongols', he said, 'believe that there is but one God in whom we live and in whom we die, and towards him we have an upright heart.' Spreading his hand, he added: 'But just as God has given different digits to the palm, so he has given different religions to men.'

The malleability of Mongol religion made it both attractive and resistant to missionaries from potentially universal faiths. Mongol courts dallied with Christianity, Buddhism and Islam, even with ancient Zoroastrianism in its Persian homeland; yet Mongols remained faithful to their own god, Tengri, usually translated as 'Heaven'. Traditional shamanism persisted, under the authority of a priestly elite who invoked the spirits of ancestors in their ritual trances.

Accommodating other faiths and traditions but firmly attached to their own, the Mongols were well suited to their position at the heart of an expanding empire. Inexorably, that expansion took them ever further eastwards: to China.

THE DECADENCE OF XANADU

The Mongols' traditional cavalry tactics were of no use in taking on China. To advance into this land, scored by paddy-fields and rivers, they had to master new techniques and technologies: amassing huge infantry forces; mobilising complex logistical support; floating riverborne navies; organising siege trains; and exploiting conquered lands to raise the funds to pay for the campaign through taxation. Adept as ever at harnessing foreign knowledge to their purposes, they hired Arab artillerymen, who operated a new kind of siege engine capable of flinging a 300-pound stone. A thousand engineers accompanied the Mongol armies. By the time China fell to the invaders, the Mongols had turned themselves into masters of siege warfare.

The Mongols brought the same gift for adaptation to the job of ruling China. Here the khans could adopt the official rites of imperial piety, ancestor worship and Confucian ethics without abandoning their own traditions. They interpreted the Chinese concept of the 'mandate of heaven' as an echo of their own ideology of command conferred by the enveloping sky. They showed reverence, or at least tolerance, for religions established among the Chinese – Buddhism, Taoism, Islam and Christianity – while reserving a privileged level of patronage for the sceptical majority of the scholar class. This kind of flexibility came naturally to the Mongol court.

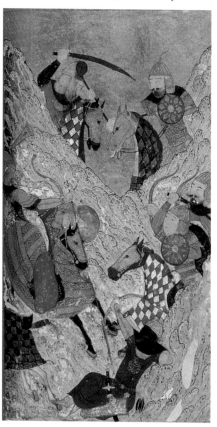

Genghis Khan and his warriors in battle, from a fifteenth-century illuminated manuscript.

The Mongols intended not to replace imperial rule in China but to renew it. At first, their choice of ministers of all races looked like a scheme to repress the Chinese elite. The Chinese, it was reported, hated the government of the Great Khan, because he set over them steppelanders, most of whom were Muslims, and they could not endure it, since it made them feel they were no more than slaves. Moreover, the Great Khan had no title to rule the land of China, having acquired it by force. Gradually, however, the newcomers took on the hues of the society they ruled. History offers plenty of examples of conquerors who run out of steam, and nomad warriors who are seduced by the soft life of the peoples they conquer; the Mongols were tamed by their own success.

The century that opened under the doughty Genghis Khan drew towards a close under the gouty Kublai Khan. Genghis got about on a pony's back and fought under the shadow of a yak's-tail banner; his grandson Kublai got fat beneath the shade of a parasol and needed four elephants to transport him. And whereas a simple tent was good enough to house his ancestors, Kublai Khan had built a 'huge palace of marble and other ornamental stones' – and alongside it the 'stately pleasure-dome' of Shantung, evoked in all its splendour as Xanadu by Samuel Taylor Coleridge's poem 'Kubla Khan' 500 years later:

Mongol troops capture a town. Originally mounted archers, they soon acquired other military technologies including boat-bridges and siege engines.

In Xanadu did Kubla Khan
A stately pleasure-dome decree
Where Alph the sacred river ran
Through caverns measureless to man
Down to a sunless sea.
So twice five miles of fertile ground
With walls and towers were girdled round
And there were gardens bright with sinuous rills
Where blossomed many an incense-bearing tree;
And here were forests ancient as the hills,
Enfolding sunny spots of greenery.

MARCO POLO

Marco Polo was, by his own account, born in 1254 into a Venetian merchant family. At the time of his birth his father and uncle were travelling on business in China, where they had been received at the court of Kublai Khan. There the Great Khan commissioned them as envoys to the pope to ask that he send to China 100 Europeans skilled in the arts and sciences – a mission they unsuccessfully tried to complete in 1269. In 1271 they left Venice to return to the court of Kublai Khan, this time taking with them the young Marco.

Travelling through Mosul, Baghdad, Khourasan, Khasgar, the Gobi desert, Tangut and Shangtu, the party finally arrived in China in 1275. Kublai Khan was impressed by the young Marco and sent him as envoy to many places, including Yunnan in northern Burma, Karakorum and southern India. For three years he served as governor of Yang Chow.

After many years of service, the Polos were eventually ready to return to their own country. Though the khan was initially unwilling to let them leave his court, they finally arrived back in Venice in 1295, bringing with them great wealth and unprecedented knowledge of the east.

In 1298 Marco Polo was taken prisoner during the sea-battle of Curzola, where the Venetians were defeated by the Genoese. He was held captive in Genoa for a year, and it was during this time that he is said to have written, in collaboration with his cellmate, a celebrated writer, his famous account of

Headless monsters and the Sciapod, said to inhabit the steppe.

his travels, which he called Divisament dou Monde – a work to dazzle the peoples of Europe with tales of the unknown. Readers flocked to him and, at a time when all books had to be copied by hand, Marco Polo's travels became the best-seller of the age. So fabulous-seeming was the world he described that, though widely read in his lifetime, it was frequently dismissed as fantasy. It is nowadays more commonly regarded as a mixture of fact and fictional embellishments.

Certainly, unadorned truth was never part of Marco's literary agenda. He collected wonder-stories designed to make the reader feel the delicious thrill of suspended belief or the frisson of moral superiority. Hence the relish with which he described Tibetan sexual hospitality and ritual cannibalism, the medicinal use of serpents' gall, social nudity, tailed men ('not at all hairy'), dog-headed men, unicorns and twin islands respectively of men and women who consorted periodically in order to breed.

Among the multitude of wonders he reported on was the Chinese use of paper money: 'All his [the emperor's] subjects received it [paper money] without hesitation because, wherever their business may call them, they can dispose of it again in the purchase of merchandise they require.' He is also credited with bringing to Europe the recipe for ice-cream, which certainly existed in the China of his day. He died in Venice in 1324.

The description on which Coleridge drew for his depiction of Kublai's extravaganza, and which over the centuries made Xanadu the epitome of the dream-palace, was the work of that problematical Venetian traveller of the thirteenth century, Marco Polo. Doubts have been cast on the authenticity of his travels in China, but there is nothing inherently improbable in them: he followed the standard intercontinental itineraries of his time. When it came to describing Kublai's life and environment at Shantung, his account is plausible in its detail.

The Khan has four consorts, all lawful wives. Each holds her own court with no less than 3,000 ladies in waiting and 7,000 other attendants.

By his wives he has twenty-two male children; by his mistresses he has a further twenty-five sons.

The Khan also has many concubines. They are divided into groups of six who serve him for three days and three nights at a time in his chamber and his bed, and he uses them for his pleasure.

But when he wishes to lie with his wife, he goes to his wife's chamber.

The halls and chambers of the palace were all gilded. Sixteen miles of game-filled parkland enclosed a pavilion

built entirely of canes but with the interior all gilt and decorated with beasts and birds of very skilful workmanship. It is reared on gilt and varnished pillars, on each of which stands a dragon, entwining the pillar with his tail and supporting the roof on his outstretched limbs. The roof is also made of canes, so well varnished that it is quite waterproof . . . And the Great Khan has had it so designed that it can be moved whenever he fancies; for it is held in place by more than two hundred cords of silk.

Marco Polo with his father and his uncle and their party, in an illustration from the fourteenth-century Catalan Atlas.

At Shantung there was abundant evidence of the khan's abiding Mongol taste: in the white mares grazing the grounds, whose milk was reserved for his exclusive use; in the portability of the parkland pavilion; in the offerings of mares' milk with which he honoured his ancestral gods; in the unvarying diet of meat served at his banquets; in the freedom with which he chose upper servants from outside the traditional Confucian elite – indeed, from outside China; and in the religious mix of his court. His reliance on women for political advice, too, owed more to steppeland tradition than to that of China: he deferred to his notoriously formidable mother, Sorghatan, and formed what seems to have been a policy-making partnership with his senior wife, Chabi.

Kublai was also, emphatically, a Chinese emperor. He performed the due rites dressed in the Chinese manner, learned the language, patronised the arts, protected the traditions and promoted the interests of his Chinese subjects. Today the imprint of his passage through Chinese history is most marked in modern-day Beijing, where Kublai created his capital. He wrenched the centre of gravity of government northwards and inland from the Yellow River valley towards his inherited power-base in Mongolia, establishing it in the dusty, windy city, difficult to provision, which has remained the capital, with interruptions, ever since. This was a construction project on a vast scale. Three million labourers dug the new city's Grand Canal, linking it to the sea; at its heart was Kublai's imperial palace, its hall alone capable of holding 6,000 visitors. Visiting merchants were serviced by 20,000 prostitutes. No building of Kublai's day survives, but the rectangular shape of the old town is as his immigrant Muslim architects designed it. The layout of the streets, in geometrical regularity, with avenues wide enough for nine horsemen abreast, reflects his instructions. The rampart of rammed earth has disappeared but the subway follows its course, marked for all to see by the ring of fifteen-storey apartment blocks above it. The former imperial palace is still where Kublai put it, though the structures he erected are long gone and the park is bereft of the tents with which he dotted it in nostalgia for the Mongols' nomadic past and fidelity to the tradition of conquest.

What Kublai wanted from China was not just culture, but cash for more campaigns. There was certainly plenty of it – especially when judged by the modest standards Marco Polo brought from his remote and peripheral homeland. In the eyes of a Christian westerner, not only China but Asia generally seemed to command dauntingly vast populations of humans and horses, and the resources to support them. In China, he noted, 'no land is left idle that might be cultivated' under rice or millet, crops which were converted into efficient food in the form of noodles, or simply boiled, without being turned into bread.

Master of this populous and prosperous land, Kublai applied its riches to the old Mongol ambition of universal conquest. It was to be a disillusioning experience.

MONGOLS AND MAMLUKS

Kublai Khan's forces registered only fleeting success. Slowed by resistance and by the vastness of the world, after 1277 Mongol conquests gradually reached their limits on all fronts. In Vietnam, the invaders levied tribute at a rate insufficient to reimburse the cost of the campaigns. In Java, one native prince was made to replace another, with no permanent gains for Kublai. Java was protected by the monsoon, Japan by the 'divine typhoons' which made lee shores a summer death-trap. Western Europe remained safe because of its remoteness and lack of appeal. In 1296 a Mongol army attempted an invasion of India and clogged the cities with refugees, but was turned back with many losses. In Africa, meanwhile, the Mongols were kept out by the Mamluk slaves selected to be soldiers in the service of an Egyptian sultan.

On 3 June 1260 'the sun had just risen', reported the Egyptian chronicler Al-Maqrizi:

> On all sides the wailings of the peasants of the villages could be heard
> and the unceasing sound of the drums of the sultan and the amirs. The
> Mongols mounted. The battle was joined. One wing of the sultan's
> army was routed and broken but at that moment the sultan flung his

Mamluk soldiers. Originally slaves trained for war, the Mamluks produced a dynasty that ruled Egypt for over 200 years.

83

The camel market, Cairo, no doubt much as in Baybars' time, when the city flourished and not only camels but humans changed hands.

helmet from his head and cried, 'Oh, Islam!' God helped him. The Mongol chief was killed in the encounter. God made the rest of their men run before the Muslims, who followed them, sword in hand, massacred them in great number and took prisoners in droves.

The hero of the battle was Baybars the Great – the 'panther of Islam'. Baybars had been a slave himself, acquired by traders as a boy, when he was probably fleeing for his life from Mongol marauders. Bought for a sultan's household at the age of fourteen, he rose to command the royal bodyguard. Success in battle gave him a reputation; military victories gave him a following; ruthlessness cleared his path to the throne. Court propagandists found his ascent easy to justify: 'Fortune made him king,' wrote one. 'Force', another explained, 'was a virtue in a ruler responsible for the wellbeing of Islam.' Above all, Baybars was justified by success, which his followers represented as evidence of divine election revealed to one of his followers in a prophetic dream: '. . . as if an unseen speaker had said, "This commander will break the Mongols." '

At first the Mongols were unimpressed by Baybars. 'When our khan left the East,' they warned in an official letter,

> he conquered the whole world; anyone who disobeyed him was killed. Therefore, whether you ascend to the sky or come down to earth you cannot escape him . . . You are a slave who was sold in a market-place, so how can you dispute the authority of the kings of the earth?

Baybars deflected these threats by preparing and training an invincible Mamluk army. Al-Maqrizi explained the routine of a cadet in the new military school under the severe discipline imposed by eunuch overseers:

> He began by acquiring knowledge of the Quran. When he approached adulthood, he learned the profession of arms, that is to say how to manage the bow, lance and other weapons. During the hours devoted to training for war, neither soldier nor scholar was allowed to speak to the pupils or even to approach them.

After building his academy, Baybars inspected it daily. He was credited with inspiring so much enthusiasm 'that there was hardly a Mamluk who did not devote himself wholeheartedly to improving his proficiency'. His was a hands-on empire: of personal rule, of energy and efficiency. His boast was that he could play polo in Cairo and Damascus in a single week, or rise naked from his bath to answer a dispatch and get his reply from one city to the other in four days. Yet while his military prowess was readily accepted as sufficient justification for his possession of power, it could not confer true legitimacy. In pursuit of this elusive ingredient of kingship, Baybars claimed a role as defender of Islam, against Christians as well as against the pagan Mongols. He designed himself a mosque outside the walls of Cairo; today it stands, battered, abused, adapted and partly restored, in a dusty suburb, away from the other great monumental buildings – but still striking an imperial pose. The stone columns represent the plunder of ancient buildings from all over Egypt; the timbers and marble were brought from Jaffa, seized from a crusader garrison in 1268.

For two and a half centuries after Baybars' famous victory, until they were conquered by the Ottoman Turks, Mamluk sultans continued to rule Egypt, adorning Cairo with mosques, hospitals and schools in witness of their piety, turning the city into the cultural and intellectual centre of the Islamic world of which they claimed to be the hub. Yet the image of Baybars that lives on in tradition is not a religious but a martial one, descended from his own propaganda: 'the lion who crushes the breath out of demons' and proclaimed 'the day of hardships and killing'. Today, his legacy to Egypt is celebrated in an epic song that takes a week to sing.

The manner of Baybars' death shows that although he kept Mongol armies at bay he was not immune from their cultural influence: he died in 1277 after a surfeit of mares' milk.

THE WEALTH OF VENICE

Armies are agents not just of slaughter but of change: along with their weapons they carry cultural influences. Goods, crafts and ideas followed the routes Mongol armies explored and established, with transforming effects on the peoples and places they reached.

The European end of the Mongol road, where trade routes of east and west met, was Marco Polo's starting place: Venice. This handful of salty, marshy islands, sinking into their lagoon, is one of the great miracles of civilisation. With the help of great oak piles grounded in shifting sand, the isles precariously support a fabulous city of stone, where no reasonable person would ever think of putting one.

The earliest buildings which survive in the Venetian archipelago imitate those of Byzantium – the old Roman metropolis of the eastern Mediterranean, later called Constantinople, now Istanbul. In politics and commerce, Venice's face was turned eastward, towards and across the sea. Geographically, however, the city was well placed for some of the natural trade routes across western Europe: the river Po and the passes across the Alps. Venice therefore adopted the role which would mark its history for the best part of a thousand years: that of a clearing-house for trade between western Europe and the eastern Mediterranean. In consequence, though the city never lost its exotic looks, it became a meeting place of cultural influences from both directions and fused them in a distinctive civilisation.

The citizens' medieval vocation for trade was a direct consequence of their lack of other means to wealth. Venetians' consciousness of their dependence on commerce was symbolised in the annual ceremony of marrying the city to the sea, which still takes place every year on the Sunday after Ascension Day. The chief magistrate of the republic, the doge, was borne in procession among the islands to cast a gold ring into the waters, as if appeasing an old pagan sea-god. Painted in the eighteenth century by Canaletto or Carlevaris, the ceremony appears as a calm assertion of the indestructibility of Venice's power. Its origins, however, lie in a constant anxiety to secure the favour of the restless waters with which Venice was surrounded, and which always threatened to overwhelm it. On the whole, Venice's bargain with the sea worked. The Adriatic bore its trade and swallowed up its enemies – as the Red Sea swallowed Pharaoh, so Venetians liked to think – and the city never fell to seaborne attack.

The sea, too, brought much of Venice's wealth. The route between Venice and Alexandria carried the most valuable traffic in medieval Europe: pepper imports, on the final stage of their journey from the far east. Gradually Venice became rich enough to assert ambitions of its own. Formerly the client of Byzantium, in 1204 it became one of the city's conquerors. A crusader army, carried by Venetian ships, hoisted the doge to the top of the city walls, though it seems unlikely he was able to enjoy the view: he was reputedly ninety years old and blind. Byzantium's riches were divided among the victors. 'One quarter and one half of one quarter' fell to Venice's share.

Venice became an imperial capital, with colonial territories scattered around the eastern Mediterranean. The spoils of Byzantium decorated the city's cathedral and its public spaces. Unlike Florence or Rome, Venice could not claim to have been founded in ancient times by classical heroes; but the loot it plundered gave it the ornaments of antiquity. The great bronze horses above the cathedral doors stamp and snort in victory. Below, a Hercules looted from Byzantium carries off, in his turn, a prize of his labours: the Erymanthaean boar. On the south side Roman emperors, carved in porphyry, guard the treasury, while pillars wrought by a Syrian hand 1,500 years ago lead into the baptistery. To wealth from trade in exotic products Venice could now add the profits of empire, exploiting conquered territories to produce more of the rare supplies demanded by its customers in western and northern Europe: sugar, sweet wines, olive oil and specialist dyes.

Through Venice, the trade of the east was funnelled into the west. Intellectual traffic, however, tended to diffuse from Paris, with its great university, the second oldest in Europe. Here, since the early twelfth century, scholars had received and pondered traditions of thought transmitted from antiquity – especially the thought of Aristotle, the Greek philosopher of the fourth century BC whose writings had survived in the west and whose ideas still dominate the way in which we try to tell truth from falsehood. The end products of this study were marvellously comprehensive schemes of knowledge and faith elaborated by the encyclopaedists of the thirteenth century. Though controlled by faith, theirs was a genuinely scientific way of understanding the world, reflected in a new realism in art and devotion, and supported by a developing tradition of experiment. The cosmos was measurable – portrayed by a French artist between the dividers of Christ the geometer.

Roger Bacon, an English professor who worked in Paris in the 1240s, insisted that scientific observations could help to validate holy writ and that medical experiments could both increase knowledge and save life. He cited the lenses with which the Greek mathematician Archimedes reputedly kindled fire to destroy a Roman fleet in the third century BC, and argued that the power of science could be used over infidels not only to cow but also to convert them. Bacon was, however, an idiosyncratic character, regarded askance by many of his contemporaries who were suspicious of his study of pagan and Muslim books, and of his enthusiasm for consulting ordinary people beyond the confines of church and academy. Like many of the scientists he befriended in his day, he admired practical expertise – of the peasant on grains, of the herdsman on livestock, of the wise woman on herbs. His work on optics, however, was even more revolutionary in its implications, reflecting the determination of the age to see the world afresh. Vision, Bacon said, 'is the channel of experimental knowledge; therefore the sense of vision becomes the subject of a special science which cannot be understood without a knowledge of the structure of the eye.' True to his principles of practical experimentation, he dissected the eyes of corpses to find out how they worked; his findings helped lead to the invention of spectacles.

But science, for Bacon, did not end with optics; it gave him a vision of the future. In 1268 he wrote, with breathtaking foresight:

> Now machines of navigation can be constructed without rowers, which are borne under the guidance of one man at a greater speed than if they were full of men. Also a chariot . . . that will move with incalculable speed without any draft animal . . . and flying machines . . . that a man may sit in the midst of it turning a certain instrument, by means of which wings artificially constructed would beat the air after the manner of a bird flying.

Bacon's image of the scientist as the wise falconer who learns by experience appealed to the most restless experimenter of the age: Frederick II, Holy Roman Emperor from 1194 to 1250, and an expert on falconry who prided himself on knowing more about it than Aristotle. Frederick's contempt for convention earned him the label 'stupefier of the world'. He was said to have had two men disembowelled to show the varying effects of sleep and exercise on the digestion; reputedly, too, he had children brought up in silence, 'in order to settle the question whether they would speak Hebrew, which was the first language, or Greek or Arabic or at least the language of their parents; but he laboured in vain, for the children all died'.

The emperor Frederick II with a falcon, in an illustration from his own book on falconry.

None of this work brought western science abreast of the technologies and skills China could boast; but the thirteenth century was a critical period in which much of the knowledge hitherto exclusive to the east was communicated, and the Mongol roads were the means by which it was transferred.

The world-view fostered by thirteenth-century science overlapped with other forms of sensibility new in the west. Considered from one point of view, the realism increasingly favoured in western painting was a tribute to the new respect accorded to the senses: to paint what one's eyes could see was to confer dignity on a subject not previously thought worthy of art. Realism and naturalism also appealed to the piety of the period. The devotion of the rosary, introduced early in the thirteenth century, encouraged the faithful to imagine sacred mysteries with the vividness of everyday life, as if witnessed in person: observation was also the key tool of a new trend in religion.

No mind felt the pain of Christian realism more acutely than that of Francis of Assisi. Embracing the poverty of Christ and the apostles, he founded a monastic order, the Franciscans, which embodied the same ideal, and consecrated his followers to spreading a sparingly bright awareness – among people previously untouched by the gospel in under-evangelised Christendom or beyond its frontiers – of the love and suffering of God.

The science and piety of the age were linked by art. The works which the Franciscan Order commissioned for their churches draw the onlooker into sacred spaces, as if in eye-witness of the lives of Christ and the saints. They stir the emotions of the devout by unprecedented realism, looking at the world with eyes as unblinking as those of the new scientific thinkers. In the previous century, the church had feared and hated nature as the abode of pagan gods and demons. Francis now enfolded the whole of nature in love: the ravens to whom he preached, the creatures, landscapes, sun and moon whom he called sisters and brothers – and 'sister death' herself.

> May thou be praised, my Lord, with all Thy creatures,
> Especially mister brother sun,
> May thou be praised, my Lord, for sister water who is very useful, and
>   humble and precious and chaste,
> May thou be praised, my Lord, for brother fire through whom thou
>   illumines the night,
> May thou be praised, my Lord, for
> Our sister, bodily death, whom no
> Man living can escape.

The welcome Francis gave to death was timely. In the next century, on a scale never recorded before, cold and plague would scythe lands and lives out of western Christendom. The last world-shaping influence to emerge from the steppe was to be the plague known as the Black Death.

ST FRANCIS OF ASSISI

Born Giovanni Pica in Assisi in 1183, the young St Francis learned to speak French at his merchant father's knee, and it was this that earned him the name of Francesco, or Francis – 'little Frenchman'. His religious fervour seems to have arisen from two crises in his early manhood: the first his year-long captivity during the war between Perugia and Assisi, the second a long illness. On recovering from the latter, according to legend, Francis set out from his parents' house wearing a new set of clothes. On the road he met a man reduced to poverty and, taking pity on him, exchanged clothes with him, returning home dressed in rags. That night he dreamt of a glorious palace full of weapons and decorated with the Cross of Christ, and a voice told him that he and his fellow soldiers should take up arms under the banner of the Lord.

He entered the church of Portiuncula and it was here that he heard in a sermon the words from the Gospel of St Matthew: 'Do not carry gold, or silver, or scrip for your journey, or two coats, or a staff.' Inspired by this message of humility, Francis gave away his money, shoes, staff and leather girdle, keeping only a poor coat tied about with cord. This code of dress was to become the habit for the order that he founded in 1209 and that still bears his name.

In 1224 St Francis is said to have undergone a mystical experience, receiving while in an ecstasy of prayer the marks – stigmata – of the crucified Jesus Christ. In 1225 he wrote the 'Canticle of the Sun', often considered to be the start of vernacular literature in Italy, in which he speaks of his belief in the kinship of animals and man. In one of the most famous scenes from his life, as painted by Giotto, he is depicted preaching to the birds, who, understanding the piety of his words, acknowledged his message by flying off in the form of a cross. He was canonised on 6 July 1228.

CHAPTER 4

Century of the
SCYTHE

THE FOURTEENTH CENTURY

CIVILISATIONS DEFY NATURE. Sometimes nature takes revenge. In the fourteenth century plague, famine and crises of climate scythed through the great civilisations of Eurasia and north Africa. And according to rumours picked up in Europe, 'in China, which is the greatest country in the world, horrible and terrifying signs appeared. Serpents and toads fell in a thick rain, entered dwellings and devoured numberless people, injecting them with poison and gnawing them with their teeth. In the south in the Indies earthquakes cast down whole towns and cities were burnt up by fire from heaven. The hot fumes of the fire burnt up infinite numbers of people and in some places it rained blood, and stones fell from the sky.'

Peasant revolutionaries mobilised in their millions, desperate to bring on the end of the world by violence. They struck states and cities like another natural disaster. In China, Islam and Christendom the progress of the previous century was reversed. Formerly marginal cultures in Africa and south-east Asia became, for a while, more promising, with dynamic empires, expanding economies and undiminished riches.

The Black Death. In an anonymous Catalan fresco, Death rides in triumph over the rich and powerful.

91

THE BLACK DEATH

'I arrived at length in Cairo, mother of cities,' wrote Ibn Battuta, pilgrim, in 1325:

> . . . mistress of broad provinces and fruitful lands, boundless in multitude of buildings, peerless in beauty and splendour, the meeting-place of those who come and those who go . . . of learned and simple, grave and gay, prudent and foolish . . . She surges with folk . . . and is of generous soil . . . and abundance of bread.

He quoted well-known praises of the city, which was still pre-eminent in Islam and vastly superior to anything in Europe in terms of size and wealth:

> No common town is Cairo, by thy life! Nay she
> Is heaven on earth for those with eyes to see.

The city, he said, was full of money and things to spend it on, including young cupbearers 'like seeded pearls' and 'maids with lustrous eyes', who reminded the poet of the houris of paradise. More prosaically, he reckoned up the statistics of prosperity. There were 12,000 water-carriers and 30,000 donkey-hirers. 'As for the places of learning in Cairo, they are too many to count.'

When he returned, twenty-four years later, the city, and the mood of its people, had been transformed. No one knows quite how many people fell victim to the Black Death; but around 200,000 were already dead, and fear clutched at those left alive. 'I found that all the shaikhs I had known there were dead. May God Most High have mercy on them!'

The plague had reached north Africa and Egypt in 1347. Its arrival, and the desolation it spread around it, was described by Cairo's poets, among them Al-Salah Al-Safadi:

> There is no possible refuge from the plague. We have all been hit. The disease dwells in the chest and melts the liver . . . The plague has spread fear and misery in the hearts of women. It has raised high the flag of death, and broken into every home like a wild bunch of thieves.
>
> Many have sought refuge in God and taken heed of the prophet's words: If you rise in the morning, do not count on being alive by nightfall.
>
> The plague has offered us the wine glass of total extinction and my soul is as drunk as could be. God has not just subdued Egypt: he has made her crawl on her knees. People's souls have become so cheap that they can be bought for nothing more than a single grain.

Ibn Battuta had seen the beginnings of the Black Death in Syria, on his way home from the far east. 'I went to Homs and found the plague already there; about 300 persons died on the day of my arrival.' At Damascus deaths numbered

CAIRO

In 1384 the Florentine traveller Leonardo Frescobaldi wrote that more people dwelled in a single Cairo street than in all Florence, and the number of ships in the port of Bulaq was three times that to be found in the harbours of Venice. Before the plague of 1347–8 the population of Cairo was said to be 500,000; even at the end of the fourteenth century it was still the largest city in the western world. Streets of only a few yards in width were dominated by buildings of ten or even fourteen storeys. So populous were the houses that the chronicles record the case of two schoolfriends who met by chance after thirty years, only to discover that they had been living in the same building for all that time.

Cairo was the greatest commercial centre of the age, a New York of its day. Goods were brought overland from Syria, Sudan, Arabia and Libya, by ship from across the Red Sea and the Mediterranean. In a city of eighty-seven markets everything the heart desired could be found: firs, ivory, arms, musical instruments, saddlery, cloth, songbirds, gold and silver swords; it is reputed that ten thousand slaves changed hands each year. Al-Maqrizi, Cairo's medieval chronicler, claimed to have counted 12,000 shops on the four-mile stretch of the Qasabah. In 1324 Mansa Musa, king of Mali, arrived with 500 slaves, each carrying a tube of gold weighing 5 pounds. His caravan was followed by 100 camels each carrying a further 100 pounds of the precious metal. But even he found the temptations of Cairo too much, and on his departure was forced to borrow 50,000 dinars from an Egyptian spice merchant to pay the debts he had run up during his stay.

Egyptian hospitality; host and guests.

2,400 a day before the citizens appeared to win divine mercy with a three-day fast. Ghaza was almost deserted. At Alexandria he was told that 1,000 people a day had died. He reached Jerusalem as the pandemic receded, to find an old friend giving a banquet: 'I asked him the reason for it. He told me that during the plague he had sworn he would give a banquet if a day were to pass during which he did not pray over a corpse. Then he said, "Yesterday I did not pray over a corpse." ' Of all the enemies Islam had absorbed, only plague was invincible.

The plague's transmission was sordid, its effects relentless, its treatment unknown. It was spread, at first, by animal carriers. Fleas ingested the bacillus from rats' blood and then regurgitated it into the bloodstream of human victims. Or they communicated infection by defecating into their bites. Death was often one of the first symptoms; in other cases, it might be deferred by the appearance of ugly swellings – small and bulbous, like brazil nuts, or big and fleshy like grapefruit – over the neck and groin or behind the ears: the buboes from which the affliction took its name. Trembling, retching, dizziness and pain might follow, often accompanied by repugnance from light, before fainting and final collapse.

Monks suffering from the plague, showing the dreaded buboes.

Like so many human invaders, the Black Death came from the plains of Asia, where a permanent reservoir of infection still exists among the rats. As for how the pest-borne contagion came to be passed on from one human to another, most contemporaries who considered the matter traced it to an encounter outside the Genoese colony of Caffa on the north shore of the Black Sea. A physician in northern Italy, who wrote the most detailed and well-informed eye-witness account, recorded the commonest belief about how it started:

> Oh God, behold how the tribes of pagan Mongols, streaming in from every side, laid siege one day to the city of Caffa and held the Christians trapped there for nearly three years . . . Look! the whole army was smitten with a

sickness which overtook the Mongols and killed thousands upon thousands every day. It was as though arrows were hurtling from heaven to strike and pierce the Mongols' arrogance. All the counsel and care of the physicians was good for nothing. The Mongols died as soon as the first marks of the disease appeared on their bodies: swellings in the armpit or groin caused by coagulating humours, followed by festering and fever . . . They ordered corpses to be placed in catapults and lobbed into the city, expecting the unbearable exhalations to kill everybody inside . . . One infected man could carry the virus to others and infect people and places with the disease just by looking at them . . . This was how almost everyone who had been in the orient or in the regions to the north and south of it fell victim to sudden death . . . Death struck on such a scale and in such a form that those who lived, weeping and wailing, through the bitter events of 1346 to 1348 – Chinese, Indians, Persians, Medes, Ethiopians, Arabs, Saracens and Greeks, for almost all the east had been affected – were convinced that the Last Judgement had come.

When a new disease evolves, people panic. Just as doctors in our own time were helpless when faced by Aids, the Ebola virus, Lassa fever and legionnaires' disease, so the medical science of the fourteenth century was baffled by the Black Death. There was no shortage of attempted cures. In Cairo, doctors smeared the buboes with Armenian clay. In Andalusia, they advised abstention from corn, cheese, mushrooms and garlic. Barley water and syrup of basil were frequently recommended. The Turks sliced off the heads of the boils and extracted 'green glands'. 'The plans and efforts of kings', as an Indian writer of the time observed, 'are quite ineffective in case of epidemics.'

In the Christian west, the plague was widely interpreted as divine punishment for human sinfulness, and penance was the most widely prescribed remedy.

Eighty thousand pilgrims, it was said, crossed Europe scourging themselves. Each wore a hood and carried in his right hand a whip with three thongs. Each thong had a knot in it with something sharp like a needle. 'The blood which flows from our wounds', they claimed in obedience to a revelation from an angel, 'mingles with Christ's whether we go to heaven or hell.' Scapegoats were sought as men tried to appease God by sacrifices, burning and bloody: Jews were massacred, heretics consigned to the pyre. 'Everywhere', a clerical critic observed, 'they think they can appease God by exterminating Jews, but the real reason why they want to kill them is that they regard them as the cause of this great mortality.'

As devastating as the physical affliction was the way this mysterious disease, rationally inexplicable, wrecked morale. It seemed to an Egyptian observer that 'everything died, even the year itself'. The glorious metropolis of Cairo never fully recovered its greatness. Ibn Khaldun – north Africa's greatest ever historian, who witnessed the effects of the plague – described the terrible havoc in famously ringing terms:

> Civilisation shrank with the decrease of mankind. Cities and buildings were bared, roads and signposts were abandoned, villages and palaces were deserted; tribes and dynasties were expunged. It was as if the voice of existence in the world had called out for oblivion, and the world had responded to the call.

In 1348 the plague began to slice through the west, heading north from the Mediterranean to reach Scotland and Scandinavia by 1350. The same Italian physician tracked its progress:

The spread of the Black Death. The terrible disease originated somewhere in central Asia and was probably carried along the trade routes. It reached Egypt and north Africa in 1347 and then spread westward, ravaging Europe in 1348 and reaching Scotland and Scandinavia in 1350.

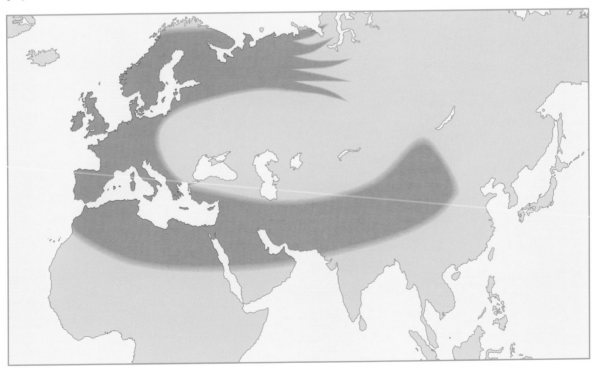

As it turned out, among the refugees who escaped from Caffa were a few seamen who had been infected with that virulent plague. Some of their boats were bound for Genoa, others sailed to Venice and to other parts of Christendom . . . 'Genoa, confess your deed. Describe, Sicily and you isles of the sea, the judgements of God. Venice, Tuscany and the whole of Italy, tell what you have done.'

'It is we Genoese and Venetians who have to make known the judgements of God. Alas, our ships had brought us to port . . . carrying the darts of death. While our kinsmen . . . embraced us and welcomed us with kisses, we were spreading poison from our lips even as we uttered.'

Images of fear and death evoke the horror felt by sufferers and survivors alike:

The mortality in Siena began in May. They would swell beneath the armpits and in their groins, and fall over while talking. And so they died. Great pits were dug. I, Agnolo di Tura, buried my five children with my own hands. So many died that all believed it was the end of the world . . .

When the plague reached Florence, the great poet Giovanni Boccaccio contemplated it with a scientific and a moralising eye, but his account of its transmission was essentially similar:

Dance of Death. Corpses in progressive stages of decomposition in a fresco from the Campo Santo, Pisa.

the noble city of Florence, which for its beauty exceeds all others in Italy, was visited by the deadly pestilence. Some say that it descended on the human race through the influence of the heavenly bodies,

BOCCACCIO AND THE BLACK DEATH

Among the witnesses of the Black Death in Europe was Giovanni Boccaccio: one of the supreme figures of European literary history; virtual creator, with Dante and his friend and older contemporary Petrarch, of literature in the Italian language; and one of the most profound influences throughout Europe on the approach to life and literature we now call Renaissance humanism.

Boccaccio was born in 1313. His father was an associate of the great banking house of the Bardi, and it was to their office in Naples that Giovanni was sent as a boy to learn business and to study canon law. His own claim that he felt himself destined for a literary life from birth may be exaggerated, but it is certainly true that he had begun to write at an early age, and freed himself from a commercial career as soon as he could. In the culturally rich city of Naples he moved between the world of the old nobility, whose chivalric values he admired, and that of the new aristocracy of commerce, who were to form the chief audience for his work; he also began to acquire that combination of profound classical learning and exposure to everyday life in all its vivid detail which characterises his greatest writing. Before he returned to his home city of Florence in or around 1340 he had written a great deal of both prose and poetry,

much of it centred, in late medieval fashion, on his love for a young woman, Fiametta.

The work for which he is most famous, the Decameron, was probably begun in 1348, the worst year of the Black Death, and it is with the plague that it opens. Ten young people have fled its onslaught in Florence and retired to a safe and comfortable place in the countryside, where for a fortnight they divert one another with conversation, storytelling and songs. The 100 tales that dominate the work are grave and gay, earthy and spiritual. If Dante's great work is the Divine Comedy, Boccaccio's is the 'Human Comedy'. Like the Canterbury Tales of Geoffrey Chaucer, who knew his Boccaccio, it celebrates life, not death. Swinging between folk tales and elegant classical models, it shows the young people of a confident new class striving to pit virtue, intelligence and courage against fortune, maintaining their spirituality but confining their desires to what is humanly possible – the very essence of humanism.

Boccaccio straddles what we think of as the medieval and what we think of as the early modern world. Although it is only the starting point of his great work, it is possible that the Black Death, like the Great War at the start of our own century, is the real watershed between an old world and a new.

others that it was a punishment signifying God's righteous anger at our iniquitous way of life. But whatever its cause, it had originated some years earlier in the east, where it had claimed countless lives before it unhappily spread westward, growing in strength as it swept relentlessly on from one place to the next.

Some villages in Provence lost four-fifths of their population; half the villages of Sicily were abandoned, as were a quarter of those around Rome. Mortality levels were lower elsewhere, but always significant, especially among the young. The undiscriminating nature of the pestilence struck observers with particular force, inducing a mood of resigned contempt for the privileges of rank.

In both Christendom and Islam, outbreaks of plague were commonplace for the rest of the Middle Ages and into the late seventeenth century. It does seem, however, that the effects were more persistent, more enduring and more often lethal in Islam: Europe recovered faster and, in the long term, resisted better. The slow shift of the balance of the world's resources and means in favour of Christendom began in the century of the scythe.

MALI: EMPIRE OF GOLD

If a cosmic observer, gazing down from an astral height, had sought the cultures most likely to succeed in the world of the fourteenth century, his eye would have been drawn away from the Eurasian land mass to sub-Saharan Africa and the edges of the Indian Ocean. In particular, his gaze would have been caught by the gleam of gold from one of the richest states, which controlled the flow of most of the world's supply of this most precious metal from mines deep in west Africa: the empire of Mali.

The fourteenth-century Malians were like the Venetians, a commercial and imperial people, strong in war and in wares. The heartlands of their prosperous state lay in a land-locked realm bounded by the Niger and Upper Senegal rivers, stretching across grazing lands from the desert in the north to the rainforest in the south. Across this territory, through the hands of canny monopolists, gold passed on its way north to the Saharan merchants whose caravans bore it to Mediterranean ports.

Camels carried the salt that would be exchanged for Mali's gold.

In 1352 Ibn Battuta, by now the most travelled individual in the Muslim world, set off from Tangier on his last great journey, across the Sahara desert, to see this empire for himself. By this time he had already been to east Africa, India, Arabia, Persia, the lands of the Golden Horde and, allegedly, to China. His powers of observation were at their height. His stories, received with stupefaction at his patron's court in Fez, were embellished with repetition; the account which survives from his own hand, however, is almost entirely convincing.

Ibn Battuta planned to travel south to Mali across the desert with the salt caravans which crossed the Sahara in a continuous stream: one writer recorded over 12,000 camels on just one of the roads in a single year. The first stage of his journey took him through Sijilmassa to Taghaza, 'an unattractive little town with the curious feature that its houses and mosques are built of blocks of salt'. From here he had an arduous journey ahead of him. The desert had to be crossed by marches of ten nights at a stretch without water, eating 'desert truffles swarming with lice' in a land 'haunted by demons . . . There is no visible road or track in these parts – nothing but sand blown hither and thither by the wind.' This marathon trek was made bearable by one powerful incentive: the prospect of swapping salt for gold.

The provenance of Mali's gold was a closely guarded secret. Procured, according to all accounts – written, perhaps, from convention rather than conviction – by 'dumb' trade, in which goods were exchanged by being left exposed for collection, the gold generated bizarre theories about its origins. It grew like carrots; it was brought up by ants in the form of nuggets; it was dug from the ground by naked men who lived in holes. In reality, it probably came from mines around the upper reaches of the Niger and the headwaters of the Gambia and Senegal rivers. Some may also have come from the Volta valley.

The middlemen of Mali never succeeded in controlling the production of the gold: any attempt by the country's rulers to exert direct political authority in the mining lands was met by the inhabitants with a form of 'passive resistance' or 'industrial action': the suspension of mining operations. But Mali controlled access from the south to the emporia of Walata and Timbuktu on the fringes of the Sahara. Marketing was therefore in the power of the rulers, who took the nuggets for tribute, leaving the gold dust to the traders.

Ibn Battuta's first encounter with Malian officialdom came at the outpost of Walata, in what is now the Mauretanian Sahara. 'It was then', he complained, 'that I repented of having come to their country, because of their lack of manners and their contempt for white men.' Culture shock struck quickly. The visitor was disgusted by the food, not realising at what cost precious millet was brought from far away. Outraged by a spectator when he relieved himself in the Niger, he subsequently discovered that the man was on guard to protect him from a crocodile. Nor was this the only surprise the river held for him:

> When we arrived at the arm of the river, I saw sixteen beasts with
> enormous bodies. I said to Abu Bakr, 'What beasts are these?' And he
> said, 'These are horses of the river – hippopotami.' The boatmen feared
> them and came in close to the shore so as not to be drowned by them.

The brazen womenfolk and the sexual freedom alarmed him, but he was impressed to find children chained until they learned their Quran, and he praised the blacks' 'abhorrence of injustice'.

A similar ambivalence is noticeable in Ibn Battuta's responses to what he found at the court of the Malian king, Mansa Musa. He was annoyed by the contrast between the copious displays of gold and the ruler's personal meanness. A gold bird bestrode the Mansa's parasol; his skullcap, quivers and scabbards were of gold; but he had to be shamed into generosity: 'What am I to say of you before other rulers?' complained Ibn Battuta. Some of the opulent rituals seemed silly, especially the antics of the poets dressed in thrushes' feathers 'with wooden head and red beak'. Other practices were more alarming. Cannibal envoys, whom the Mansa had presented with a slave girl, appeared at court to thank him, daubed with the blood of the gift they had just consumed. Fortunately, 'they say the white man is indigestible, because he is unripe'.

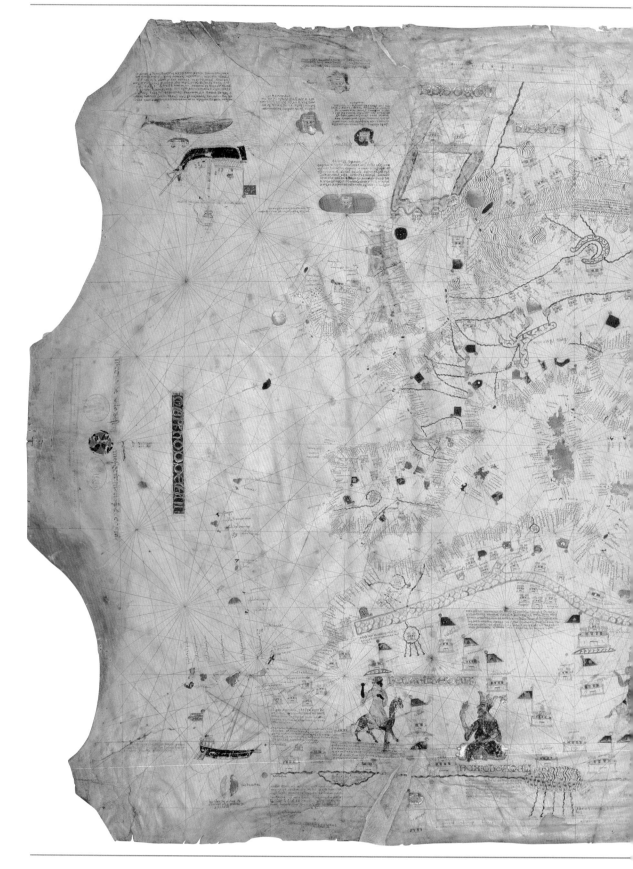

A medieval map shows the king of Mali crowned like a Christian monarch.

One of Mali's mounted warriors depicted in terracotta.

Yet in spite of himself, Ibn Battuta could not help being impressed by the ceremonial magnificence of the court of Mali. The Mansa, he found, commanded more devotion from his subjects than any other prince in the world. Black states did not normally attract respect from Arab writers: this makes the goggle-eyed awe of Ibn Battuta and his fellow observers in this case all the more impressive. Everything about the Mansa exuded majesty: his stately gait; his hundreds of attendants, bearing gilded staves; his indirect method of address through an intermediary; the acts of humiliation – prostration and throwing dust on the head – to which his interlocutors submitted; the reverberant hum of strummed bowstrings and murmured approval with which his words were greeted at audience; the capricious taboos which enjoined death for those who entered his presence in sandals or sneezed in his hearing. And this exotic theatre of power had a suitably dignified stage setting. The Mansa's audience chamber was a domed pavilion in which an Andalusian poet sang. His bushland capital had a brick-built mosque.

The position of the Malian king was buttressed by a renowned army; and the strength of this army was cavalry. Images of Mali's mounted soldiery survive in terracotta. Heavy-lidded aristocrats with protuberant lips and haughtily uptilted heads, crowned with crested helmets, sit rigidly on elaborately bridled horses. Some have cuirasses or shields upon their backs, or strips of leather armour worn apron-fashion. Their mounts wear halters of garlands and have decoration incised into their flanks. The riders control them with short reins and outstretched arms.

By the middle of the fourteenth century, the power of these warriors had established the Mansas' rule from the Gambia and lower Senegal in the west to the Niger valley below Gao in the east, and from the upper Niger in the south to the Sahara in the north. Traders followed in their wake – and overtook them, thrusting beyond the reach of the ruler's direct authority to found colonial settlements, for instance, on the forest-edge, where gold could be bought.

Yet, like many empires of promise in out-of-the-way corners of the late medieval world, Mali became a victim of its own relative isolation. Eroded by rebellions and incursions at its edges, it was weakened by rivalries at its heart. From about 1360, a power struggle pitted the descendants of Mansa Musa against those of his brother, Mansa Sulayman. At about the end of the century the Songhay, the people lowest down the Niger, broke away and Gao slipped from Mali's grasp. This was a serious blow, for Gao was one of the great entrepôts between the forest and the desert, and losing it meant losing the monopoly over trade passing through. In the 1430s, Tuaregs from the desert seized Walata and Timbuktu. Two decades later, when European explorers made contact with Mali for the first time, the Mansa's power was virtually confined to the old heartlands.

The accident of timing which deprived the European interlopers of the opportunity of seeing a great black empire at the height of its glory seems, in retrospect, one of the most tragic ironies of history. While known only by report, fourteenth-century Mali had projected a splendid image. In European maps from the 1320s onwards – and most lavishly in the Catalan Atlas of about 1375–85 – the ruler of Mali was portrayed like a Latin monarch, save only for his black face. Bearded, crowned and throned, with panoply of orb and sceptre, he was perceived and presented as a sophisticate, not a savage: a sovereign equal in standing to any Christian prince. Against this background of expectation, the discovery of Mali in decline was a source of bitter disillusionment. Familiarity bred contempt, and the heirs of the Mansa came to be seen as crude racial stereotypes, dangling simian sexual organs.

The brick-built mosque at Mali's capital, Djenne.

TIMUR AND THE SURVIVAL OF ISLAM

Timur's mausoleum in his favourite city of Samarkand.

Under Malian protection in west Africa, Islam remained robust. On other fronts it survived because the opportunities to recruit warriors from the steppeland were not yet exhausted.

The new influx of nomad strength in these years was led by Turkish sultans who founded great empires across the Islamic world. In the west, what started as a small principality in Turkey became the empire of the Ottomans: rulers who claimed to be God's choice as custodians of Islamic orthodoxy. Meanwhile, at the eastern end of Islam, the Muslim sultanate was planted in the midst of India. And in the lands between those giant empires, Islam was championed – at least in name – by the most feared conqueror of the age: Timur the Lame, known to many later as Tamberlaine.

Almost everything currently believed about Timur is false. Western writers have seen him as the embodiment of a pastoral ideal, evidence of the superior virtue of a 'shepherd king'; in reality, he was a high-born townsman. He claimed descent from Genghis Khan, and married into his dynasty; his real forebears, however, seem all to have been Turks. His clever self-projection as a devout practitioner of *jihad* – holy war – ensured him an enthusiastic press from co-religionists; but most victims of his wars were fellow Muslims, and his real role models were the pagans Alexander the Great and Genghis Khan. His court historian proclaimed him 'the being nearest to perfection' and he called himself 'the Auspicious Amir'; but his victories were, in most of their effects, destructive or short-lived. On the one hand, he appealed to the Mongol tradition, invoking the name and upholding the law code of Genghis Khan (he demanded submission with a Mongol-style formula: 'Almighty God has subjugated the world to our domination and the will of the Creator has entrusted the countries of the earth to our power'); on the other, he exploited his Islamic credentials, quoting the Quran – especially on the subject of holy war – and denouncing his enemies as lukewarm Muslims or outright pagans. Nevertheless, he imagined himself a world conqueror and almost became one.

Timur was born in 1336, a cadet of the line of lords of Kesh in Transoxania. Service to the Mongol khanate brought him promotion, over the heads of relatives better qualified by blood, to control of the family domains. He then turned against his masters, joining other nobles of the region in an 'independence movement'. Armed with a swelling band of followers, he progressed from robber tactics, rustling and guerrilla campaigns to conventional warfare. As his victories accumulated, he deftly eliminated his allies, leaving himself, by 1370, as sole ruler of Transoxania. He placed a royal diadem on his own head and 'girded himself with the imperial belt'; but his legitimacy was always doubtful, even at the height of his military success. His empire was an adventure and his strategy was opportunism. The state he created by war and subjection was a personal monarchy, which could not survive him. Even in his lifetime it was held together only by the momentum of conquest, which continually renewed the treasury from which warrior-followers could be rewarded.

The empire of Timur. When he died at the age of seventy-four he had conquered Iran, destroyed the khanate of the Golden Horde, reduced the Mongol state to a rump, invaded Syria and India, and halted the growth of the Ottoman empire. But his empire was sustained only by the momentum of his conquests and did not survive him.

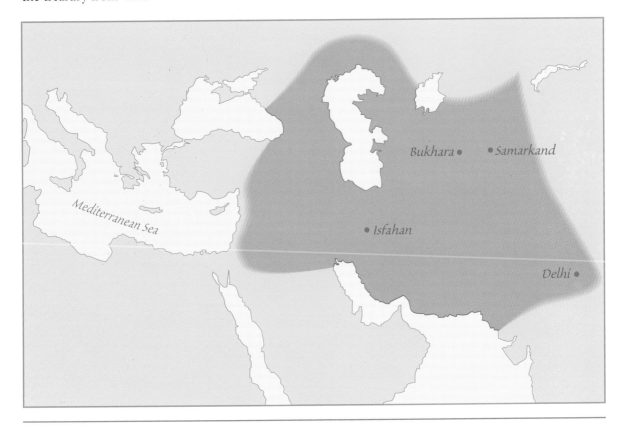

When Timur died at the age of seventy-four, in 1410, he had conquered Iran, wrecked the khanate of the Golden Horde to the north, reduced the Mongol state to a rump, invaded Syria and India, projected the conquest of China, halted the growth of the Ottoman empire and imprisoned its sultan in a cage. The marks of his passing, wherever he went, were the heaped-up skulls and towers of corpses of citizens injudicious enough to attempt to withstand his sieges. His success was by no means uniform, but at the time it was so impressive in its cumulative effect as to seem decreed by God or by the hand of fate. And yet the day after his death, as the legatees of his divided inheritance turned on each other, his ambitions seemed hollow and his achievements ephemeral.

Timur's impact on Islam is often seen as negative: had it not been for him, it is argued, the strength of Islam could have been directed concertedly against external enemies. By fighting the Ottomans, he gave Byzantium a reprieve; by humbling the Golden Horde of the northern steppe, he encouraged the Christians of Russia; by ravaging the sultanate of Delhi, he delivered millions of Hindus from the threat of Muslim rule. These criticisms, however, ignore two legacies: Timur's services to Muslim education – embodied in the magnificent mosques and religious schools which stand in his favourite city of Samarkand in what is now Uzbekistan; and the power of his image as a champion of Islamic orthodoxy and an exemplar of the power of holy war. He was the last great conqueror in the nomadic tradition and represented the consummation – forceful and terrible – of the process by which the nomads had been converted from the scourge of Islam to the spearhead of the *jihad*. Everywhere, in the late Middle Ages, the survival and success of Islam depended on its capacity to tame the alien forces which challenged it from the deserts and the steppes. Except in what are now Hungary and Bulgaria, no fully nomadic people had been successfully absorbed by Christendom. India was a victim of Turkic invaders who rejected Hinduism. China had assimilated the Mongol conquerors, but emasculated them in the process, instead of channelling their energies – as Islam did – in the service of the host civilisation.

This was how Islam survived the century of the scythe. Despite the shift of population in favour of Christendom, Islam remained the fastest-growing world civilisation into the second half of the millennium. The whole of what is conventionally called the 'early modern' period, from the sixteenth century to the eighteenth, was really an age of transition. If the resurgence of Islam today continues into the next millennium, the intervening centuries of unchallenged western supremacy will disappear from the view of future generations or shrivel, in their perceptions, to the dimensions of a curious but ultimately unimportant blip.

Islam's fourteenth-century transformation of the Turks and Mongols guaranteed that central Asia would stay Muslim, while helping to ensure that the Indian Ocean would link mainly Muslim shores, and that the ancient trade routes which crossed both spaces would be controlled by Muslim hands.

OPPOSITE *Timur heaps up the corpses. Like his Mongol predecessors he used terror as a propaganda weapon, building towers of skulls.*

THE WEALTH OF THE INDIAN OCEAN

The Indian Ocean was – and had long been – the world's most active arena of commerce. The summer monsoons blew ships from the African coast to India and the spice islands, where they idled in port, waiting for the winter monsoons to blow them back. The prestige and wealth of the ocean in the fourteenth century were displayed in the concentrations of power and prosperity dotted around its shores – on the Malabar coast of India, where small, rich sultanates could defy the might of the empire of Delhi; on the shores of the Arabian Sea; and as far away as Kilwa of the Shirazi, off the coast of what is now Tanzania, where the gold of the inland civilisation of Great Zimbabwe was brought into the circuit of Indian Ocean trade.

Ibn Battuta was afraid of the Indian Ocean when he first saw it, but – if his claims are unexaggerated – he soon became a seasoned traveller on its tides, and at every stop on his tours of the ocean's rim he found riches to titillate his senses and arts to excite his mind. One trip took him from Aden to the port of Zeila, in what is now Eritrea, which did business with Ethiopia, 'a large city with a great bazaar, but it is the dirtiest, most disagreeable and most stinking town in the world. The reason for its stench is the quantity of its fish and the blood of the camels they slaughter in the street.' Mogadishu was agreeable, with merchants 'possessed of vast resources', great stocks of

The monsoons. The monsoon trade winds offered rapid and relatively easy crossings between east Africa, India and the spice islands of the east. In the fourteenth century these were the world's busiest and most profitable trade routes, offering few incentives to voyage outside the wind-system.

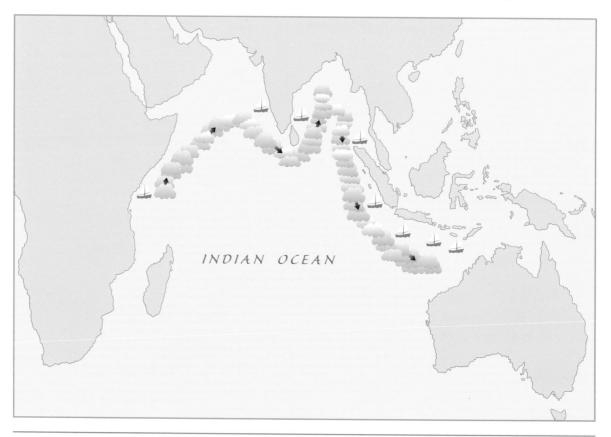

camels and sheep, canny business practices and textile factories. Here Ibn Battuta was moved to single out for comment the comfortable corpulence of the inhabitants, a marked feature of local culture, and the strange food that took him unawares: he was served with bananas, cooked in milk, and mangoes, which he described as resembling apples with stones. Further south off the African coast, at Kilwa, Ibn Battuta found 'one of the finest and most substantially built of towns', whose splendours are today just detectable amid the grim ruins. The dome of the mosque was lined with blue-and-white porcelain bowls from China in an engaging display of the economic unity of the ocean. Even more to his taste, the pilgrim found a sultan of fabled largesse.

In this vast region, lapped by the ocean and united by the monsoon, the most upwardly mobile state was in Java. The island was already famous as the source of some of the world's most valuable products: incense, cloves, aloes and camphor – which, according to Ibn Battuta, would not ripen unless a blood-sacrifice was made at its root. In Latin Christendom, Java was renowned as the place where all the spices in the east were grown or traded.

Surviving temple reliefs from the time depict neat hamlets of wooden houses perched on pillars over stone terraces. Peasants plough inundated rice fields or tease water buffalo over them to break and fertilise the ground. Women harvest and cook the rice. Orchestras beat gongs with sticks to inspire masked dancers. Java's fourteenth-century self-image, therefore, was not that of a state founded exclusively or primarily on commerce – like, say, Hong Kong or Singapore in our own times – but rather that of an agrarian society, settled in long-established rhythms and rituals. Nevertheless, the island's growing volume of trade was given impetus by elite appetites already whetted by foreign luxuries. The shipyards of the northern ports, whose products dominated Indonesian waters when the first European intruders arrived, were probably already in existence at this time.

Java was also home to a kingdom of dazzling ambitions, ruled by the self-conscious imperialist King Hayan Wuruk. His mental world is captured in a poem by his childhood playmate, Winada-Prapanaca, a Buddhist scholar of the royal chancery. The *Nagara-Kertagama* of 1365 is propaganda in praise of the ruler, an exercise in the intimidation of neighbours, and a manifesto of a dynamic and aggressive polity. The poet lovingly describes the wonders of the realm. The royal compound of Majapahit, in the eastern part of the island, had iron gates and a 'diamond-plastered' watch-tower. Majapahit was said to be like the moon and sun; the rest of the towns of the kingdom 'in great numbers' were 'of the aspect of stars'. Hayan Wuruk travelled about the country on his royal progresses in numberless carts, or was borne through the capital, attired in gold, on his lion-throne palanquin, to the music of tambourines and battle-drums, conches, trumpets and singers, to receive tributes in Sanskrit verse from foreign courts.

Ruler and subjects in a land of plenty; temple relief from Kediri in East Java.

The king's rule over the land of Java having grown firmer and firmer, victorious over other regions, it is here in Majapahit that he receives homage, bringing about the welfare of the world . . . In vast numbers he has created rest-houses, pious foundations and temples, to bring happiness to others. And officials, priests and scholars are the ones given the authority to join in performing meritorious acts in the world.

Hayan Wuruk's hospitality, graded according to the demands of caste and hospitality, was legendary:

The superior dishes arrived, the trays made of gold. Promptly those bringing them took up positions before the king. His food consisted of mutton, buffalo, poultry, venison, wild boar, bees, fish, duck . . . Dog, donkey, worms and rats are forbidden, as well as frogs which are very low.

Artistic performance was both a way of entertaining and a way of honouring the gods. Hayan Wuruk, like many other Javanese and Balinese monarchs, was a well-respected performer, and portrayed himself in his theatrical appearances as a living god. Taking upon himself the divine attributes of both Buddhism and Hinduism, he called himself 'Buddha in the body' and 'Shiva incarnate'. His territorial ambitions were no less extensive than his spiritual claims, though his realm (which, according to the poet, was incomparable for renown in all the world, except with India) actually occupied little more than half the island of Java. The poet's list of tributaries includes names scattered through what are now Indonesia and the Philippines and islands way beyond, as far north as the China Sea and as far south as Timor. 'Protectorates' are claimed all over south-east Asia; the poet even makes China and India sub-servient to his lord. 'Already the continents', he boasts, 'are getting ready to show deference to the Illustrious Prince.' And indeed, commercial rival realms in the nearby island of Sumatra do seem to have been annihilated by Majapahit. The neighbouring smaller island of Bali was conquered in about the middle of the century and its elite ruthlessly exterminated.

Curiously, as a result of later migrations, the Balinese today regard them-selves as the heirs of Majapahit and treat Hayan Wuruk as their culture-hero. They honour him with songs 'like the cries of a peacock . . . like creaking bamboos in their awesomeness, breaking one's heart'. 'His heroism has no end,' the songsters still proclaim, 'while his majesty soars as high as the sky . . . Those who are constantly in his presence are freed of their impurities if he should happen to see them and especially if he should speak to them.'

But the Majapahit legend is not the whole story. The unique culture of Bali is the legacy of an earlier era, when the island was one of the last overseas territories to be incorporated into the Hindu world. In most areas of south-east Asia, colonised earlier, Hinduism was the preserve of small elites, but in Bali the missionaries are said deliberately to have laid the basis of a pro-foundly popular religion, commanding the erection of three temples in every settlement. All over the island to this day, the triple nest of temples can be seen in every village, while a profusion of shrines embellishes every home and public building.

Javanese imperialism could not interrupt the continuity of this history; indeed, it probably did not much outlast the fourteenth century. For while trade is, on the whole, good for peace, a sudden expansion of trade whets territorial appetites – both within and outside the region; and sure enough, south-east Asia's late medieval boom set the states of the region at each other's throats as well as attracting Chinese conquistadores and colonists. Indian Ocean economies were victims of their own success: Java's ships were as big as those of any trading state in the world, but there was so much commerce near at hand that all the island's shipping seems to have been fully subscribed in local trade throughout the century; despite their technical prowess, there was no incentive to explore or venture further afield in search of markets, and in any case the zone of storms which edged their ocean to the south made naviga-tion outwards unattractive. In the long run, therefore, the future lay not with kingdoms like Hayan Wuruk's, clogged with prosperity in the fourteenth cen-tury, but with lands on the other side of the world – where plague raged and climate killed.

CHRISTENDOM: COLD AND HUNGRY

According to the established pattern of politics in world history up to this time, it was normal for a single state to rule an entire civilisation. China was reunited under Ming rule; the Ottoman Turks were striving for unity in Islam. The Mongol empire, while it held together, was a loose dynastic federation, but its component parts all continued to subscribe to the ideal of a single, world-encompassing stage. There was a similar lack of restraint about the ambitions of the sultans of Delhi, who united most of the Indian culture-area.

Western Christendom, on its smaller scale, had similar aspirants. Some looked back to the legacy of the Roman empire; others looked forward to the role of Last World Emperor – a figure of prophecies popular at the time, whose cosmic struggle with the Antichrist was expected to precede the end of the world. Many kings commissioned propaganda to exploit a prevalent mood of millenarianism; all, under the spectral shadow of Rome and the remote goad of the apocalypse, got on with their own business and concentrated sovereign power within their frontiers. As a result, Christendom was full of increasingly powerful, increasingly competitive states. Images of rulers, like all art, grew lively and realistic: the earliest recognisable French portrait is of King John the Good, done in the mid-fourteenth century. At the same time, kings were made to look like saints: John, for instance, is shown in profile, as if on a classical medallion, against a field of gold, as if an icon of the Eastern church. In sculpture, monarchs were displayed at church doors, as if they were the janitors of heaven.

King John II, 'the Good', of France. His is the earliest recognisable French portrait.

The fashion for individual portraits of majesty had already attained its greatest splendour when it reached the court of Richard II in England in the last quarter of the century. In the famous travelling altar known as the Wilton diptych the king kneels before the Virgin, attended by angels who wear his livery badge: the gesture he flutters in her direction has been variously interpreted, but he seems to be opening his hands to receive the Christ-child, whom the Virgin appears to be about to hand to him, in allusion to holy communion and advertisement of the closeness of the king's relationship to God.

Richard's portrait sat permanently in his choir-stall at Westminster Abbey, as if perpetuating his presence, staring with priestly dignity from a shimmer of gold leaf. One can imagine the coronation scene, as the order of service described it:

> 'With this sword exercise thou the force of equity and mightily destroy the growth of iniquity, protect the Holy Church of God and his faithful people and pursue heretics no less than infidels; defend and keep widows and orphans, restore the things that are gone to decay, maintain the things that are restored . . .' Then shall the metropolitan

OPPOSITE King Richard II of England, portrayed in the travelling altar known as the Wilton diptych.

or bishop say, 'Receive this pall, which is found with four corners, to let you know that the four corners of the world are subject to the power of God and that no man can happily reign, who has not received authority from heaven. Amen.

'Receive the sceptre of kingly power, . . . punish the wicked and protect the just . . . Receive the rod of virtue and equity . . . to terrify the wicked . . .' Then shall the crown be blessed by the metropolitan or bishop . . . Then shall holy water be sprinkled on the crown, and then the metropolitan or bishop shall cense the crown and put it on the king's head, saying, 'God crown thee with a crown of glory . . .'

The upward revaluation of majesty can be detected in the pronouncement of one of Richard's ministers to Parliament some years into his reign:

There must be one king over all . . . one king and one governor and by no other manner can any kingdom be governed. And . . . to the good governance of each king, three things are needed: first, that the king must be powerful to govern; secondly, that the laws by which he ought to govern be kept and justly executed; thirdly, that the subjects of the realm should duly obey the king and his laws . . . that the king may be in his liberty and power as his progenitors before him . . . a king to all. And he will govern them.

Ambrogio Lorenzetti's idealised portrayal of the peace and prosperity that followed from 'good government', painted for the Signorie of Siena.

As the powers and importance of monarchs increased, so too the functions of states changed. Growing in size and complexity, expanding their technical resources, enhancing the reach and power of government to communicate and enforce its commands, they extended the range of their stewardship over the vistas of common life and public welfare. Ambrogio Lorenzetti painted a panorama of good government on to the walls of the Signorie of Siena. Accompanying the enlarged vision of the scope of the state, laws and admin- istrative regulations multiplied. From the fourteenth century, the use of paper slashed the cost and boosted the turnover of bureaucracies.

And yet, as the conditions of life for the many deteriorated in the four- teenth century, the limits of contemporary ideals of good government were sharply exposed. The awe that monarchs were so assiduous in cultivating proved hard to sustain in a period plagued by pestilence, pinched by famines, chilled by cold. In 1315–17, the dead of exceptionally lethal winters of famine and flood were mourned from the Elbe to the Loire. The 'little ice age', of which this was an episode, forced settlers down from the hills and back from the northern corners of Christendom. Frontiersmen gradually withdrew from their outposts in Greenland and the Baltic, while in the heart- lands of the continent hill farms became untenable. John Trokelowe, an English monk, saw what happened in his own country:

> In the year of our Lord 1315 . . . famine arose in the land, as if God
> were displeased with our statutes . . . For summer rains abounded to
> such a degree that the corn could not ripen . . . Nor had bread any
> longer such power to nourish, or such essential virtue, as it usually has,
> because the grain got none of the benefit of the rays of summer sun.
> Therefore noblemen and religious communities alike cut down on their
> rolls of employment, spent less on charity and shrank their households.
> Servants who lost their jobs, after getting used to the sweet life, did not
> know how to dig and would not deign to beg, but, their morale
> undermined by want of food and drink, they hungered and thirsted for
> other people's goods and inclined to murder and rapine. And Jews, no
> less, were affected, because the faithful would not suffer them to live in
> peace . . . Therefore, as this hunger came to grip the whole land,
> mortality followed. For so many of the needy died that the living were
> hardly enough to bury the dead. The evil called Dysentery – caused by
> rotten food – killed almost all of them, with acute fever followed by a
> plague of the throat. Nor during this pestilence could the physicians
> find any remedy by wisdom or art, as they used to be able to do in the
> old days. For medicinal herbs, which used to confer relief on the
> sufferer in time of mortality, had decayed and become de-natured,
> because of the intemperate weather and the unprecedented conflict in
> the elements, and instead of potency bred poison . . .

*The Peasants' Revolt.
John Ball and Wat Tyler
lead the rebels in a
somewhat fanciful
fifteenth-century
illustration.*

Ordinary meats, indeed, and lawful to eat, grew too costly; horseflesh was too pricey for some who stole fat dogs for meat. And – so many claimed – furtively, in various places, men and women ate their little children, and even other people's. And – what will horrify future readers who learn of it – thieves newly committed to prison were devoured instantly, half-alive, by the inmates.

On the frontiers the impersonal enemies – plague, famine and cold – were supplemented by human foes. In 1354 a violent earthquake demolished the walls of Gallipoli, a Christian enclave on the Turkish coast: Turks were waiting to take over the ruins. Meanwhile, on northern fronts, pagan enemies roamed as the allies of winter: mysterious raiders called Skraelingar wiped out the westernmost settlement of Christendom in Greenland; on the north-east extremity pagan Lithuanians forced Christians back. On most fronts, the late medieval west was a civilisation in contraction or stagnation.

Insecurity bred violence. Jews, foreigners, food-hoarders at times of famine and scapegoats at times of plague: these were the common victims of mass brutality. At other times the rage to destroy was turned against the followers of particular great families. In 1358 the city of Paris, in collective revolt against the crown, made a brief alliance with peasants on the rampage in the countryside. Occasionally, low-born revolutionaries were heard – or claimed – to demand the abolition of rank; but nowhere did these outbreaks of disaffection achieve more than temporary notoriety. In 1381 in England, for instance, the 'Peasants' Revolt' saw rebellious workers hanging tax-gatherers, burning records of debts and dues, and boldly asserting that 'all men be free and of one rank'. John Bull, a priest preaching at this time, demanded the creation of a new Eden:

> In what way are those whom we call lords greater masters than
> ourselves? How have they deserved it? Why do they hold us in
> bondage? If we all spring from a single father and mother, Adam and
> Eve, how can they claim or prove that they are lords more than us,
> except by making us produce and grow the wealth which they spend?
> They are clad in velvet and camlet lined with squirrel and ermine while
> we go dressed in coarse cloth. We are called serfs and beaten if we are
> slow in our service to them, yet we have no sovereign lord we can
> complain to . . . let us go to the king – he is young – and show him
> how we are oppressed and tell him that we want things changed or
> else we will change them ourselves.

Resentful day-labourers from inside the city opened the gates of London to them. But the fear and contempt felt by the well-to-do for the rebels swarming menacingly in the capital turned to pity when the wretches were defeated, slaughtered and dispersed:

> *In Kent this curse began*
> *In rout the rioters ran*
> *For folly fears no man*
> *And churls make chiefs as can.*
>
> *The hoodlums hooted loud,*
> *'Fit shriver to his shroud!*
> *Leave bravoes bathed in blood!'*
> *The realm gained little good.*

In a continent pounded and impoverished by disaster, the wealthy saw peasant rebellion as another natural catastrophe – but one that could at least be suppressed. In the fourteenth century, the demands of the poor for justice and equality fell on deaf ears.

Tristan et yseult

Irlande

CHAPTER 5

Century of the
SAIL

THE FIFTEENTH CENTURY

A MAP MADE BY Fra Mauro for the Venetian state in the 1440s depicted an inviting world, smothered with riches and streaked with threads of gold, like the spilled contents of a jewel-casket; a world open with opportunities and dense with dynamic states. China, Islam, parts of eastern Christendom and parts of what would become the Americas all seemed ripe to burst into long-range expansion. As the disasters of the previous century began to recede, civilisations all over the world started or resumed careers of growth and even aggression at their neighbours' expense. Some had the potential to explore, and perhaps to conquer, the rest of the world.

The most impressive and mature sea-going technologies belonged to the coastal states of maritime Asia. The fastest-growing empires, encompassing the widest range of terrain and habitat, were in the Americas. In the Old World they were rivalled, in speed and scale of growth, by the Ottoman and Muscovite empires, both of which made spectacular leaps into new environments: the Russians into the frozen north and the White Sea, the Ottomans into the waters of the Mediterranean.

All over Eurasia there were states with ambitions to conquer and dominate the world. Most of the planet is covered by water: the conquerors of the world had first to be masters of the seas, and in the age of sail the only routes capable of linking civilisations separated by the great oceans were at the mercy of winds and currents. For most of the fifteenth century, the state that seemed best equipped to realise aims of global dominion was China, armed with practical achievements in exploration, navigation, colonisation and warfare that exceeded those of all possible rivals.

Towards the end of the century, however, almost without warning, a few poor and peripheral communities on the Atlantic side of Europe suddenly emerged as potential global powers, wielding an impressive and far-reaching maritime capability. It was from these western harbours that sail-borne expeditions set out to master the wind-systems of the world.

Illustration from a fifteenth-century French version of the tale of Tristan and Iseult. In ships like these, mariners from western Europe ventured forth to master the wind-systems of the world.

CHINA'S BRIEF EXCURSION

When the galactic museum-keepers look back on the history of our planet, they will surely see the Chinese as the most colonial-minded people on earth. Even today, London's Chinatown, and its counterparts in San Francisco, New York and countless other modern cities all over the world, bear witness to the formidable potential of the Chinese as long-range seafarers, travellers and colonists. For most of history, Chinese empires have been built up on land. Overseas colonialism has usually been left to private enterprise – the kind of private enterprise which reached across the Indian Ocean in the Middle Ages and left hundreds of blue-and-white porcelain bowls to line the domes of Kilwa, off the east African coast, and thousands of shards of jade-green Sung pots to be turned up by archaeologists in the earth of Tanzania. However, there was a moment in the fifteenth century when it looked as though the Chinese state would sponsor maritime imperialism.

One summer day in 1415 the emperor of China, accompanied by a vast retinue, hurried with as much speed as was consistent with the dignity of the occasion to welcome to his court a distinguished foreign arrival, brought by a Chinese fleet all the way from Malindi, on the far shore of the Indian Ocean. Had the guest been merely human, the occasion would not have been so auspicious, but this time the newcomer was a creature of reputedly divine provenance: a Huih-lin, symbol of good luck.

A giraffe brought from Africa to the Chinese emperor. Chinese of the time confused it with a Huih-lin or unicorn, symbol of good fortune.

An eye-witness described the fabulous animal: 'It has the body of a deer and the tail of an ox and a fleshy, boneless horn, with luminous spots like red or purple mist. It walks in a stately fashion, and its every motion observes a rhythm. Its harmonious voice sounds like a bell or a musical tube.' In fact, it was a giraffe – one of a host of strange new creatures which enriched the imperial menagerie in the early fifteenth century: lions, leopards, ostriches, dromedaries, zebras, rhinoceroses and antelopes. Truly, it seemed, 'all the creatures that spell good fortune arrive.'

This dazzling zoo was a side-effect of a new policy of sending official naval expeditions towards the remotest regions of the world known to Chinese geography, under one of the most expansionist, aggressive and maritime-minded emperors in Chinese history. The Emperor Yung-lo revived much of the tone and some of the projects of the reign of Kublai Khan (see above, p. 78). He restored the capital to Beijing, invaded Vietnam and became engaged in the politics of the Malacca region and beyond. For a time, even Japan was drawn out of isolation by pressing offers of trading opportunities.

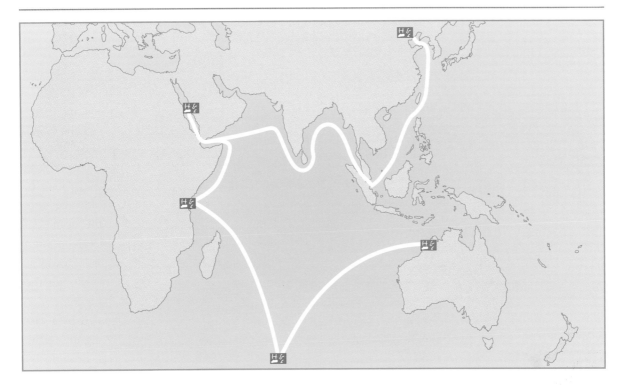

Initially at least, Yung-lo's aim was not conquest but the gathering of intelligence and the demonstration to the world of China's superiority, and his chosen instrument for this campaign was an admiral of legendary presence and charisma: Zheng He. Zheng cut an impressive figure: 'He stood seven feet tall and five feet wide. He had swarthy skin as rough as an orange, and his eyes sparkled like light on a fast-moving river.'

A Muslim of Mongol descent and a eunuch, Zheng He's outsider status made him an ideal choice for the imperial mission. An outsider in an inward-looking court, he enjoyed the support of factions whose interests offended the Confucian scholar-elite: the commercial lobby, which wanted to mobilise naval support for long-range traders; the imperialist lobby, which wanted to renew Mongol visions of conquest; the religious lobbies, which wanted to keep state funds out of anti-clerical Confucian hands by diverting them to other enterprises; and the eunuch lobby, which wanted more offices for its own members.

Between 1405 and 1433 Zheng He led seven expeditions, six of them under Yung-lo's patronage. The scale and range of these voyages were massive. They penetrated the furthest reaches of the Indian Ocean – even, according to some reports, to the Southern Ocean and Australia; according to the best available estimate, the seventh expedition – which probably journeyed to the furthest point from home – sailed 12,618 miles. The voyages lasted, on average, two years each and visited at least thirty countries around the rim of the ocean, as far south as Zanzibar, as far north as Mecca and as far west as Jiddah. The first fleet to set out was said to comprise over 300 ships, including 62 junks of the largest class ever built and 225 support vessels, and nearly 28,000 men.

The voyages of Zheng He. Between 1405 and 1433 Zheng He led massive maritime expeditions under the patronage of the emperor Yung-lo. They penetrated the furthest reaches of the Indian Ocean and, according to some reports, may have reached the Southern Ocean and Australia; Zheng He's enormous ships were certainly capable of such a venture. Each voyage lasted on average two years; the longest was of 12,618 miles.

Zheng He's 'treasure junks' were the largest wooden ships ever built, giants that dwarfed the comparatively tiny European caravels. Over 400 feet long and 180 feet wide, each was driven along by twelve bamboo sails, set on nine masts, that could be set at any angle to the wind. The hulls were of an equally revolutionary design. The compass room, admiral's quarters and galley were at the stern, with crew, animals and cargo down below, and the ship was kept afloat by thirteen watertight compartments, each of which could be individually flooded as required for use as a fish tank or washing area. This technology was 500 years ahead of the west, where it was used in the building of the *Titanic*.

Shipbuilding skill was matched by navigational prowess. In plotting their course, the Chinese sailors understood the difference between true and magnetic north. They checked latitude by measuring the positions of the sun and stars in relation to the horizon, and had a mechanism for measuring the speed of their vessel. Time was kept using calibrated joss-sticks. Zheng He himself had a confident respect for the abilities of his pilots: 'However far the seas and lands beyond the horizon, their distances can be reckoned, their routes recorded.'

Despite their formidable strength, these voyages were intended to show the flag, not erect it permanently; primarily, at least, to demonstrate superiority rather than exercise dominion. If the account given by the admiral's surveyor, Ma Huan, is to be believed, they made the desired impression:

The coastal towns are full of rare spices and beasts that evoke a sigh of admiration . . . Everywhere we went the natives looked with longing on our gracious gifts, felt our transforming power and duly presented their tribute . . . Rubies, lions, pearls the size of plums were all given to return to the central country.

For all their outwardly diplomatic character, however, these lordly visitations effectively demonstrated China's potential as the launch-bay of a seaborne empire – the capacity and productivity of its shipyards; the ability to mount expeditions of crushing dimensions and despatch them over vast distances. Nor was Zheng He reluctant to use force when circumstances seemed to call for it. On his first two expeditions he suppressed a pirate kingdom in Sumatra and set up a satellite state in Malacca. On the third he overthrew the king of Ceylon and installed a substitute. On the fourth he captured a Sumatran chief who refused to cooperate in the usual exchange of tribute for Chinese gifts.

Zheng He's own perception of his role seems to have combined an imperialist impulse with the peaceful inspiration of commerce and scholarship. An inscription he set up in 1432 began in jingoistic vein: 'In the unifying of the seas and continents the countries beyond the horizon and from the ends of the earth have become subjects.' The voyage on which he was engaged at the time, however, was to be his last, and the last of China's official maritime programme. For in the power struggles at court the balance was tipping in favour of the isolationists and against the expansionists; and in the 1430s the former achieved a decisive triumph.

China at this period was governed by a coterie of Confucian scholars, contemptuous of barbarism, and of gentlemen, indifferent to trade. By 1430 these elements, convinced that the outside world had nothing to offer China, had persuaded the emperor to abandon his global ambitions. 'Barbarian kings', wrote one scholar, 'should be treated like harmless seagulls.' The renunciation of overseas expansion, the demotion of commercial values and the abandonment of shipbuilding became such important badges of identity for the scholar-elite that bureaucrats destroyed all Zheng He's records in an attempt to obliterate his memory. A promising imperial effort was abruptly aborted and never resumed. China's 'manifest destiny' was never fulfilled, and the world predominance which for a time seemed its for the taking was abandoned to other contenders from the west.

Today, Zheng He and his great enterprise are virtually unknown in his own country. Elsewhere, however, traces of his expeditions remain. A type of ginger is named after him; in Sri Lanka, a tablet records his visit. In the Philippines, pearl divers find porcelain, decorated with images of mythical beasts, including the Huih-lin. On the west coast of India, Chinese fishing nets still adorn the entrance to Cochin harbour: the last relics of a time when Chinese technology ruled these seas.

A Huih-lin or unicorn appears on a Chinese dish that found its way to the sultan's palace in Istanbul.

Bankers in an Italian counting-house. The chief centres of Italian banking were Florence, Venice, Siena and Genoa.

ART AND MONEY: THE RENAISSANCE

For most of the fifteenth century, western Europe was in recession. The German empire lost territory to pagans and heretics on its borders. Venice, in retreat in the eastern Mediterranean, fell back on exploiting its own hinterland in the Po valley. The rapid swell, puff and deflation of Lithuania and Hungary only showed how volatile were the eastern marches of Latin Christendom. England, a formerly invincible military power, lost its continental empire. The royal house of Barcelona was in decline, drawing in its far-flung Mediterranean outposts. Civil wars were commonplace – mostly the results of an aristocratic culture of violence out of control. Only the kingdom of France got significantly bigger over the course of the century and the kingdom of Castile towards its end.

But while state expansion and territorial acquisition temporarily faltered, in the wealthy cities at the heart of the continent bankers and merchants found a new source of riches with which to boost their status and proclaim their financial success: art, inspired by the ancient cultures of Greece and Rome. Their lavish investment and patronage, spurred on by intense competition among their ranks, created a reborn civilisation: the Renaissance.

Florence – the city which, more than any other, came to be regarded as the home of the Renaissance – was an arena of two kinds of fertile rivalry. The city itself strove constantly to outdo its neighbour city-states, while inside its walls institutions, families and factions contended to accumulate clients and control the government. Bankers, charging 45 per cent interest, became as powerful as warlords. One of the richest merchant dynasties, the Medici, established an ascendancy in Florence – but it was always precarious and had to be won and defended in the face of the rival claims of other families whose badges and monuments decorate areas and quarters of the city to this day: the name of the Ruccellai blazes from the façade of the church of Santa Maria Novella, the emblems of the Albrizzi decorate street corners in their own quarter and the Pazzi Chapel represents an attempt to outdo the Medici in the erection of a family pantheon in classicising taste. Florentine palaces, like those of other urban elites of the period, are virtual fortresses.

The rivalry of the great urban bosses and clans was suspended only for huge projects of civic self-glorification undertaken in competition with other towns. Siena had, in Il Mangia, a tower far higher than any in Florence; but Florence, thanks to Filippo Brunelleschi's engineering genius, was eventually able to acquire a cathedral dome more capacious than Siena's. The city's wealthy patrons competed and cooperated to give Florence a style and skyline to match their individual and communal pride, imagining their town as the ideal polis, perfectly laid out in accordance with divinely ordained rules of proportion.

Florence and its cathedral. Striving to outdo rival city-states in lavishness, its wealthy merchants provided the patronage that made it the chief birthplace of the Renaissance.

For all its glorious monuments to artistic skill and endeavour and to the rediscovery of classical scholarship, what drove fifteenth-century Florence was money. In its hothouse environment of commercial, social and political intrigue, cash bought votes, big spending brought prestige. Secular patrons were in the business of buying conspicuous display. Those who were merchants, like the Medici, were keen on value for money, and money was evoked more by lavish use of gold and precious stones than by intellectual preferences for mathematics and monumental simplicity. The women of Florentine high society wore their wealth on their sleeves: 'Their cloaks were embellished with silver and pearls, enamelled flowers and gold leaf, corals and 800 peacock feathers.' Attempts were made to keep such ostentation within bounds – officials policed the streets for those wearing too many buttons and furs – but they had little chance of success, with money, social status and power in the same hands.

The Medici were the ultimate political party-givers. When in 1439 Florence was chosen as host to the council of churches of east and west, the Medici picked up the bill. Successive heads of the family ruled the city as though it were their private property, relying on the methods advocated by their adviser, Niccolò Machiavelli, bequeathed to us in his famous treatise *The Prince*. Machiavelli neither had nor encouraged illusions about human nature: 'It is far better to be feared than loved if you cannot be both. One can make this generalisation about men; they are ungrateful, fickle liars, and deceivers, they shun danger and are greedy for profit; while you treat them well they are yours . . .'

The Medici treated their artists very well indeed, paying them lavishly: but their expectations were clear. In a society so conscious of fashion and status, artists were expected not only to produce works which by their quality would enhance the standing of their patrons, but to adapt established religious themes to personal requirements. Members of the Medici family were painted into key roles in sacred scenes; needless to say, they were depicted clad in the latest modes, and these fabrics did not come cheap. Leading Florentine merchants readily spent as much on a single outfit as on a large town-house; a set of brocade wall hangings could cost more than a country estate. If the objects of this expenditure were to be properly appreciated, they had to be painted realistically, and artists who could do this commanded handsome fees: the more exact the illusion of reality, the richer the artist's purse.

Just like the textiles they painted, so the artist's materials relied on rare and costly colourings. Before the artist began work, a contract was drawn up stipulating how and where each tint was to be used. The most expensive of all was ultramarine, a deep blue made from lapis lazuli, a mineral found only in Afghanistan. There was also Kermes Red, made from crushed Turkish spiders; Orpiment Orange from the mountains of Bavaria; Burnt Sienna; Yellow Ochre . . . on the number and quantity of such pigments depended the value of the painting.

The priorities of the merchant patrons had an inevitably distorting effect on much produced in Florence at this period. The Medici Chapel painted by

Benozzo Gozzoli is closer in feel to a Gothic painted manuscript than to the Renaissance ideal. The Medici spent far more on jewels and antique gems, which represented sound investments, than they did on new art. As collectors of classical bric-à-brac, which lined the atrium of their palace, they were acting, in a sense, like medieval relic-collectors, amassing objects of power and influence.

Yet from these antiques they developed an interest in the pagan world that was stimulated by humanist scholars. Venus, Cupid or the Three Graces – subjects painted for the raffish villa society over which the Medici heirs presided – could be enjoyed as titillating excitants or interpreted as philosophical allegories. Irrespective of the mercenary and earthly preoccupations of their patrons, Florentine artists, drawing on the classical heritage, sought beauty and harmony in nature; focusing on the human form, they created ideal images, establishing an idea of beauty that lives on in western aesthetics today.

Preoccupation with the human body brought art and science together. In his quest to understand nature as well as to represent beauty, Leonardo da Vinci examined the intimate workings of the human organism. An artist who approached his subjects with the mind of an engineer, he designed fortifications and guns, imagined bicycles and parachutes. 'Science is the captain, practice is the soldier. Those who fall in love with practice without science are like a sailor without helm or compass.' From the discovery of man, Renaissance curiosity turned

FOLLOWING PAGES
Cosimi de' Medici depicted as one of the three Magi in a painting by Gozzoli. Other members of the Medici family also appear in the painting. Gozzoli took pains to show in intricate detail the jewelled magnificence of his patrons' costumes and accoutrements.

Leonardo da Vinci's scientific curiosity embraced anatomy, mechanics, hydraulics, ballistics, fortifications – and the possibilities of manned flight.

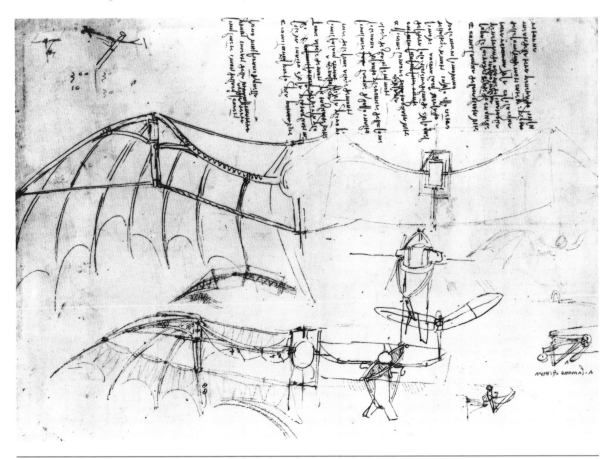

RENAISSANCE ART AND THE INVENTION OF PERSPECTIVE

One of the most influential and ground-breaking developments of the period we know as the Renaissance was the discovery of linear perspective.

Perspective, the creation of the illusion of three-dimensional volumes and spatial relationships on a flat picture plane, can be found in medieval art, but it was judged only by the artist's eye. At the beginning of the fifteenth century Italian painters began to make perspective drawing an exact science, based on the principles that objects appear to diminish in size and parallel lines to converge towards vanishing points as they approach the horizon. It was the Florentine architect Filippo Brunelleschi who formulated and published the geometric principles of architectural perspective in the Costruzione Legittima. One of the earliest exponents was Masaccio, who introduced architectural exteriors and interiors as backgrounds for religious paintings in Florentine churches, giving an illusion of great three-dimensional spatial depth. The laws of linear perspective as they applied to painting were codified by the great Renaissance genius Leon Battista Alberti in his Della pitturu (1436).

Another kind of perspective is aerial perspective, which creates the illusion of depth and distance by modulating colour, shading and chiaroscuro (light and dark). This can be seen combined with linear perspective in such High Renaissance works as Leonardo da Vinci's Virgin of the Rocks.

Perspective drawing device in a woodcut by Albrecht Dürer.

to the discovery of the world, and in Leonardo's case to the sky – and his dominating obsession, flight: 'The screw creates a helix in the air that rises rapidly . . .'

In Florence at this period the Renaissance was a minority movement, and the fifteenth century closed with a puritanical and clerical reaction against these secular, pagan and erotic trends. But history is directed less by the reality of events than by the way they are perceived. Reputation made Florence the hub from which Renaissance influence radiated, and that influence reached a long way. In 1460 a king of Hungary built a palace inspired by literary accounts of a Roman country villa. In 1472 the Grand Princess Zoe took Italian architects and engineers to Moscow. In 1495 the German artist Albrecht Dürer returned home from study in Italy. In the first half of the next century, centres of diffusion of Renaissance style were established in Spanish, Czech and Austrian cities and at the royal courts of England, France, Poland and Lithuania.

The Renaissance cannot be said to have made westerners more likely to conquer the rest of the world, but it did help to define the civilisation they took with them: a civilisation modelled on an ideal image of classical antiquity, a scale of values in which virtue was ennobling, harmony and proportion were beautiful, and the individuality of man was asserted along with a sense of human superiority over the rest of creation.

BLOOD AND PLUNDER: THE AZTECS AND INCA

Today, Mexico City is the biggest, busiest city in the world. Hidden inside and under it are the few traces that remain of another great metropolis that stood there 500 years ago: Tenochtitlán, the capital of the Aztec empire.

The Aztec and Inca empires are usually represented as easy victims for the militarily superior European invaders. In fact they were impressively aggressive and dynamic civilisations, hard to defeat. They may have lacked the means to compete in empire-building on a global scale; but measured by their ability to sustain huge populations, at a density unrepeated in their respective regions for hundreds of years, they were remarkably efficient. Judged by their works – especially the art works of the Aztecs and the engineering feats of the Inca – they were dazzlingly accomplished.

Almost nothing of the Aztec world remained above ground when its conquerors had finished dismantling it. But the Aztecs' remembered vision of themselves can be recovered from a manuscript preserved in the Bodleian Library in Oxford, copied or recalled from fifteenth-century sources: the Codex Mendoza. The first leaf depicts the foundation of the Aztec capital, whose name, Tenochtitlán, means 'place of the cactus and the stone'. Here the image of a prickly pear growing from a stone is surmounted by a huge eagle, with wings

Tenochtitlán, capital of the Aztec empire, as it appeared when the Spaniards first saw it. What is left of it today lies hidden inside and under Mexico City.

131

In a symbol of the founding of Tenochtitlán, an eagle surmounts a prickly pear growing from a stone, on the first leaf of the Codex Mendoza.

outspread, beak parted, head poised to strike and talons rampant, guarding the bones of its prey. According to the foundation myth of the city, the Mexican hero Tenuch was guided by such an eagle to the spot chosen by the gods.

Tenochtitlán was indeed an eagles' nest, and a place for swooping down from. Perched 7,500 feet above sea level, it was surrounded by a huge lake and crossed by intersecting canals. The Aztecs' drawings in the Codex Mendoza show marshy plants, and the humble structures of mud and reed with which the city started. Yet by the time European observers first saw it, a few years after the century's end, they were awestruck by the prospect of vast, gaudy, angular, menacing palaces and temples, including 'the principal one, whose size and magnificence no tongue could describe, for . . . within the precincts . . . a town of five hundred inhabitants could easily be built . . . These great buildings rising from the water, all made of stone, seemed like a city made by a sorcerer.'

This metropolis sustained a huge population; 8,000 dancers performed in its main square. Causeways four miles long linked it to the mainland. Bridges wide enough for ten horsemen crossed the canals. In the marshes around the city, gardens were raised. Many arcaded squares enclosed permanent markets, and streets were dedicated to specialist trades:

> There are streets of herbalists where all the medicinal herbs and roots found in the land are sold. There are shops like apothecaries', where they sell ready-made medicines as well as liquid ointments and plasters. There are shops like barbers' where they have their hair washed and shaved, and shops where they sell food and drink.

The abundance of food was a sign of prodigious wealth: specialists dealt in eighteen sorts of game, 'every sort of vegetable', honey, wax and maize cane syrup, eggs, pies and tortillas, along with 'much fresh and salted fish'; there were also 'ornaments of gold and silver, lead, brass, copper, tin, stones, shells, bones and feathers', builders' materials in brick, stone and wood, fine cotton, skins, good-quality earthenware – and more 'that because of their great number and because I cannot remember many of them nor do I know what they are called I shall not mention them'.

How could a community crowded on to a small island in a brackish lake at an inhospitable altitude get so rich? The codex suggests the answer in the martial symbols that adorn its depiction of the city: a shield decorated with clumps of eagle feathers, a stack of barbed throwing-spears and a skull-rack for the display of the heads of captured sacrifice victims. All the Aztecs' wealth came from war: this was a vast robber-empire which bred warriors and lived off plunder. For the Aztec heartland was in a hostile environment: too high for the cotton which was essential for clothing and quilted armour; too cold for the cacao to make the drink that conferred high social status; too waterlogged to produce maize in sufficient quantities for the densely packed population; too remote from the places where other vital ingredients of civilisation in the region were produced, such as gold and jade, rubber for the ritual ball game, incense for other rituals, jaguar pelts, gulf-coast conches and rich tropical plumage for the divine disguises worn by warriors, priests and ball-players.

From every land they conquered, the Aztecs forced tribute. Tenochtitlán received annually, in units, probably of about a bushel and a half, 140,000 of maize, 105,000 of beans, 105,000 of sage and 90,000 of purslane; 4,000 loaves of salt, 980 loads of cacao and 320,000 baskets of maize flour and other powdered foods. The palace of the allied city of Texcoco was said to have absorbed daily, in the mid-fifteenth century, tribute amounting to up to 1,200 kilograms of maize and 143 of beans, 32,000 cacao beans, 100 turkeys, 20 loaves of salt, 40 baskets of chillies, 10 baskets of tomatoes and 10 squashes with, reputedly, 400,000 tortillas. Cacao was turned into chocolate: the elite drink enjoyed by the city's nobility and priesthood, taken at a thick, viscous consistency and mixed, according to surviving recipes, with all

AZTEC ART

Aztec society was complex, imperialistic and dynamic, with a highly ritualistic religious life and a stylised and iconographic art developed to meet its demands. At the time of the Spanish arrival in 1519 most central Mexican states were subsidiaries of a powerful triple alliance centred on the city of Tenochtitlán. Each city-state operated with some independence and displayed distinctive features, but a unified cultural tradition had prevailed throughout the region for the preceding three centuries.

Central to Aztec culture, and to much of Aztec art, was the importance of blood sacrifice. One Spanish soldier, Andrés de Tapia, recalled the experience of seeing a horrifying sculpture encrusted with gold, jewels and human blood. He may have been describing the statue of Coatlicue, accidentally rediscovered in 1790, considered so terrifying that it was systematically re-interred several times, but surviving today. The head of Coatlicue, 'she of the serpent skin', has been severed and in its place are two snakes, symbolising flowing blood; a third descends from her groin, suggesting both phallus and menses.

Around her neck is a necklace of the severed heads and hearts of sacrificial victims; her hands and feet are claws. Daubed with the blood of a human sacrifice, she must have been a terrifying sight to the newly landed Spanish conquistadores.

In the exuberant geometry of Aztec architecture, multi-roomed palaces, laid out around a central patio, and temples built as staged pyramids were elaborately decorated with stone sculpture and richly coloured painting. Huge statues such as that of Coatlicue, elaborate sculptures of animals, eagles and rattlesnakes, and of plants in the form of cacti and squash dominated the temples and household shrines. Vivid wall-paintings, pictographic manuscripts on skin, cloth and paper, featherwork shields and head-dresses, jewellery of jade, amethyst, opal, jet and amber, ornamental metalwork of gold, silver and copper: all reflect the vibrant and elaborate, if bloodthirsty, culture that was to be swept away by the arrival of the armed might of Christendom.

Xuihtechtli, Lord of Fire.

the flavours of the tributary lands: honey, rose water, maize, the blood of game animals, nuts, herbs, purslane, chillies, eggs and tomatoes.

To maintain this vast empire of plunder, the Aztecs needed to nurture warriors above all else, and the upbringing of children was ruthless to this end. Discipline was severe: disobedient girls were made to inhale chilli smoke, while boys were pierced with cactus spikes.

Above all, the hegemony of the Aztecs depended on divine favour bought with human sacrifice. Their world, they believed, was renewed by fire, the sun kept in the sky by blood. 'All their struggles and battles', according to memories recorded in the sixteenth century, were

> to fight in order to seize captives, each side from the other, for the
> purposes of sacrifice . . . more to take captives than to kill each other
> on the battlefield . . . only to bear food to the idols and those evil
> butchers whose hunger was for human flesh . . . And after sacrifice, all
> well smeared with human blood, and having anointed all the façades of
> the temples and houses of the gods with it and the faces of the idols,
> all the young men and women, dressed up . . . with garlands and
> sartales with necklets of dried maize, drawn up in order and in rings,
> would dance and sing to the beat of a tambor . . .

Prisoners taken by the Aztecs knew what their fate would be, and considered it an honour: 'There is nothing like death in war, nothing like flowery death so precious to the Giver of Life. My heart yearns for it.' They died in their thousands to feed the warriors' gods: the Aztecs' most celebrated ruler, Ahuitzotzin, was credited (in the Aztecs' own probably exaggerated records) with the conquest of forty-five communities in nineteen years' campaigns and with the erection of a temple to the war-god that was inaugurated in 1487 with the sacrifice of 80,400 captives.

The Inca empire also functioned by terror and tribute, but its structure was determined by the long spine of mountains along which it took shape. It was an enterprise both vaster and more tightly regulated than that of the Aztecs, and both features are apparent in the relics of the extraordinary road system with which they scarred the length of the range. Stretching over 12,000 miles and 30 degrees of latitude, this extraordinary network of highways climbed over passes 16,700 feet high. The system was studded with way-stations at altitudes of up to 13,000 feet, in which workers were housed and rewarded with feasts and pain-numbing doses of maize-beer, and linked by prodigious bridges like the famous Huaca-chacha ('Holy Bridge'), which stretched 250 feet on cables thick as a man's body, high above the gorge of the Apurimac river at Curahasi.

To implement projects on this scale, and to maximise production of essential commodities, the Inca were masters of the art of organising labour. A few years before the arrival of the Spanish conquistadores early in the sixteenth century, the Supreme Inca Huayna Capac colonised the Cochabama valley

for maize production with 14,000 forced settlers from all over the empire. The Inca state was enriched by tribute in goods as well as labour: from just one source, for example, they took coca, chillies, mate for making tea, dried birds, fruit and crayfish. Awestruck Spanish accounts of the Inca capital, Cuzco, dwelt on the garden of the Temple of the Sun, 'in which the earth was lumps of gold and it was cunningly planted with stalks of corn that were of gold'. Spanish soldiers reckoned the fortress of Sacsahuamán was big enough for a garrison of 5,000 men: a single stone, still standing in the ruins of the lowest terrace, is 28 feet high and reckoned to weigh 361 tonnes.

Like the Aztecs, the Inca empire enforced its law by terror and fed its gods with human sacrifice. Also like the Aztec system, it had structural weaknesses. The Inca condemned themselves to internecine conflicts by immobilising huge resources in the cults of dead Supreme Incas at Cuzco: this increasingly burdensome tradition fuelled disaffection in the powerful frontier capital of Quito and helped to cause a civil war which the Spanish conquistadores were able to exploit. The Aztec realm was made vulnerable by the complex network of tributary relationships which sustained it: when subject communities began to refuse tribute with Spanish encouragement, Tenochtitlán could not survive.

Inca ruins at Sacsahuaman. The Spaniards were profoundly impressed by the massiveness and precision of Inca structures.

135

AN EMPIRE OF FRUSTRATION: THE OTTOMANS

In the spring of 1453 the skies over eastern Europe darkened. The thousand-year-old walls of Constantinople, for centuries the centre of the eastern Christian world, were besieged by Muslim forces – an army 100,000 strong, led by a prince aged just twenty-one, the Ottoman Mehmet II, known as Mehmet Khan.

The final assault, launched in the middle of the night, is still described by Turkish puppet-masters, who enact in their shows the story of the city's fall: 'You know how difficult it was to capture Istanbul? Thousands of people died on both sides. Let's now close our eyes and imagine how it happened.' On that last night the defending Christians, outnumbered fourteen to one, withstood the onslaught until dawn; but then, seeing the Ottoman flag flying from the battlements, they retreated in despair, allowing the besieging army to flood over the ramparts. Their acknowledgement of defeat had been premature: the invaders' standard had been raised by a small group of Ottoman soldiers who had swum through the sewers to the citadel in a successful attempt to demoralise resistance.

In the ensuing carnage, the last Byzantine emperor died as the Ottoman armies took revenge on his subjects for their reluctance to surrender. In the great Orthodox cathedral of Hagia Sophia, where many Christians had taken refuge, seeking God's protection, priests were decapitated as they celebrated the mass; women were butchered as they knelt; young boys and girls were violated on the altars.

Mehmet Khan, entering the city on a white horse, rode straight to the cathedral. Seeing the devastation wrought by his troops, he wept, commanding that the destruction be halted. Hagia Sophia became a mosque, the cornerstone of the new Islamic capital, which he determined should be built on charity and tolerance. To each new mosque, a soup kitchen was attached that could feed 10,000 people every day. Mehmet encouraged people from all nations to come and live in his city, proclaiming: 'The empire of the world I say must be one. To make this unity, there is no place more worthy than Constantinople.'

In fact, the Turks already had the city under control long before they took it over; but the final loss of Constantinople was a terrible trauma to Christendom. Its importance was more symbolic than real: it was the capital of Rome's first Christian emperor and the seat of Christian Orthodoxy. Its rulers had inherited a sense of being Roman and of preserving cultural traditions which went back to primitive Christianity and classical antiquity. By the fifteenth century, their empire was a rump and their authority was exercised under Turkish sufferance; but they had never renounced their ancient claim to rule the world by divine election.

OPPOSITE *The siege of Constantinople. The Turkish forces greatly outnumbered the defending Christians and made use of the most powerful military technology of the day, including massive cannon.*

Mehmet Khan in the hippodrome in Constantinople.

In 1403, a visiting Castilian ambassador had at his own request been given a conducted tour of Constantinople 'to visit and view the city, churches and relics'. His first impression was of wealth, induced by the columns and wall-claddings of marble and jasper, the hangings of silk, the richly wrought mosaics, the relics mounted in gem-spangled gold and the sheer scale of Hagia Sophia, such that 'even should the visitor return day by day, seeing all he could, there would always be new sights on the morrow'. His next impression was of the defensive strength of the site, enclosed 'within a stout and lofty wall, defended by many strong towers'. But he also spotted many signs of decline: the depopulated quarters abandoned to cornfields and orchards; the many monumental buildings now ruined. 'It is, however, plain', he concluded, 'that in former times when Constantinople was in its pristine state it was one of the noblest capitals in the world.'

The independence of this waning metropolis was little more than nominal. When the Turks lost patience with it, the blow came quickly and inevitably. The accession of Mehmet II as sultan in 1451, at the age of nineteen, marked the end of counsels of prudence. He resented foreign control of a stronghold that dominated a strait vital for the communications of his empire; and he resented the way the people of Constantinople believed in their own myths of their valour against the Turks and their preservation by divine protectors. He was also growing anxious about Constantinople's overtures to potential Christian allies in western Europe. Above all, he fancied himself as a Roman emperor.

The great church of Hagia Sophia, built by the emperor Justinian in the sixth century, became a mosque after the Ottoman conquest.

The fall of the city was prepared by every contrivance of the siege engineer's craft. Huge forts, known respectively as the Castles of Europe and Asia, were erected on either shore to command access to the Bosphorus. The heaviest artillery ever founded was used to shatter the walls. Ships were transported overland in kit form to outflank the defenders' boom. In the end, it was sheer weight of numbers that proved decisive.

In just eighty years after Mehmet's victory, the city's population rose tenfold, Christians, Muslims and Jews living side by side. In an embodiment of his tolerance for religious expression, Mehmet also built a prayer hall for the Whirling Dervishes. Here these devout mystics worshipped God through music, spinning themselves into ecstasy. At the centre of his capital, Mehmet built his palace: 'I give orders for the erection of a palace on the point of old Byzantium. It will leave nothing to be desired, a palace that should outshine all in looks, size and gracefulness.' This palace, the Topkapi Saray, best evokes the character of the Ottoman world in the second half of the century, when it became the sultanate's political nerve-centre. The throne room is a pavilion and many apartments are kiosks scattered through the grounds, like the tents of a camp. For this was an empire which preserved memories of its nomadic origins through long centuries of sedentary solidity. In the warren of the harem, with its lavish alleys and secretive culs-de-sac, the arcane methods by which the empire was regulated can be sensed: here pillow talk was of politics, and women and eunuchs conspired to secure the succession for a potential patron from among the sultan's brood.

From this epicentre the Ottoman empire grew to straddle Europe and Asia, from the Danube in the west to the Euphrates in the east. The rich trade routes that crossed these lands bore back to the capital the ingredients of an Ottoman obsession: food. In the vast kitchens of Mehmet's palace, the cooks were challenged to invent new dishes to show to best advantage the ever-increasing array of produce flowing in from the corners of the expanding empire: aubergines from Persia, oranges from Jordan, dates from Egypt – and from Yemen a new and exotic bean: coffee. 'You fry the beans in a pan. You cook them yourself. They come from plants a long way away.' This new delicacy had a particular practical use: Islam forbade the consumption of alcohol, and the stimulating properties of the coffee bean were highly valued by Muslim merchants on their journeys across the imperial lands.

Like the products for the kitchens, the personnel of the palace came from all over the empire. The harem was an ethnic melting-pot and the elite corps of warriors, the Janissaries, was drawn from infidel minorities, mostly Christians forcibly recruited in childhood and re-educated as Muslims.

Though western visitors to Istanbul went away heady with exotic scents of palace life, any impression of self-indulgent hedonism was likely to lead to mistaken assessments of the power of the Ottoman state. For all its eastern ambience it could outstrip in efficiency and match for adaptability its western competitors, many of whose traditions it shared. Mehmet II saw his capital

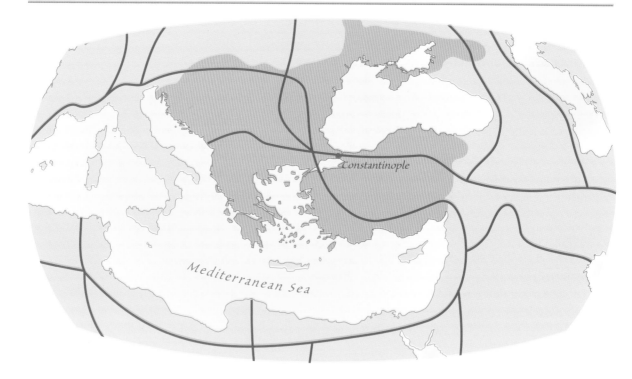

Trade routes of the Ottoman empire. Constantinople, which the Ottomans captured in 1453, was at a vital junction between Europe and Asia. Controlling it, they profited from trade routes that extended far beyond their empire. But though the Turks now controlled the eastern Mediterranean, their maritime expertise was insufficient to carry them into the great oceans where new empires would be made and unmade.

on one level as a continuation of that of Rome, and in his portrait by Bellini he displays the profile of a Renaissance prince. Other empires of nomadic origins failed when faced with the need to adapt to new military and naval technologies; the Ottomans could batter Byzantine walls or blow away Persian cavalry, thanks largely to their engineers' quick grasp of gunnery. And the direction and balance of their conquests, which in the fifteenth century tilted heavily towards the heart of Europe, gave them access to huge numbers of Christian subjects, reared in distant successor-states of Rome.

Today, Turkish poets celebrate Mehmet's life in their songs: 'My story is famous in history. I have honour and glory. I gave dignity to my people. I chose the right way. I ended one era and began a new one. I am the Fatih Sultan Mehmet Khan.'

Though the capture of Constantinople looms very large in the history of fifteenth-century Europe, in Ottoman history of this period it is dwarfed by the transformation that came about when their quest for power took to the sea: for despite their nomadic origins and nostalgia for the life of the tent, the Ottomans proved remarkably adept at launching a navy.

The Turkish vocation for the sea did not spring suddenly and fully armed into existence. From the early fourteenth century, pirate-nests on the Levantine shores of the Mediterranean were run by Turkish chieftains, some of whom allegedly had fleets of hundreds of vessels at their command. The greater the extent of coastline conquered by their land forces, as Ottoman imperialism stole west, the greater the opportunities for Turkish corsairs to stay at sea, with access to watering-stations and supplies on shore. Throughout the fourteenth century, however, these were unambitious enterprises, limited to small ships using hit-and-run tactics. It was only from the 1390s that the sultan Bayezid I began to build up a permanent fleet of his own, though even then without embracing a radically different strategy from the independent operators who preceded him. Set-piece battles usually occurred in spite of Turkish intentions and resulted in Turkish defeats. As late as 1466, a Venetian merchant in Constantinople claimed that for a successful engagement Turkish ships needed to outnumber Venetians by four or five to one. By that date, however, Ottoman investment in naval strength was probably higher than that of any Christian state. Far-seeing sultans realised that if the momentum of their conquests by land was to be sustained, it had to be supported by power at sea.

After the long generations of unsuccessful experiment in pitched battles, Bayezid's navy humiliated that of Venice, formerly the eastern Mediterranean's greatest naval power, in the war that broke out in 1499. Turkish ships fought their way through combined French and Venetian fleets to enter the Gulf of Corinth and capture Lepanto, gaining a seaborne empire and lasting hegemony in the eastern Mediterranean. Never, since the Romans reluctantly took to the sea against Carthage, had a naval vocation been so successfully embraced by so unlikely a power. The balance of naval strength between Christendom and Islam that had prevailed for 400 years was reversed, at least in this crucial region, and a new era can be said to have begun.

Their new naval expertise, however, was insufficient to carry the Turks into the oceanic arenas where the great empires of modern history would be made and unmade.

Turkish ships off Lepanto. Victory there gave them control of the eastern Mediterranean.

THE OCEANS TAMED

Seamen on the Atlantic fringe of Europe stared out from a corner of the continent over an unexplored ocean. Their lands were on the very edge of the civilised world; they were the poor relations of their wealthy Mediterranean neighbours. For them the sea, traditionally the domain of monsters and serpents, was the source of a living to be wrested by piracy and slave-trading.

There was, however, another source of inspiration, embedded in a culture familiar to them, which contributed to making this unpromising corner of the world into a nursery of imperial ambitions: the chivalric romances which offered the tantalising prospect of elevation to the status of knightly conqueror. These tales were the universally popular 'pulp fiction' of the age, providing its heroes and role-models. In the classic version, the hero starts life as a poor son, sails across the world, duels with giants and monsters, marries a princess and ends up ruling some enchanted island. When such fantasies came to be embellished with stories of the gold of Africa and the spices of the east, the seafarers of Spain and Portugal – most of whom had little to lose and much to gain – were spurred to set off on their exploration of the world to the west.

There were other features of western society which helped to entice it seawards: a social structure prolific in ambitious outcasts who were prepared to take risks; a militant, evangelising religious faith; a consciousness of inferiority; an anxiety to escape from the threat of expanding Islam; a competitive state-system which encouraged a long-range search for resources; and an economy neither too poor to generate venture capital nor too rich to suffer from complacency. Unlike their counterparts at the eastern end of Eurasia, west Europeans had to look far afield for the products and outlets they wanted or needed. None of these elements would have been sufficient, however, without the highly motivated manpower mobilised by images of seaborne knight-errantry.

If there was a 'secret ingredient' in western culture which peculiarly fitted it for worldwide out-thrust, this was it. In fifteenth-century Malacca, Muslim traders used Malay titles of nobility and Hindi merchants used the lesser, Sanskrit-derived title of *nina*; but the limits of social ambition for those in trade were strict. In China, merchants and eunuchs were willing to risk the social obloquy of a seaborne life. But seafaring generally was seen in the east as a source of dishonour, a means of 'losing caste'. In the west, by contrast, it could elevate a weaver's boy like Columbus to the rank of viceroy and hereditary Admiral of the Ocean Sea. Whereas in China merchants and seafarers were condemned to lowly status by the landlubber-values of the mandarins, a Portuguese king called himself 'Lord of Commerce and Navigation' and Prince Henry of Portugal came to be known as Henry the Navigator.

The transformation of the Roman hero-figure from knight to saint and back to knight in chivalric tales is echoed in the double lives of some of the heroes of early European maritime expansion: of Prince Henry himself, for instance, the explorers' patron who took pride in his chastity and his hair shirt; or of Christopher Columbus, who affected almost simultaneously the roles of 'a captain of cavaliers and conquests' and of a prophetic, almost priestly figure, clad in a friar's habit. Other aspects, too, of the popular romances were imitated in many real-life careers of explorers and conquerors in the fifteenth-century Atlantic. Prince Henry's retinue of so-called knights and squires was full, in fact, of thugs and pirates; but they gave themselves island-fiefs and story-book names like 'Tristram of the Island'. Columbus, who imagined himself in the same role, married the daughter of one of them, who ruled the tiny Atlantic island of Porto Santo.

Before the key transatlantic voyages of the 1490s took Europeans to the New World, the seafarers' efforts focused on finding a route to the spice islands of the east. The tables of the rich cried out for a constant supply of the exotic flavourings which conferred both taste and status; and yet the overland route from their sources was long, laborious and expensive. At every stage of the journey from east to west, taxes were levied on the precious cargoes as they passed through the hands of countless middlemen, maintaining inflated prices. Merchants and kings alike hired geographers in the quest to pinpoint new routes that would enable them to circumvent this system. But the journeys themselves had to be attempted by sailors.

In search of this tantalising source of wealth, Portuguese navigators sailed south to Africa, along dangerous coasts which their rivals feared: 'Beyond was a green sea of darkness: a ship would stick fast in gelatinous slime, loathsome monsters hovered in the depths, and men turned black beneath the scorching sun.' As each expedition ventured a little further south, the navigators meticulously mapped the newly discovered coast. At each new landfall, the limit of the voyage was marked with a cross – an affirmation and a challenge to those who would follow.

Eventually, this painstaking progress down the shoreline of Africa brought the Portuguese to the tip of the continent and the greatest obstacle of all: the Cape of Storms. In 1488 it was rounded, and renamed the Cape of Good Hope: the navigators had reached the gateway to the Indian Ocean. But the currents and winds effectively kept it shut, and they could go no further. It was another ten years before Vasco da Gama changed the world by finding the key to the puzzle: the winds that carried him around the Cape and into the Indian Ocean. At a stroke, the Arab stranglehold on the spice trade was broken. Within a few years, the prizes of the islands were arriving in the Portuguese harbours by the shipload.

By the time da Gama returned to Lisbon with his first bags of spices, a break-through had also been achieved in the opposite direction – albeit by mistake. When Christopher Columbus set off from the Portuguese capital to head west into the Atlantic, he did so with the same object as his fellow adventurers searching east: to find the spice islands of South-East Asia. 'Travelling leagues you will reach the most fertile of lands abundant with every type of spice, jewel, and precious stone. I call the location of these species the west, although commonly it is said that they are found in the east.' Columbus argued that the Eurasian continent stretched halfway across the world, and that the coast of Japan lay in the

Columbus's ship, the Santa Maria, *in a contemporary engraving.*

middle of the Atlantic in the path of winds that no one had yet followed. If he could get there, he reasoned, he would find the riches of the 'east' at his mercy.

The really revolutionary part of Columbus's scheme was not his idea that there was nothing but ocean between Europe and Asia, but that he could sail with the wind on his outward voyage. Previous explorers from Portugal had always sailed into the wind on their way out, knowing that the same wind would bring them home again. Columbus, on the contrary, intended to sail west, believing the winds would eventually swing north and carry him home. It was a gamble; but he was right.

Columbus made landfall on 12 October 1492 on what he believed to be an island off the coast of China. In fact, it was the Caribbean. He claimed he saw fabulous creatures of the east, dog-headed men and griffins' footprints – and 'great numbers of birds all different from those of Spain except for the Nightingales, who entertained us with their songs'. But his burning desire to reach the eastern lands had blinded him to the facts of nature as well as of geography: nightingales are not found in the New World.

Once the codes of the Atlantic wind system had been cracked, the ocean was transformed from an obstacle to the expansion of European peoples into a means of access to previously unimaginable empires and trades. The Atlantic became the axis of communication around which western civilisation has taken shape; for good or ill, the world of sundered cultures was set to become ever more closely interlinked, enmeshed by routes of mutual access, borne on winds and currents.

Wolf-headed people of the Andaman Islands, as depicted in a fifteenth-century manuscript. Columbus claimed he saw creatures like these in the islands of the Caribbean.

CHAPTER 6

Century of the
COMPASS

I N THE SIXTEENTH CENTURY the world became an arena of imperial and religious competition as aggressive empires intent on expansion and equally aggressive religions intent on making converts – the secular and the spiritual enterprises frequently working hand in hand – set out to conquer and subjugate.

The new long-range contacts made across the oceans by imperialists and missionaries alike created superstates, transformed cultures, shifted migrants – and changed the course of evolution. Through the whole history of the planet before this period, the living things of each continent had evolved in isolation from those on other land masses; now, as the ships traversing the seas between continents bore with them – accidentally as well as by design – plants, animals and microbes from their homelands and their destinations, the direction of evolution was reversed. Where formerly the life forms of each continent had been growing more different from those of all the others, they now began to converge.

The frontispiece of a book by a Spaniard on his country's conquests, published in the last year of the century, showed the author pinching a globe between a pair of dividers, over the motto

> To compass and to sword the score
> Is more and more and more and more.

This sense of the manageable size of the globe, and of a new human capacity to encompass the entire world, was reflected in the map-rooms of gentlemen all over Europe, where visitors could experience the worldwide grasp of the new ocean-borne imperialism and the opportunities for exploration. Writing a thank-you letter to his uncle for the gift of a globe, St Francis Borgia's nephew admitted that he had never realised how small the world was before.

In an engraving based on a sixteenth-century painting a scholar ponders the mystery of the lodestone, whose magnetic power lay at the heart of the compass. A lodestone floats in the vessel in the left foreground.

DIEGO DE LANDA

For all the technological skill and military power of the new maritime empires, none of them had the resources or the mastery of communications to impose its will at long range. Consequently, the only way to run a far-flung empire in the sixteenth century was by means of collaboration with local elites; and indeed, imperialists from far away were often welcomed in environments where objective arbitration was helpful or where allies were wanted in local squabbles. Thus elements, at least, of the peoples colonised by the European invaders participated in their subjection; but the exploitation was not all one way. The complexity of the relationships between conqueror and colonised is perhaps nowhere better illustrated than by the curious case of Diego de Landa and the Maya Indians of Yucatán in Central America.

Diego de Landa, portrayed in a statue from modern Yucatán.

De Landa, a Spanish friar of the Franciscan Order, was a spiritual conquistador, a frontier missionary whose small band of friars held perhaps a quarter of a million Maya in awe in late sixteenth-century Yucatán (now an area of Mexico). The most notorious episode in his story involved the torture of thousands of allegedly recalcitrant natives suspected of reverting to their pagan rituals. The ferocity of this assault was the more surprising because de Landa was well known as a spokesman for and admirer of Mayan culture; he had spent time in the villages, learned to speak the dialects of the Mayan language and attempted to master the local customs. He was the first European to be initiated into the secrets of the Mayan past. Later, he argued that even in their paganism these people enjoyed a partial revelation of the truths of God; but as a devout Catholic, he believed that without being formally received into the Christian church they had no hope of salvation, and so he and his fellow friars presided over mass baptisms of the natives, often thousands in a single day and after minimal instruction in the tenets of the faith.

One day in 1562 the dangers of this hasty approach to inculcating Christianity became only too clear when idols were found in a cave. The Franciscans embarked on an investigation, rounding up and interrogating the villagers. The Maya, unaware that their new religion was supposed entirely to supplant the old, readily admitted to owning idols and worshipping them to bring rain and success in hunting. In just three months, 4,500 natives were put to torture. Confessions multiplied. It was, in the memory of victim-communities, recorded in 1567:

A persecution of the worst that can be imagined; and it was in the year '62, on the part of the religious of St Francis, who had taken us to indoctrinate us, but instead of doing that, they began to torture us, hanging us by the hands and flogging us cruelly, hanging weights of stone on our feet, torturing many of us on the rack, pouring a great quantity of water into our bodies, from which tortures many of us died or were maimed.

The campaign of terror culminated in a Grand Inquisition: a single night during which hundreds were tried, punished and ritually shamed. The Maya were particularly distressed that their chiefs and elders were not spared this onslaught.

Precious writings were also consigned to the flames in a holocaust which almost wiped out the traditional Mayan literature. 'We found', de Landa explained, 'a great number of these books in Indian characters and because they contained nothing but superstition and the Devil's falsehoods we burned them all; and this they felt most bitterly and it caused them great grief.'

At one level, these ferocious acts of intimidation help to explain the Indians' awestruck attitude, but they also raise a question: why were the friars, who were not numerous, who were unarmed and who had little secular support, not massacred by their indignant congregations? It seems strange that so few could exercise such power over so many. But the friars were obeyed for several reasons. For one thing, the appeal of the holy man from afar is strong in cultures under stress from conflict or change, as the Maya were at this period. For another, the Indians appreciated that the friars were more benign masters, on the whole, than secular Spaniards – 'foreign dogs', in Maya eyes, 'empowered by steel to lift skirts'. And yet, as became only too evident, when they felt the occasion demanded it they were willing to use terror tactics equal to anything in the repertoire of lay conquerors. As for why the supposedly peaceful Franciscans could resort to such appalling means, they too were under terrible strain: far from home in a remote, fearsome and challenging world, they cast themselves as God's terrorists against the devil.

The force of de Landa's motives began to emerge when Francisco de Toral, the newly appointed bishop, arrived in Yucatán to act as arbiter between the friars and their critics and victims. Native writers remembered him as 'the master who will put us to the test . . . the sacrificer . . . the bishop . . . whom they call the Holy Inquisition . . . in Saul's company to demand faith and Christianity'. He confronted the zealous missionary directly:

De Toral: Fray de Landa, did you ever torture or kill these people?
De Landa: No one died nor was badly wounded. There were a few scourges and stripes, only laid on with great moderation; if it is true that some died during the Inquisition it is that they did not see or understand Christ, strangling themselves so as not to give up their idols or heathenism.

The bishop found that worthless confessions had been extracted under torture. The Maya were proclaimed blameless of idol worship, and de Landa was summoned to Spain to face trial himself. Ironically, he later returned to Yucatán, having cleared his name, to succeed de Toral as bishop. To this day he is vilified in the area for his betrayal and the destruction he wrought.

And yet the mystery remained. Whose lies were to blame? Were the friars neurotically deluded? Or had some of the Maya – de Landa's supporters and informants – used him in pursuit of their own agenda?

At the root of the Maya's docility, which not only tolerated excesses of missionary violence but accepted subjection to representatives of a foreign religion with evidently little reserve, were the warring interests of established factions in a bitterly divided indigenous society. The Maya world was divided between lineages who hated each other so much that they could not unite even against the Spaniards. On the one hand, the communities of de Landa's victims wrote to the king of Spain:

> Though we truly love Fray Diego de Landa and the other fathers who
> tortured us, only to hear them named causes our entrails to revolt.
> May they do penance there for the evils they did us and may our
> descendants to the fourth generation be recompensed for the great
> persecution that came to us from them.

On the other, there were collaborator communities who begged for the return of 'that Fray Diego de Landa, through whose really great benevolence and goodness in the eyes of our Lord God we truly owe to him alone our Christianity'.

De Landa was well aware of these divisions. His tutor and friend in his quest to learn about the Maya was Chief Nachi Cocom, whose family had once ruled the city of Chichen Itza and who taught de Landa about the warring dynasties of his land. 'Between the three houses of these principal lords,' Landa remarked,

> who were called the Cocom, the Xiu and the Chel, there were great
> feuds and enmities which continue to this day although they have now
> become Christians. The Cocom accused the Xiu of being foreigners and
> traitors who had killed their natural lord and stolen his land. The Xiu
> said that they were as good as the Cocom and just as ancient and lordly
> and that they were not traitors but had liberated their country by killing
> a tyrant. The Chel said that his lineage was as good as theirs because he
> was the grandson of the most highly regarded priest in the old capital
> city of Mayapan, and as for himself he was a greater man than they.

This is not, however, to say that docility, let alone acquiescence in Spanish rule, was the universal result of these internal conflicts. Some Mayan communities cordially hated all Spaniards and Diego de Landa in particular. Mixing history with prophecy, one of their sacred texts foretold:

Your white raiment will be bloodied when the accursed bearded foreigners come . . . Their priests adore an incarnate God, when . . . he spreads his power over the fatherless orphans, the motherless orphans. His head will be a jaguar's, his body a deer's . . . The bird of prophecy will be there. The horsemen of fear will arrive when Christ arrives. Tribute will then be hidden in . . . the place of wells . . . The red-beards, the sons of the sun, the men of pale skin: woe to us at their arrival! . . . It will be the climax of greed, the climax of the seizing of goods, the climax of the wretchedness of the world.

The Maya oppressed. A Maya drawing shows the hard labour imposed and the beatings inflicted by the conquistadores on the native peoples.

Yet, if views such as these had prevailed generally, early colonial Yucatán would have been ungovernable. Many indigenous communities, pursuing ancient tribal vendettas against neighbours and rivals, or celebrating liberation from tyrannies which pre-dated the Spanish conquest, repeatedly declared themselves on the Spaniards' side. Their leaders revelled in the title of 'Maya conquistador' and saw themselves as redeemers of more benighted natives in helping the friars to spread Christianity. De Landa's Inquisition resulted in a significant shift in the Mayan power structure: the elders taken into custody were soon replaced and a new balance of power emerged in the villages. The scandal of idol worship and pagan sacrifice may well have been the means of working out an agenda entirely different from that of the Catholic friars: it is at least possible that Diego de Landa, the conqueror of souls, was the unwitting agent of a Mayan plot.

'THE WIDE EMPIRE OF THE MUSCOVITE'

Given the difficulties of running seaborne empires, it is not surprising that some of the greatest imperial efforts of the sixteenth century were made across land. Land-bound empires of this period – strangely neglected by historians – registered growth rates as spectacular in their way as those of ocean-going imperialists. Morocco, which succeeded in beating off the Portuguese invaders from the north, launched an imperial effort of its own in 1588, across the sea of sand to the south which separated it from the gold of west Africa (see p. 98). The east African empire of Mwene Mutapa, which ruled lands from the Zambezi towards the Limpopo, was also strong enough to repel Portuguese conquistadores. The Ottoman dominions continued to grow: Suleiman the Magnificent shunted armies between Austria and eastern Persia, and pushed the western frontier of his empire along the north African coast to the Moroccan border. As for the Europeans, of all the empires they founded around the world in the sixteenth century, the only one still intact – and it is still the largest – is Russia's.

SULEIMAN THE MAGNIFICENT

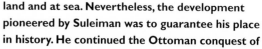

'I who am Sultan of Sultans, the sovereign of sovereigns, the dispenser of crowns to the monarchs on the face of the earth, the shadow of God on earth, the Sultan lord of the White Sea and of the Black Sea ...'

So began a letter from Suleiman to Francis I, king of France. It is perhaps no surprise, then, that he became known as 'the Magnificent' in Europe; to his own people in the Ottoman empire he was known as 'Kanuni' – the lawgiver. Suleiman instituted a programme of internal reforms, granting freedom of religion and raising standards of justice and administration. He also did much to improve his capital, and other Ottoman cities, with an ambitious programme of public building, producing mosques, aqueducts, bridges and public baths. Many of these are attributed to his chief architect, Sinan, whose greatest project was the mosque, Sulaymaniyah, immortalising his master.

The empire Suleiman the Magnificent inherited from his father, Selim I, in 1520 was strong both on

land and at sea. Nevertheless, the development pioneered by Suleiman was to guarantee his place in history. He continued the Ottoman conquest of the Mediterranean, extending the empire both east and west. In 1521 he captured Belgrade, in 1522 Rhodes; he took Mesopotamia from the Persians, and annexed Hungary.

Suleiman's expansionism continued under his successors, but increasing withdrawal of central control and personal direction of government was ultimately to weaken the empire. Another factor in its long, slow decline was the paranoid suspicion of the Ottoman rulers, fathers living in fear of the machinations, real or imagined, of their ambitious children. Suleiman himself ordered his eldest and most able son strangled in front of him, and many sultans banished their children to 'gilded cages' to keep them out of the way until their own deaths.

As in Spain and Portugal, so in Russia the secular and the spiritual powers embarked on conquest, and celebrated it, hand in hand. St Saviour's cathedral in Moscow, destroyed by Stalin and now being painstakingly rebuilt, symbolises Moscow's success story, founded on the role it claimed as centre of the eastern Orthodox church, a status which brought the city, and the Russian state, a power and a prestige that radiated throughout the vast lands beyond. In St Saviour's and in other lavishly appointed cathedrals and churches, the grandeur and growth of the Muscovite empire in the sixteenth century gleam from icons, holy images, which commemorate conquests: against backgrounds of celestial gold, armies led by denizens of heaven – saints and ancient heroes and emperors – leave pagan cities in flames. In the Icon of the Hosts of the Heavenly King, made in the third quarter of the century, a royal army, led by Solomon and David and guarded at the rear by saints, marches across a fantastic landscape of mountains and rivers, from a city of infidels, ringed by fire, towards a shrine of the Virgin. The earthly army is flanked by heavenly hosts, and featuring prominently in the ghostly cavalry are the founder-emperors of the Russian Orthodox tradition of Christianity, Volodomir and Constantine. 'Although the martyrs were born on earth,' reads the commentary, 'they succeeded in attaining the rank of angels . . . for thanks to their suffering they became partakers in the honour due to incorporeal heavenly beings.'

The breakthrough in the Russian imperialism which inspired this art was the conquest by Tsar Ivan IV – Ivan the Terrible – of Kazan, a Muslim empire to the south-east of the Russian heartlands around Moscow, which had hitherto blocked any expansion into Siberia. To commemorate this achievement, Ivan commissioned St Basil's cathedral, its famous domes designed to represent Kazan turbans, one for each chieftain killed in the siege. Legend has it that Ivan had the architects blinded so that they would never be able to surpass their achievement in designing this monument.

Victory over Kazan gave Ivan and his successors command of the entire length of the river Volga, the great artery of commerce at the western edge of Asia, and of the apparently limitless riches of the Siberian fur trade. For, just as gold lured the Spaniards to the Americas and spices captivated the Portuguese in the Indies, so furs summoned Russians to feats of conquest and colonisation in the north Asian wilderness. And it was fur that put Russia on the international stage, drawing in a wave of foreign traders. An empire which now extended from the White Sea in the Arctic to the Caspian Sea far to the south-east had every incentive to expand to the north and east.

'Expensive sables,' reported a merchant's handbook of 1575, 'unripped, with bellies and feet, are valued in all countries.' Native hunters could land an arrow on a sable's nose; the Russians had to resort to a more laborious procedure. They cut a hole big enough for the animal's head in a tree trunk and connected a log by a balance to the bait. When the sable put its head in the

An icon celebrates Ivan the Terrible's conquest over the Tartars of Kazan. The Muscovite forces are shown as crusaders, aided by the saints and warriors of Russia's past.

hole, the log crushed the skull, 'without injuring in the slightest the valuable parts of his skin'. In 1595 Russia's ruler sent a present of furs to help pay for a proposed crusade against the Turks: skins worth 44,645 roubles at Moscow prices had risen in value to 400,000 roubles by the time they reached Prague – exclusive of 120 sables reckoned so rare as to be priceless. The furs filled twenty chambers in the emperor's palace; tens of thousands of squirrel skins had to be left in wagons outside.

The tsar's next task was to conquer Siberia itself – perhaps the harshest terrain on earth – and control the production as well as the trade in fur. In 1555 Ivan IV began to call himself 'Lord of Siberia'. Three years later, he cut a deal with the Stroganoff family, the biggest merchant dynasty in the world of furs, who were willing to pay to turn that title into reality – and reap the rewards. The language of a chronicler's account reflects the typical mind-set of white imperialists in all the new worlds assailed by Europeans, with the assertion that pagans have no rights; that their lands are 'empty'; that colonisation can be promoted by fiscal privileges; and that the work is holy.

In the year 1558 on the 4th of April the Pious Sovereign the Tsar and Great Prince Ivan Vasilyevich of all Russia granted Grigorey, son of Anika Stroganoff, the empty lands below the Great Ural . . . In those regions where Grigorey might choose a strong and well guarded place, we have commanded him to establish a stronghold and build fortresses and by his own authority to appoint cannoneers and fortress gunners and musketeers and artillery-men for defence against the Siberian peoples . . . and the peoples of other hordes. We have also commanded the same Grigorey to recruit freely to himself those who are untaxed and unregistered in those lands.

From the 1570s, colonisation made detectable inroads. Treatment of the native peoples was uncompromising. Those who paid tribute in furs were accorded the protection of Russian armies 'against the fighting men of Siberia'. No attempt was made to rule the 'savage' tribes directly: they just had to take oaths of submission. The Ostyaks were made to swear on a bearskin on which a knife, an axe and a loaf were spread: the oath-breaker would choke to death or be cut to pieces in battle with men or bears. The Yakuts had to pass between the quarters of a dismembered dog.

Ivan the Terrible's rule was no kinder to his own people than to the tribes of Siberia. Unhinged by the strain of empire, trusting no one, Ivan set up a new force to protect himself against real and imagined threats: the Oprichnina or 'Men Apart'. Empowered to arrest, torture and execute on the tsar's slightest whim, these agents of terror were the first Russian secret police. People were rounded up and executed, or skinned alive and fed to the dogs.

On the field of conquest, too, Ivan sought out the most brutal tools to carry through his plans. The manpower for the Siberian conquest was supplied by the crack troops of the old frontier with Kazan: the Volga Cossacks. In 1579, the Russians' prospects were transformed when 540 Cossacks under a chief (ataman) of stupendous prowess joined the campaign: for Yermak Povolskoy was to the Siberian enterprise what Cortés and Pizarro had been to the Iberian conquistadores in the Americas. The Stroganoffs welcomed these paragons with open arms,

> received them with honour and gave them many gifts and provided food and drink in abundance for their enjoyment. The atamans and cossacks stood against the godless infidels, daring and united, together with the men living there in the strongholds, and they fought the godless infidels fiercely and unmercifully.

Characteristically of European military operations on remote frontiers, the Russians ascribed their success to the intimidating effect of unfamiliar technology. From their firearms mounted on river barges, the waterborne

The empire of Ivan the Terrible. In his reign what was once the principality of Moscow began the process that would eventually take the Russian empire to the shores of the Pacific. Before him, expansion had always been blocked by Kazan, a Muslim empire to the east; once Ivan had captured Kazan the way east was finally opened.

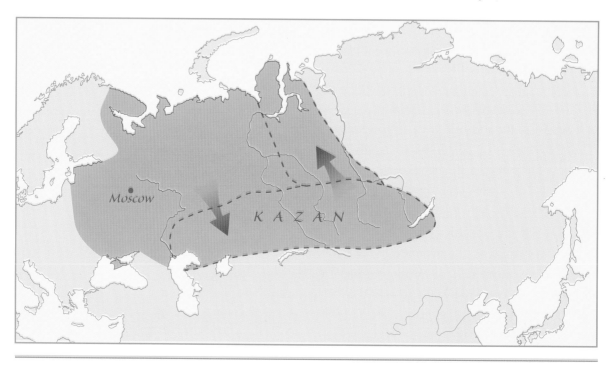

invaders exchanged bullets for bowshots with defenders on the banks. One Siberian khan was said to be dismayed to hear from a spy that

> the Russian troops are so powerful: when they shoot from their bows, then there is a flash of fire and a great smoke issues and there is a loud report like thunder in the sky. One does not see arrows coming out of them. They inflict wounds and injure fatally, and it is impossible to shield oneself from them by any trappings of war. Our scale armour, armour of plates and rings, cuirasses and chain-mail do not hold them; they pierce all of them right through.

The object of the campaign spearheaded by Povolskoy's Cossacks was not to colonise the ice-bound wastes but to eliminate the only state capable of challenging Russia in the region: the khanate of Sibir, which dominated the eastern tributaries of the Irtysh river. The khan, Kuchum, was a Muslim, and so the expedition of conquest was sold as a crusade, and depicted symbolically by representations of gospel-rays spreading from the eyes of Christ between colonists' cities. Russian propagandists put a prophetic vision into the mind of their target: 'The skies burst open and terrifying warriors with shining wings appeared from the four cardinal points. Descending to the earth they encircled Kuchum's army and cried to him, "Depart from this land, you infidel son of the dark demon, Muhammad, because now it belongs to the Almighty." '

An illustration from a contemporary chronicle shows Ivan at the scene of a battle. His troops are depicted in late classical costume as heirs of Christian Byzantium.

Muslim resistance was soon reduced to the level of guerrilla activity; but it was not finally crushed until 1598. Meanwhile, Povolskoy met his death one rainy night on the Irtysh:

> The pagans, like a viper breathing fury against Yermak and his company, were preparing their swords for vengeance, were hoping to regain their inheritance . . . The time was about midnight. Yermak and his company were sleeping in their camps, beneath the curtains of their beds. The pagans, breathing fury as if mad, prepared themselves for the shedding of blood, and understood that it was already time to achieve their wish . . . And so all were killed there and only one escaped; and the most wise, brave and eloquent Yermak was killed.

Or perhaps, according to another version, drowned in the effort to reach his boat.

Portrait sculpture of Hideyoshi.

HIDEYOSHI, 'THE BALD RAT'

Of all the imperial efforts launched seaward in the sixteenth century, the least well known is Japan's. It began in the home islands, with a project to reunify a country that for two centuries had been riven into ever smaller units by bitter and constant conflict among competing barons. For a time, an overarching order was imposed not by one of the rival aristocratic warlords, but by a former peasant soldier become warrior dictator: Toyotomi Hideyoshi, 'the Bald Rat'.

In the 1580s Hideyoshi proposed to undertake an ambitious survey of his entire country, encompassing 'the deepest caves of the mountains and the reach of oars at sea'. It was to include the dimensions and soil quality of every rice field and the location of every irrigation channel. Villagers who withheld information would be crucified; landowners who failed to cooperate would be put to the sword. The surveyors were warned that sake (rice wine) is strictly forbidden while surveying. You shall go out in the morning at the hour of the Rabbit [5 a.m.] and return in the evening at last third of the hour of the Monkey [6.30 p.m.]. Do your calculations at your lodgings . . . You may not accept any gift, large or small . . . Should there be any inappropriate act by yourselves, needless to say, or your underlings, you shall be brought to judgement as soon as we hear of it.

Begun in 1583, driven by demonic energy and hurried along by pitiless force, the job was finished in 1598.

The very idea of such a comprehensive survey would have been barely conceivable a generation before: in just twenty-odd years from 1560 Hideyoshi had brought his country to the point where he could not only gaze upon it as a single realm but could look beyond its confines to project the conquest of the world. 'With 500 or 1,000 men,' he boasted, 'I succeeded in uniting Japan, a country of warriors and furious internecine struggles . . . the land of the gods.'

Some of his subjects hoped for an era of peace. 'What a marvellous age!' exclaimed Miura Joshin. 'Even peasants like me enjoy tranquillity and happiness and there are wonderful things to be heard and seen.' Hideyoshi became the 'Most Bright God of Our Beautiful Country'. In his hands the nation bloomed for the first time in over a century. Temples and palaces ravaged by civil war were restored and covered with gold. According to Ota Gyuichi, the foremost chronicler of the era,

> Ever since the advent of Hideyoshi, gold and silver have gushed from the mountains and plains in the land of Japan. Moreover, silks, damasks and crepes and golden brocades . . . Men vie with each other in presenting ever new and rarer things to his Highness, so that it has been like piling up mountains of treasure. In the old days, no one so much as laid an eye on gold. But in this age there are none, even among peasants and rustics, no matter how humble, who have not handled gold and silver aplenty. Our empire enjoys peace and prosperity: on the roads not one beggar or outcast is to be seen, all on account of the Taiko.

He praised Hideyoshi's devotion to acts of compassion and mercy. 'By his deeds you shall know the quality of the prince. His power and glory made his a blessed reign.' Peace at home, indeed, was Hideyoshi's first priority – and again a secular policy was infused with a spiritual significance. 'The farmers and the vassals', he decreed in 1588,

> are strictly forbidden to keep sword, spears, firearms and other implements, lest they be tempted to evade their taxes and plot rebellion . . . So that the long swords and short swords collected shall not be wasted, they shall be reforged as rivets and clamps in the forthcoming construction of the Great Buddha. This will be an act by which the farmers will be saved in this life, needless to say, and in the

life to come. If the farmers possess agricultural tools alone and engage completely in cultivation, they shall unto eternity. It is with compassion to the farmers that we rule in this manner.

Eager to be seen as an agent of the 'civilising process', Hideyoshi incorporated ritual and spectacle in his art of government alongside naked brutality. His use of the tea ceremony, which evolved in this period as a piece of political theatre, both illustrated his methods and revealed the insecurity bred by his lowly origins. In espousing the cult he was imitating his predecessor, the master of his youth, whom he had always aspired to emulate: Oda Nobunaga, who, 'lacking no gold or silver mine or cash', had started to collect costly tea vessels in 1569. Hideyoshi was thrilled when the right to have his own ceremony was conferred on him in 1578; by the standards of the scale of values which prevailed at the Japanese court, the high point of his career came when he entertained the emperor to a tea party in 1585. Such events, for all their esoteric and aesthetic trappings, were occasions of political business. The decree commanding such an occasion in 1588 read:

> We order that a grand tea party be held . . . so that the ceremonial vessels can be displayed to serious persons . . . The Japanese, even the Chinese, anyone with a connoisseur's interest, should join in. As for dress, it should be at one's pleasure and diverse . . . those who fail to come for this occasion shall be regarded in offence should they prepare even barley tea . . . We order that practitioners of the cult, whoever they are and from whatever distant place, shall be served tea from the hand of Hideyoshi.

On this occasion Hideyoshi did indeed serve 803 individuals – and took the opportunity to impose a humiliating oath on aristocrats suspected of recalcitrance: 'We solemnly swear that we were moved to tears of gratitude . . . We commit ourselves and our children and our children's children . . . to obey the Lord Regent in everything and we shall not violate his orders in the slightest.'

Not all the glories of his exalted position could defend Hideyoshi against his insecurity or obliterate his despotic instincts. Gradually he came to suspect that Rikyu, his tutor in the art of the tea ceremony, had exploited him. 'In recent years,' it was reported at court, 'Rikyu provided himself with tea implements of a new type and sold them at high prices. Hideyoshi was furious . . . calling it the ultimate in sharp practice.' The tea-master's disgrace was surrounded by other rumours. He had glorified himself with a portrait sculpture. He had dabbled in Christianity and corruption. Lapses of taste – the ultimate derogation for a master of ceremonies – were also alleged. Hideyoshi ordered Rikyu to commit ritual suicide.

The vicious, manic pride which so often corrodes self-made dictators drove Hideyoshi to escalating ambitions further afield. 'Originally,' he recalled,

OPPOSITE *A silk screen shows an outdoor tea gathering. The bowls in use are Korean celadon. Korean potters were brought to Japan after Hideyoshi's military conquests.*

I was a lowly subject. But when I was in my mother's womb, my mother dreamed that the sun entered her belly . . . The rays of the sun filled the room where my father and mother conceived me. The fortune teller said, 'When the child grows up, his glory will radiate in ten thousand directions and the four seas will know his fame . . . Because of this strange fact . . . when I fight, I always win.'

For the first time in the millennium, Japan looked abroad. Hideyoshi sent demands for submission to the kings of Indo-China and the Spanish governor of the Philippines. He proclaimed himself the gods' choice for mastery of the world. By 1587 he was planning the conquests of Korea and China. After early successes power tipped over into megalomania and, his passion for conquest becoming an obsession reminiscent of the world-wide vocation of a thirteenth-century Mongol khan, Hideyoshi proclaimed himself master of the world.

In some ways, foreign adventure was a rational policy in the circumstances. The long civil wars had militarised Japan; professional warriors needed employment; the arms industry needed markets; the energies of the warlords had to be redirected. Hideyoshi's ambitions, however, exceeded rational bounds. 'To take by force this virgin of a country,' he said of China, 'will be as easy as to crush an egg.' Future conquests would form not just personal trophies but a

SONS OF HEAVEN

Shinto, 'the way of the gods', is the indigenous religion of Japan, according to which the imperial family are direct descendants of the sun goddess Ameratsu-Omikami. Its most sacred shrine is at Ise, where the inner temple, dedicated to Ameratsu, contains the mirror that she is supposed to have given to the first emperor, Jimmu, in the seventh century BC. Shinto lacks a single founder or central body of scripture, but its long tradition continues to the present day.

Shinto revolves around elaborate ceremonies to the kami – disembodied forces of nature, non-moral manifestations of power. They can be appealed to through ritual and offerings to provide their blessing for a good rice harvest, protection from fire or famine, the blessing of children, and so on. Equally they can be displeased by inattention, insufficient offerings or the pollution of blood, dirt or death; and they are feared for their power to curse families or villages.

The Shinto ritual, known as Daijosai, which is performed after the official enthronement of a new emperor in the grounds of the imperial palace, takes place in specially erected wooden buildings, which are destroyed soon afterwards. The ritual culminates in a secret late-night ceremony in which the new emperor shares the first fruits of the harvest with the kami. During the fifteenth century the ceremony was discontinued, but it was revived in 1687 by the Tokugawa shogunate. After the defeat of Japan at the end of the Second World War Emperor Hirohito was made to renounce his divinity, but at the enthronement of Emperor Akihito, the first post-war coronation, the Daijosai was once again performed, the Japanese government taking the controversial step of funding the ceremony at a cost of £10,000.

Despite the divinity of the emperor, from the late twelfth century political control of Japan remained in the hands of the shoguns, military dictators such as Hideyoshi, who arose from a number of locally powerful clans, reducing the role of the emperor to that of a symbolic figurehead. It was not until 1867, and the rule of Meiji Mutsuhito, that control of the country's destiny was restored to the emperors.

A computerised reconstruction of a Korean turtle boat, an armoured tank of the seas.

thoroughbred empire. The Koreans and Chinese would be 'taught Japanese customs'. The land would be partitioned among Japan's nobles. The Japanese emperor would take over from China the 'mandate of heaven', the divinely conferred right to rule the world.

The imperial plan of campaign began with an invasion of Korea. While Japan had been steeled by war, Korea had enjoyed two centuries of peace; and while its rulers dismissed Hideyoshi's threats as incredible, its generals, at first, submitted to them as irresistible. The Japanese task force, 300,000 strong, reached the Korean capital, Seoul, in twenty days. Yet Hideyoshi had miscalculated the problems of maintaining a seaborne force far from home. Though the 'Black Ocean' which separated Korea from Japan looked small on the map, the hazards of navigation there made it almost as daunting a space as the Atlantic vastnesses traversed by the Spanish and Portuguese conquistadores of the time. Reinforcements and supplies were held up. 'The waves', Hideyoshi fretted in 1592, 'are very rough on the sea to Korea.' More threatening even than the elements alone was the secret weapon of the Korean navy: the turtle boat, an armoured tank of the seas. Armed with these terrifying vehicles, the Koreans blew the Japanese out of the water, while the invading army became weary and demoralised, mired in foreign mud. 'Hell cannot be in any other place,' wrote the Buddhist priest Keinen, who accompanied Hideyoshi's second Korean campaign, '. . . the sight of the fiends and man-devouring demons must be like this.'

Under the strain of the war, the image Hideyoshi had constructed at home began to crumble. 'He hath so impoverished all the rude and rustic multitude,' a Jesuit visitor reported, 'that they have scarcely enough whereon to live.' What to Hideyoshi was 'the tone of a well ordered realm' was to his critics the surface glitter of the *nouveau riche*: the same observer noted that in a castle which was 'nothing else but a pump of all pleasures' he enjoyed 'such banquets, such disports and recreations as the very rehearsal would surpass all credit'. The would-be world ruler responded to the change in his fortunes by retreating into a fantasy world of his own – a mental bunker walled with two private obsessions: the Noh theatre of drama and dance, and preoccupation with his family. From his travels in 1594, he reported in a letter home, 'I have had no free time because of theatricals . . . My dramatic technique becomes more and more accomplished; whenever I present the uncostumed dances of various plays, the whole audience praises it very much . . . I shall perform plays for you. Look forward to it.' Impartial critics took a less congratulatory view of his artistic attempts: 'He danced with such an evil grace,' reported a Jesuit, 'as well argued an impotent and doting old man.'

Trivia – his chilly bottom, tummy troubles and choice of theatrical costumes – came increasingly to dominate his letters. He had remained childless until late in life, when a concubine bore him a son, named Hideyori. He transferred his frustrated ambitions on to the boy, about whom he became irrationally anxious: 'It may be beyond your understanding,' he told the boy's mother,

> that I feel such affection for Hideyori . . . It is important that you spare no attention to prevent him from catching a chill . . . While recently I have been far away, I have known only a longing for home. I cannot describe the endless tedium, as if I were guarding an empty house, when Hideyori is not here with me. I say again, be strictly vigilant against fire. Each night have someone make the rounds of the rooms two or three times. Do not fail in this.

In 1597, he reproved the five-year-old boy, nicknamed 'Lord Chunagon', with a tyrant's advice: 'Your wet-nurse is quite wrong. Should anyone try to thwart the will of Lord Chunagon, he must beat and beat such a man to death, and then nobody will be against him.' And in a typical letter written the same year, he wrote, 'I shall be back very soon . . . Then I shall kiss your lips. Your lips should be kissed by no one else, not even a little bit. I can imagine how you are growing finer and finer . . . Though I meant to write to your Mamma too, I hope she understands.'

The aged ruler was ruthless in securing Hideyori's succession, ordering his nephew to commit suicide and massacring the rest of his family. But it was all to no avail, for his last appeals for loyalty to the boy went unregarded. When Hideyoshi died in September 1598, his generals, returning defeated from Korea, immediately disputed the succession. Hideyori and his mother took their own lives, and Japan turned back in on itself. Losing both its internal unity and its global vision, it slid into an era of so-called 'isolation' which would last for over two centuries. The verses Hideyoshi wrote on his deathbed could have been the epitaph of his empire: 'My life fell like dew / And disappears like dew.'

THE MOGHULS

Alongside Russia, the most spectacular case of imperial growth in the sixteenth-century world happened in India. Vulnerability to the imperialism of outsiders is a recurrent feature of Indian history, and at this period the threat came from central Asia. Islamic invaders called Moghuls – descendants of the Mongols who had overrun Asia in the thirteenth century (see above, p. 66) – made India their empire by adapting to it: a process described in an account stretching over three generations written by Gulbadan, the daughter of the first Moghul emperor, Babur, and surviving today.

Gulbadan's family claimed descent from Genghis Khan himself; yet the Moghul empire began not as a conscious continuation of this dynastic heritage but by accident. Umar Shaikh Mirza, Gulbadan's grandfather, was more interested in pigeons than politics; but his hobby turned out to be his downfall:

> Umar Shaikh Mirza flew with his pigeons and their house, and became a falcon who took flight to the other world.

Umar's death opened the way for his more ambitious son to make his mark in the world. Babur, 'the Tiger', was an adventurer in the mould of his ancestor Timur (see above, p. 104). On succeeding his father at the age of eleven, he first attempted to take Timur's favourite city of Samarkand; unsuccessful there, he turned eastwards and established himself in Kabul, in modern Afghanistan. It was from here that he went on, through a series of eight campaigns that took him as far as Bengal, to found the Moghul empire of the Indian subcontinent.

Though Babur spent his own life on the campaign trail, the heart of the empire remained a five-month journey away, in Kabul, where the court and harem were based. A strict Muslim, Babur took only four wives; but the harem was filled with concubines, female relations, and the families of nobles who had been killed or imprisoned. Together with numerous daughters, mothers, aunts and servants, these made up a substantial population: it is likely that Babur never knew how many women he sheltered in his precincts.

Babur 'the Tiger'.

And he added to them. Gulbadan recalled in her diary a special delivery from her father, which arrived with specific instructions: 'I send some of the

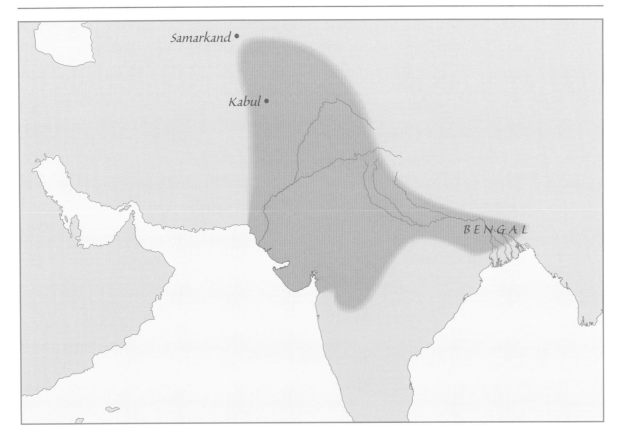

valuable presents and curiosities of Hind which fell into our hands . . . each senior woman is to be given one special dancing girl, with one gold plate full of jewels.'

Babur loved India as a source of plunder, not of cultural development: the country changed him, but only by making him more self-conscious about his own cultural heritage and strengthening his identity as a Muslim. He built gardens and baths to protect himself from heat, wind and dust. In his youth, he had held drinking parties that went on all night; but now he renounced wine better to fit himself for holy war against the warrior princes of India who combined to challenge his rule. He proclaimed: 'For the love of the faith I became the enemy of pagans and Hindus. I strove to make myself a martyr.' And yet it was dysentery, rather than a call from God, that put an end to Babur's life, two years after his victory against the Rajput princes.

Babur had conquered much of India, but it remained a foreign land to him. His grandson, Akbar the Great, upheld the martial part of his legacy and completed the conquest of the subcontinent, but India also conquered his affections. Akbar adopted Rajput dress and Indian mysticism in a pick-and-mix religion, worshipping the sun while his subjects were made to worship him. His realm was set at a crossroads of expanding religions and competing cultures, and Akbar made the most of its position, concocting a religious synthesis and creating a pluralist state. Where his predecessor had waged holy

The Moghul empire of the Indian subcontinent, founded by Babur 'the Tiger'. Thwarted in Samarkand, Babur turned his attentions east; first to Kabul, in modern Afghanistan, and then, through a series of eight campaigns, as far as Bengal.

OPPOSITE *Dancing girls perform before Akbar the Great. His grandfather Babur introduced this form of entertainment, which is still a feature of the cultural life of India today (inset).*

war, he made a virtue of toleration. The epitaph Babur had written for himself proclaimed him 'a warrior for Islam'; Akbar cultivated breadth of thinking and tried to get representatives of the vast land's various religions to discuss their beliefs and theologies with one another. He built a special house of worship in which all the different faiths were represented, intending that it should be a forum for ordered discussion and reasonable debate, from which a truly comparative theology could emerge. His optimism was soon confounded: often, the participants in these discussions could not even agree on where to sit.

These initiatives greatly distressed and disturbed his devoutly Muslim aunt Gulbadan, as did the latitude he granted himself in his domestic life: instead of the regulation four wives, Akbar kept an estimated 800 or more, establishing marriage alliances that brought him lands and loyalty. As Akbar, having conquered India, came to be possessed by it, Gulbadan fled in protest to the Muslim holy city of Mecca.

Akbar and the quarrel of the ascetics. Although a devout Muslim himself, Akbar tried to encourage peaceful debate among adherents of Indian's different religious traditions.

CABINETS OF CURIOSITIES

The world-ranging imperialism which began in the sixteenth century has been presented, so far, as a movement of political and religious allegiances. But it was also part of a wider phenomenon of inter-oceanic exchange, in which the products of art and nature were garnered and transferred from their traditional environments into the common pocket of humankind, to function as a source of wonder and of power.

The German artist Albrecht Dürer, whose life straddled the fifteenth and sixteenth centuries, jotted his reaction to the wonders of the New World in his diary:

> I have seen the things brought to the king from the new golden land: a sun, wholly of gold, wide a whole fathom, also a moon, wholly of silver and just as big; also two chambers full of their implements, and two others full of their weapons, armour, shooting engines, marvellous shields, strange garments, bedspreads and all sorts of wondrous things for many uses, much more beautiful to behold than miracles . . . In all my life I have seen nothing which gladdened my heart so much as these things. For I have seen therein wonders of art and have marvelled at the subtle wits of people in far-off lands. And I know not how to express what I have experienced thereby.

These collections were amassed and presented primarily in order to provoke wonder – an experience identified by the French philosopher René Descartes as fundamental to the age: 'I regard wonder as the first of all passions. It has no opposite, for if the object has nothing that surprises us, we consider it without passion.'

Vegetable portrait of the Emperor Rudolf II by Giuseppe Arcimboldo. The portrait was intended to be flattering; the fruits, flowers and vegetables composing it represent the four seasons in perfect harmony.

Of the artefacts amassed, those of gold were almost all melted down for bullion; but others found their way into the collections of princes or gentlemen's 'cabinets of curiosities' across Europe. The world-wide grasp of explorers' tentacles filled these proto-museums with the spoils of nature and art – some of them bizarre in the extreme. Contemporary lists included a horn that was grown on the forehead of an Englishwoman; the passion of Christ carved daintily on a plum stone; the huge boots belonging to the deformed Duke Johann Frederick II of Saxe Coburg; flies which glow at night from Virginia ('since there is often no day there for over a month'); a lock of the hair of Petra Consalves, the hairy man from Tenerife.

Like the assemblages of saints' relics which preceded them in the sequence of collectors' fads, these treasuries of marvels were testimonies to the wonders of creation. 'The ideal collection', wrote Samuel Quiccheberg, the foremost curator of the age, 'should be nothing less than a theatre of the universe . . . keys to the whole of knowledge . . . the full script of man and his maker.' The exotic items gathered in this way were linked in the collectors' minds with the projects of Renaissance magic and alchemy associated with the story of Faust, who made a pact with the devil in his ambition to master all knowledge and 'be like God'. But Quiccheberg was quick to point out the entirely respectable Christian credentials of such an enterprise: 'In making a theatre of the universe the higher purpose, of course, is to honour God's sublime creation, to show his miracles in every face.'

God's hand was indeed evident in exhibits from the natural world – minerals with magical properties, prodigious animals that were like works of art: nature stretched to the limits of creativity. But man could be God's rival in the fashioning of extraordinary objects: the Creator, it seemed, was no longer the only creator. Holy relics and natural magic shared shelf space with new science; the collections of marvels were theatres of memory and power, but they were also, at least potentially, scientific collections, which contributed to the sudden enlargement of European knowledge of the world.

The collection of the Emperor Rudolf II in Prague was, by common assent, the most prodigious of the day, with over 20,000 exhibits and specimens from all over the world packed into just four rooms. Now dispersed and beyond recovery, it can still be pictured in the descriptions recorded – bit by bit, for no one could comprehend the whole – by visitors and cataloguers. It included armadillos, chameleons, pelicans, crocodiles, iguanas, tortoises, starfish, blow-

The letter R: a hand-painted illumination, from a book of calligraphy, produced under the patronage of Rudolf II.

fish, seahorses and 'a bird of paradise with its natural wings and feet'. Dissected frogs were displayed with a hippo's teeth and seventeen claws from tigers or leopards. From ingredients in Rudolf's cabinet, his physician, Oswald Croll, compounded a plague remedy: 'Dessicated toads and pulverised chickens, the menstrual blood of a young maiden, white arsenic, pearls and emeralds from the Orient. This concoction is to be baked into a toad cake and worn next to the heart in an amulet.'

Rudolf's collection had a political as well as a scientific message. The emperor himself was carefully placed at the centre of his miniature universe, depicted as master of nature itself; visiting dignitaries, shown round the collection, would be impressed by the extent of Rudolf's world-wide reach as they marvelled at the wonders it had produced.

In the high proportion of their contents that came from across the Atlantic, the collections were also an early sign of another world-historical revolution: the enrichment of Europe

A sixteenth-century cabinet of curiosities, in a television reconstruction.

by the New World. It would take a long time for the treasures of the New World to be fully exploited to the advantage of Europeans, and it would take longer still for markets west of the Atlantic to grow sufficiently to make a big difference to the global balance of trade and production. In the sixteenth century, the advantage in the competition for world resources still lay firmly where it had always lain: at the eastern end of Eurasia and, especially, in China.

An early European window-shopper there was Fernao Mendes Pinto, a Portuguese who claimed to have sailed the east from 1521 to 1558 as a soldier of fortune, penetrating every cranny of the accessible orient, surviving en route more shipwrecks, enslavements, slaughters, storms and changes of circumstance than any reader could reasonably believe. However tendentious, his account of his adventures is a masterpiece of picaresque literature with many delicious asides, both moralising and amusing. Though his description of China is no more verifiable than the rest of his book, it fairly reflects the image of the country prevalent among his contemporaries. In the tingle of senses excited by the excess of everything, it rings true as the relation of an eye-witness, walking round the markets of Beijing, for example, 'as if in a daze' at the quantities of 'silk, lace, canvas, clothes of cotton and linen, marten and musk and ermines, delicate porcelain, gold- and silver-plate, seed-pearls and pearls, gold dust and gold bullion' – and as for the base metals, gems, ivory, spices, condiments and foods: 'Well, all these things were to be had in such abundance that I feel as if there are not enough words in the dictionary to name them all.'

But the age of the marvellous was drawing to a close. As trade and traffic spread around the globe, these objects lost their power to excite wonder. The idea that the whole world might be stored as data in a single room is only now becoming believable once more.

CHAPTER 7

Century of the
TESLESCOPE
THE SEVENTEENTH CENTURY

U NTIL NOW, western science had lagged behind that of rival cultures. For most of the Middle Ages the scientific writings of the ancient Greeks and Romans had been transmitted to European scholars through Arabic translations; scientific instruments had been copied from Arab models. The science of China, which had its own ancient tradition of observation and experiment founded by sages working centuries before the birth of Christ, had always seemed immeasurably more sophisticated than anything the west had produced. But in the seventeenth century the balance shifted, as western science began to outpace that of the far east.

The globe was enmeshed in a grid of reference, mapped to scale for the first time on the basis of verifiable observations. In the 1670s, the third floor of the west tower of the Royal Observatory in Paris was laid out as a vast map of the world, 24 feet in diameter, with lines of longitude and latitude spread over it at intervals of 10 degrees. Previously unknown places were marked in as new inventions made it possible to report their position accurately. Scientific travellers despatched reports from Goa and the Cape of Good Hope. Expeditions were sent to Guiana and Egypt, Cape Verde and Guadeloupe. Jesuit missions in Madagascar, Siam and China made observations to the same end. When the French king Louis XIV visited the work in progress,

King Louis XIV of France receives members of the Academy of Sciences, founded in 1666, among symbols of scientific enquiry including, in the background, a telescope.

he could stamp on the world and know exactly where his foot fell. Even in China, where scientific complacency was habitual, the mandarins were waking up to the threat and promise heralded by the new evidence of the ingenuity of those whom they had hitherto derided as 'barbarians'. It would still be a long time before westerners forged ahead of other civilisations, technologically or economically; but the trend of centuries was going into reverse.

The unprecedented primacy of western science was the first sign of a shift of initiative during the seventeenth century; but it was not the only one. Thanks in part to the effects of oceanic travel, the distribution of plants and people across the globe was transformed. The new balance favoured communities with access to the Atlantic, especially within Europe. Western Christendom came to span the ocean and to acquire ever-growing interests in other parts of the world. The great moments of world history in these decades happened outside Europe, but they all bore witness to the reach of European prowess: the moment when Dutch conquerors wrested control of production of some of the world's most valuable commodities in Makassar; the moment when wise men from the west took over the imperial astronomical observatory in Beijing; and the moment when English settlers planted a colony in North America, taking as they did so a decisive step in the creation of a single Atlantic-wide civilisation – the civilisation which in the long run would come, at least for a while, to dominate the world.

A telescope belonging to Sir Isaac Newton.

GENTLEMEN SCIENTISTS

The west was no richer than its rival cultures in the intellectual ingredients from which the new science of experiment and observation was brewed; but it did seem to provide a unique social framework for the study of nature. In seventeenth-century Europe, science was a fit occupation for a gentleman; honour and esteem could be gained by adventures in the laboratory as readily as on the field of battle, and minds full of curiosity about the world could also pursue dreams of wealth and rank. In England, the calm after the storm of a bloody civil war freed gentlemen from the demands of military service. Robert Boyle, who measured the volume of gases and devoted his life unwaveringly to science, was an earl. His compatriot Francis Bacon, the politician who has been hailed as the founder of modern science, became a baron. Bacon's phrase 'knowledge is power' resonated powerfully among the ruling houses of Europe: every nation wanted to be the first to gain access to the new truths. In England and France, scientific societies and academies attracted royal patronage. René Descartes, the French philosopher and great theorist of experimental method, was lured to Sweden by a royal admirer – somewhat against his inclinations: hating to rise before noon, he died in Stockholm after Queen Christina obliged him to get up at dawn to give her philosophy lessons. Isaac Newton – a farmer's son who as a boy played with fireworks attached to a kite, to see how light travelled – rose to be not only a popular hero but a knight and a companion of kings.

Sir Isaac Newton in a sculpture by Roubilliac made for his old college, Trinity, at Cambridge.

Newton's own heroes were his scientific predecessors, who sought to explain the workings of the universe. 'If I have seen further,' he said, 'it is by standing on the shoulders of giants.' The science of the seventeenth century homed in on observation, looking at how the world really works rather than relying on book-learning. Newton, educated in the classics at the University of Cambridge, had no doubts about his priorities: 'Plato is my friend,' he said, 'Aristotle is my friend; but my best friend is truth.' New technology extended the reach of the senses: unheard sounds became audible, the moons of Jupiter became visible. The order of the universe, previously known only to God, came within man's grasp. At London's Globe Theatre, the audience heard that order described in Shakespeare's wondrous verse, in *Troilus and Cressida*:

The heavens themselves, the planets and this centre
Observe degree, priority, and place,
Insisture, course, proportion, season, form,
Office, and custom, in all line of order.

Now they would be told that this order was imposed not by the mysterious hand of the divine but by simple laws intelligible to the human mind. Newton, a typical absent-minded professor, was said to be unable to find his way around his Cambridge college; but he comprehended the universe.

Newton responded to the fascination of the mundane. He broke down a beam of light entering his study window into the colours of the rainbow. He experimented with the behaviour of light and vision: 'I take a bodkin and put it betwixt my eye and the bone as near to the backside of my eye as I can and pressing my eye with the end of it there appear several white, dark and coloured circles.' He felt the force of gravity that bound the cosmos together in the weight of a dropping apple. He measured the way ordinary objects behave when they collide, and found that their movements were predictable, governed by universal laws and exact arithmetic. He saw the universe as working like a clock, set in motion by God the mathematician, the celestial engineer: 'A certain infinite spirit pervades all space and contains and vivifies the universal world. In him we live and move and have our being. Hence the omnipresent God is acknowledged.'

And yet, despite all this apparent grounding in the everyday and the verifiable, for Newton, as for most seventeenth-century scientists, science was a continuation of magic by other means; like the medieval alchemists striving to obtain the secret of creating gold, the aim remained the control of nature through knowledge. Newton himself devoted years of his life to alchemical

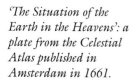

'The Situation of the Earth in the Heavens': a plate from the Celestial Atlas published in Amsterdam in 1661.

CAMERAM STELLATAM.

trials; and he never lost his childlike curiosity, or his sense of awe at the wonders of the cosmos awaiting discovery and explanation. 'I don't know what I may appear to the world but, as to myself, I seem to have been like a boy playing on the sea shore and diverting myself in now and then finding a smoother pebble or a prettier shell than the ordinary, whilst the great ocean of truth lay all before me.'

Others, too, felt the excitement of scientific investigation. The English diarist Samuel Pepys was caught up in the thrill of the chase after truth. 'At noon to the coffee house where with Dr Allen some good discourse about physick and chemistry. Thence by agreement we all of us go to the Blue Balls, whither Mr Pierce the surgeon also goes with us and anon comes Manuel and his wife.'

'I discoursed with Mr Hooke about the nature of sounds,' he recorded his friend Dr Allen saying, 'and he told me that having come to a certain number of vibrations proper to make any tone, he was thus able to tell how many times a fly beats her wings.'

And of Mr Pierce: 'I too conducted a pretty experiment of the blood of one dog let out till it died into the body of yet another, whilst his own run out. The first died but the other lives yet. I understand that the dog filled with another dog's blood is doing very well, and is likely to do so for a long time.'

Astronomers at work in the Octagon Room in the Royal Observatory, Greenwich.

ATLANTIC OPPORTUNITIES

Virginia, in a map of 1622 showing a portrait of Powhatan by John Smith.

During the seventeenth century the Atlantic trade itself was tiny by comparison with that of the Indian Ocean or the China seas – a puddle economy rather than an ocean economy, carrying relatively minute amounts of traffic. But the Atlantic seaways were already of a greater significance, as the gates to the resources of the world; for it was from these shores that vessels from all the seaborne empires of the time set out. The Atlantic, in the age of sail, was a highway that led not only to the immense, under-exploited, defenceless resource-base of the Americas, but also to wind-systems that linked up with the rest of the world. The explorers who cracked the codes of the Atlantic winds won the key to the unexplored globe.

The first consequence of the Atlantic traffic was the creation of a single civilisation which spanned the ocean. In the seventeenth century, this disparate Atlantic civilisation came to embrace North as well as Central and South America, and Africa as well as Europe. The *Mayflower* has become an American icon, evoking the heroic age of colonisation in every mind; but the first permanent settlement in what is now the United States was in Virginia, not Massachusetts, and the ships which deserve pride of place in any exhibit of transatlantic pioneers are those which took the first settlers there in 1607: the *Godspeed*, the *Susan Constant* and the *Discovery*. These ships bore a motley collection of would-be colonists – including aristocrats and soldiers, but no farmers and no women – sent on their way with the authority of the king of England, James I, who in the previous year had granted a charter to open up the Americas, proclaiming: 'They shall and may beginne their first plantation and seat of their first abode and habitation at any place on the coaste of Virginia.'

The place had been chosen less for its suitability than in the hope that no possible rival would bother to fight for it; nevertheless, the expedition's PR man, Robert Johnson, enthused about the New Britain waiting to be plucked from deadly swamp and impenetrable forest: 'Nova Britannia . . . offering most excellent fruits by planting in Virginia.' The settlers themselves echoed his praise: 'Joyful news out of the new found world, wherein is declared the rare and singular virtues of diverse and sundry herbes, trees, oils and precious stones. Without doubt a paradise found out to be true.'

Self-deception painted an alluring picture. The air was 'most sweet and wholesome, much warmer than England and very agreeable to our natures', and 'wheresoever we landed upon this river, wee saw the goodliest Woods . . . and Vines in great abundance; and all the grounds bespred with fruites – Strawberries, Mulberries, Rasberries'. However, not the most inventive propaganda could disguise one particularly irksome fact among all the awkward details: this Eden already had its own Adam. So the native inhabitants were classified, according to the colonists' convenience, in any way that rendered them fit for dispossession: first as ideally exploitable beings, then, almost in the same breath, as brutish victims unworthy of human rights:

> It is inhabited with wild and savage people . . . like herds
> of deer in a forest. They have no law but nature . . . yet . . .
> they are generally very loving and gentle and do entertain
> and relieve our people with great kindness . . . And as for
> supplanting the savages, we have no such intent . . . unless
> as unbridled beasts they procure it to themselves.

To an unprejudiced eye, the natives were by no means irredeemably barbaric. On the contrary, they had the essential rudiments of civilisation in European eyes: they built dwellings and towns; the confederacy in which their society was organised was recognisable as a sovereign state, with the same legitimacy as the white men's realms of Europe; and their ruler was evidently hedged with divinity:

Nova Britannia. *A book published in London in 1609 advertises the delights of the Virginia settlement.*

The great emperor at this time amongst them we commonly call Powhatan . . . the greatness and bounds of whose empire by reason of his powerfulness, and ambition in his youth, hath larger limits than ever had any of his predecessors in former times . . . He is a goodly old man, not yet shrinking, though well beaten with many cold and stormy winters, in which he hath been patient of many necessities and attempts of fortune, to make his name and family great, he is supposed to be a little less than eighty years old . . . And sure it is to be wondered at, how such a barbarous and uncivill prince should take unto him . . . a form and ostentation of such majesty as he expresseth, which oftentimes strikes awe and sufficient wonder into our people, presenting themselves before him, but such is (I believe) the impression of the divine nature, and howsoever these (as other) heathens forsaken by the true light, have not that portion of knowing the blessed Christian spirit, yet I am persuaded there is an infused kind of divineness, and extraordinary (appointed that it shall be so by the king of kings) to such who are his immediate instruments on earth.

The laws and customs of Christendom at the time offered no good grounds to make war on these people. The English government's advice to the colonists was larded with cant, but its rough edges are clearly visible under the slick language:

If you find it convenient, we think it reasonable you first remove from [the natives] . . . their . . . priests by a surprise of them all and detaining them prisoners, for they are so wrapped up in the fog and misery of their iniquity and so terrified with their continual tyranny, chained under the bond of death unto the devil, that while they live among them to poison and infect their minds, you shall never make any great progress in this glorious work, nor have any peace or concur with them. And in case of necessity or conveniency, we pronounce it not cruelty nor breach of charity to deal sharply with them and proceed even unto death.

The model the English had in mind in advocating this approach was obvious: they intended to imitate the conquest of Mexico by the Spaniard Hernán Cortés. As for the Indians' ruler, 'if you find it not best to make him your prisoner yet you must make him your tributary'.

At first, however, the English pioneers were impeded by their own incompetence and the unfamiliarity of the environment. They called their settlement Jamestown, after their king, and built it as a mirror image of an English village; but it was surrounded by mosquito-ridden swamps, and the drinking supply was contaminated with salt water. Disease and hunger claimed one man in two. Few of them had any useful skills in planting and building, and dependence on Native American charity was their only means of staying alive. 'The Indians did daily relieve us,' they admitted, 'with . . . such corn and flesh as they could spare.' Indeed, their hosts were consciously forbearing. 'We can plant anywhere,' they were reported as saying, '. . . and we know that you cannot live if you lack our harvest and that relief we bring you.'

This was no way to go about a conquest. Nor, in the long run, could it sustain an enduring colony. The policy of peaceful coexistence was already collapsing – torn apart by the increasing mutual resentment of the English and their hosts – when a character in the tradition of Cortés took command of the settlers and inaugurated a new approach: aggressive, ruthless and uncompromising. Captain John Smith was the first great American boss, a self-important tyrant whose real personality has been obscured by soothing myth. He claimed to be able to charm goods and girls out of the Indians; but his real means of making them feed the colony was terror. As one of his many critics among his fellow colonists put it,

> the command from England was so straight not to offend them . . . till well it chanced they meddled with Captain Smith, who without further deliberation gave them such an encounter as some he hunted up and down the Isle, some he so terrified with whipping, beating and imprisonment . . . it brought them in such fear and obedience, as his very name would sufficiently affright them.

Smith himself was frank about the mutual brutality into which his relations with the Indians degenerated, and had violent scenes incorporated into the ornamentation of a map illustrating his conquests.

He tried similar tactics on colonists who disobeyed him. 'Seeing how the authority resteth wholly in myself,' he decreed, 'you must obey this for a law, that he that will not work shall not eat, except by sickness he be disabled. For the labours of thirty or forty honest and industrious men shall not be consumed to maintain 150 idle varlets.'

When Smith was disabled in an accident and forced to return to England, his fellow colonists rejoiced. So did the Indians. 'The Savages no sooner understood Smith was gone, but they all revolted, and did spoil and murder all they encountered.' Suddenly, the colony was bereft of security, labour and food. Six months after the first landings, the original 600 settlers had been reduced to a mere sixty. New arrivals from England in May 1610

> found the palisadoes torn down, the ports open, the gates from off the hinge and empty houses (which own death had taken from them) rent up and burnt . . . And the Indians killed as fast without, if our men stirred but beyond the bounds of the blockhouse as famine and pestilence did within.

The saviour of the colony was an enterprising heavy smoker called John Rolfe. Dissatisfied with the unpleasant weed the Virginian Indians smoked, in 1611 he hit on the idea of transplanting Spanish tobacco seed from the Caribbean. It worked. In 1617, 20,000 pounds of tobacco were harvested. In 1622, it was

Slavery in the Americas. Ferdinand van Kessel's painting, Allegory of America, *1691, shows a Native American and an imported African slave.*

reported: 'All this Summer little was done, but securing themselves and planting tobacco, which passes there as current Silver.' That year – despite the recurrence of war with the Indians – 60,000 pounds were grown. By 1627 Virginia's annual production of tobacco had reached 500,000 pounds; by 1669, 15 million.

Tobacco made the colony viable, but the climate still killed the Englishmen who came to live there: out of 15,000 arrivals from 1607 to 1622, there were only 2,000 survivors. As for the Native Americans, their numbers were 'thinned' by wars with the colonists and the depredations of the unfamiliar diseases introduced from Europe. In the long run, the labour supply could only be assured by importing black slaves.

Though there were already blacks in the colony before 1619, it is in that year that first mention is made of an incoming shipment, when a Dutch warship 'sold us twenty niggers'. Over the next couple of decades, black slaves appear in the colony's records among or alongside lists of white servants, often without either name or date of arrival: the latter omission is important, as it distinguishes slaves from servants, the term of whose bondage was calculated according to length of service. The numbers of slaves remained small until the 1660s because of the steady supply of poor migrants from England. With mortality rates high among newcomers of whatever colour, it was more cost-effective to rely on the exploitation of poor whites, who could do the work and cost something under half the price of an African slave: investing in four servants rather than two slaves spread the risk. Between 1650 and 1674, 45,000 labourers arrived; by the end of that period there were probably fewer than 3,000 black slaves. Thereafter, however, the proportions began to be reversed.

THE WORLD THE SLAVES MADE

Across the New World as a whole, the 'Atlantic civilisation' which took shape in the seventeenth century was genuinely, comprehensively Atlantic – transplanted from the ocean's African shore at least as much as from Europe's. Among all the large-scale migrations facilitated for the first time in this period by the development of oceanic communications, the biggest single transference of population was from Africa to the Americas. South of Virginia, as far as southern Brazil, which by the beginning of the eighteenth century was perceived as 'another Guinea', the vast majority of transatlantic colonists were black. Moreover, in much of Atlantic-side America, the culture the Africans brought with them was overwhelmingly African, affected only lightly, if at all, by the presence of their European masters or neighbours, who left religions, languages and forms of society untouched.

In these years, most slave communities in America did not reproduce naturally, for reasons which are still little understood, but which surely include in part the consequences of the inhuman treatment to which slaves were subjected. Contraception came to be a form of resistance to oppression. The Anglican priest Morgan Godwyn, 'the Negro's advocate', denounced excesses he witnessed in the 1660s and 1670s in Virginia and Barbados, where the planters saw Africans as beasts of burden: they obstructed evangelisation, for

Punishment beating of a Brazilian slave in a nineteenth-century representation.

custom dictated that Christian slaves had to be freed after five years; they kept them hungry, and effectively massacred infants by preventing mothers from suckling them; they punished them by flogging, ear-cropping and emasculation. The rules drawn up for the guidance of a sugar-plantation overseer in 1663 recommended, for the punishment of ill-behaved slaves,

> not to beat them with a stick, nor to pelt them with stones and tiles, but, when a slave deserves it, to tie him to a cart and flog him. After being well flogged, he should be pricked with a sharp razor or knife, and the wounds rubbed with salt, lemon juice and urine, after which he should be put in chains for some days.

The Jesuit prophet and court-preacher Antonio de Vieira, whose grandmother was of mixed black and white parentage, compared the sufferings of slaves in Brazil to Christ's time on the cross; but his well-intentioned advice enjoined patience, not liberation – except in the mind:

> Christ was mistreated in every way and so are you. Of irons, prisons, lashings, wounds, and ignominious names your imitation is made, which along with patience will win you the rewards of the martyr . . . When you serve your masters, do not serve them as one who serves men but as one who serves God. Because then you will not serve as captives but as free men, and you will obey not as slaves but as sons.

The triangle of the slave trade. Slaves shipped out of Africa were sold in the Americas for sugar and other crops, which were shipped back to Europe and sold for cash to buy more African slaves.

The land was known as a purgatory for whites but a hell for blacks. The boom product of the seventeenth century was sugar, and it transformed Brazil:

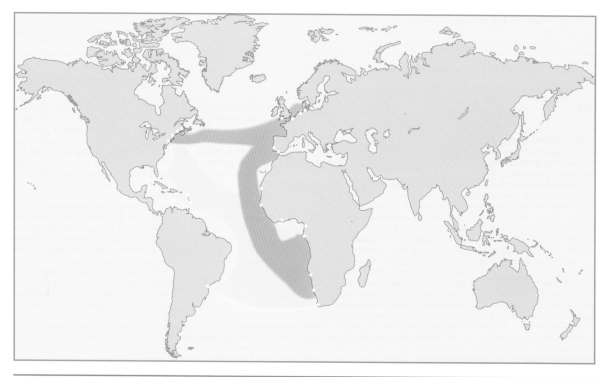

San Salvador, on the north-eastern coast of the country, became the second largest city in the Portuguese empire. On the plantations, it was the Africans who chopped and crushed the canes, and sweated over the boilers in the refineries. Slaves who survived for ten years would see almost half their fellow-workers die. According to an Italian monk who visited Bahia in Brazil in 1682, slaves were 'reckoned to live long if they hold out seven years'. Constant new imports were therefore required just to maintain labour levels. Slaves shipped out of Africa were sold in the Americas for sugar and other crops which were taken back to Europe and sold for cash to buy more Africans. Over 1.5 million black slaves reached the New World by the end of the seventeenth century. The numbers that left Africa were somewhat larger, for the voyage across the Atlantic was fatal to many, at least on the longer passages. Slaves died in their hundreds: because they could be bought cheaply and sold dear, shippers were willing to waste cargo and throw the corpses overboard.

As the trade grew, slave ports multiplied all around the Atlantic. The slaves came – in varying degrees at different times – from Africa's Atlantic coastal states, especially the Congo and Angola. The vast majority of them were sold by black overlords who had taken them prisoner in the course of war and raiding, which reached many hundreds of miles into the interior. Despite the breadth of the catchment area, the export of manpower must have affected the societies targeted by the slavers. The effects are much disputed among historians, but by any sensible estimate cannot have been other than generally dire. For a time the Angola region seems to have developed a marked excess of females over males. Some areas on the fringe of black trading states may have been depopulated. The slave market encouraged wars between blacks for human booty and encouraged kingdoms in Africa specialised in capturing slaves– like Dahomey, where the paths of the king's palace were paved with human bones, or Lunda, where virago queens challenged the cannibal kingdom in competition for captives.

At their destinations, the slaves were usually the great majority of the colonial population: Jamaica in 1700, for example, was home to 45,000 blacks and just 8,000 other people in all categories; according to a census of 1614, Lima, the most Spanish city in Peru, had over 10,000 blacks in a total population of 25,454. By the end of the seventeenth century, blacks were the biggest element in the population of parts of Mexico, coastal Peru and wherever plantation economies grew up. Most of these regions were on or near the ocean coast: English North America from Virginia southwards; the West Indies; some coastal areas of Mexico, Central America, Venezuela; and the sugar lands of Guyana and Brazil.

The most unmitigatedly African areas were maroon statelets – rebel republics or bandit kingdoms founded by runaway slaves. Freed slaves soon began to play a part in Virginian society. 'Antonio the Negro', sold as a slave in 1621, survived to become the freedman Anthony Johnson in 1650, with a black wife, slaves of his own and 250 acres of land. Francis Payne bought his freedom with 1,650 pounds of tobacco. But other blacks declined the white man's freedom and escaped to create mini-Africas in the woods. In 1672 bands of maroons excited fears of rebellion so great that whites were licensed and encouraged by law to hunt them down and kill them on sight. In 1676 the Virginian colony was convulsed by a poor farmers' rebellion, amid fears of a slave revolt in alliance with Dutch invaders. In 1691 a black guerrilla called Mingoe led a band of followers in the thefts of food and guns. In consequence, patches of Virginia more closely resembled a 'new Africa' than a 'new Europe'. At Esmeralda, in Colombia, the maroon kingdom had a treaty with the Spanish crown dating from 1599. In Surinam the first maroon community arose in 1663, when Portuguese Jews sent their slaves into the back country to avoid paying the head tax due on them.

In Palmares, in the hinterland of Pernambuco, an effectively independent black kingdom survived from the turn of the century until 1694: at its height, under King Zumbi, it could mobilise a royal guard of over 5,000 men. The culture of Palmares was hybrid: part African, part Portuguese. What most impressed visitors was the efficiency with which it was governed and the dignity with which its institutions were endowed. The king had a palace, according to a Jesuit report,

> and houses for his family and the service of all the guards and officials normally found in the house of a king. And he is treated with all ceremony due to a king and all the honours of a ruler. Those who find themselves in his presence fall to their knees in sign of recognition and in deference to his excellence. They call him 'Majesty' and their obedience is wonderful.

The black elite of Palmares were rich enough to buy slaves of their own and plenty of guns, with which they beat off Portuguese attempts at reconquest. Their capital, Macaco, developed a reputation for invincibility. Even after his death and the crushing of his kingdom, Zumbi continued to inspire black insurrections as a phantom king, a shade of Africa.

The cultures of most slave communities were pluralistic because they typically comprised groups of different peoples from different parts of Africa. But whether on plantations or in maroon enclaves, they were always African cultures, little affected by white influence. Evangelisation was enjoined by the authorities in Catholic countries: in Brazil, for instance, slaves had to be allowed to attend mass and were obliged to have their children baptised. In practice, however, regulations of this sort were evaded by the slave owners, most of whom preferred to keep their property out of the relatively humane hands of the clergy. Slaves bound for Brazil were loaded on ships with the words, 'Know that you are now children of God. You are leaving for the lands of the Portuguese, where you will learn the substance of the Holy Faith. Think no more of your native lands, and eat no dogs, horses or rats. Be happy.' But that was as close to Christian instruction as many of them came. Their entertainments were tribal music and dance; from 1681, at the feast of Our Lady of the Rosary, papal regulations allowed slave communities of Congolese origin in Brazil to elect a 'king' and 'queen' of their festivities to preside over songs and dances of their own devising. Food – the basic ingredient of any culture – was cooked and shared as it had been on the other side of the Atlantic. Oracular methods of justice often prevailed; or, especially in English colonies, the administration of justice was devolved by slave owners to the blacks' own 'governors' or elected 'kings'. Personal adornment, marriage customs and naming practices continued in their African forms in 'a near-pure African civilisation'. The practice of baptism and the role of godparent provided a framework within which ritual kinship could be perpetuated and tribal or national links preserved in the slaves' new homes. Spiritual solace was provided by spirit mediums. The black religions such as Candomblé, still practised on the beaches of Rio or Bahia at night, when the spirits replace the tourists, show how a few Christian images can be incorporated by forms of 'voodoo' directly transmitted from Africa.

Beyond the plantation world, blacks gradually became an ethnic minority, composed of domestic servants, concubines, freedmen in unpopular occupations or – if they came from the right part of Africa – technicians in mining industries. Paradoxically, the fewer they were in relation to other colonists and natives, the easier it was for them to integrate or introduce offspring into the white and mixed-race elites. Under the Spanish and Portuguese crowns, at least, the

Memories of Africa. In the ceremony of Yemanja, modern Brazilians set afloat beautifully decorated small boats for a return voyage to the ancestral homeland.

descendants of free blacks enjoyed equality with whites before the law. Spectacular cases of the exploitation of these rights include those of Dom Henrique Dias and Dom Joao Fernandes Vieira, ennobled for their services in Brazil's 'War of Divine Liberty' against Dutch invaders from 1644 to 1654. Generally, however, administrative discrimination and automatic racism kept them repressed.

Even today, a sense of African identity remains powerful in modern black Brazilians. One of the most poignant of the Candomblé ceremonies is that of Yemanja, the sea goddess, in which, every New Year, exquisitely decorated small boats are made and set afloat, to sail back to Mother Africa.

THE GOLDEN AGE OF AMSTERDAM

Amsterdam burghers in a joint portrait by Rembrandt. Such men, wealthy but sober in their dress, were the patrons of a Golden Age of Dutch painting.

The seventeenth-century Netherlands was a damp smear of a country barely rising from the sea, waterlogged or frozen according to the season: according to an English poet around the middle of the century it 'scarce deserves the name of land'. It was 'the indigested vomit of the sea' – a place no reasonable man would want to live in, full of Europe's refuse and refugees. But it was the success story of seventeenth-century world history. It became the centre of the furthest-flung empire the world had ever known, where the profits of a world-wide transfer of resources were banked. 'God has taken their riches from other cities,' said an Amsterdam guidebook of 1662, 'and spilled them into our bosom.' A new economy and society took shape within a new political order, as some of the provinces of the Netherlands renounced their hereditary ruler and joined in a republic. Fidelity to the sovereign was replaced by a new ethic of virtuous prosperity. Dutch propaganda claimed wealth as the wages God paid to piety and thrift. It became glorious to grow rich.

The means of making money were brought from the remote orient by a new route, opened in the second decade of the century by Dutch navigators desperate to break into the world's richest commerce: the spice trade of the Indian Ocean. Formerly, shipment by sea of the highest-value exotic condiments – nutmeg, cloves, mace – had followed the monsoons and had been carried to Europe around the Cape of Good Hope at the southern tip of Africa by Portuguese ships. Now the Dutch created a new approach, non-stop from Europe, across the mouth of the south-east trade winds of the southern Indian oceans, through a belt of perilous storms, to the Sunda strait and the spice islands. The trading advantage conferred by this faster route on its own was considerable, but as their resources grew the Dutch boosted it further by using force to divert trade into their hands. They seized the emporia of European rivals and bombarded native states into cooperation. Eventually they embarked on a hugely significant change of policy, taking over spice production directly and inventing a form of colonial exploitation that would be a model for white powers overseas for the rest of the millennium.

The decisive moment came with the fall of Makassar (in modern-day Indonesia), where mace and nutmeg grew – ounce for ounce, the costliest goods in the world. In 1659 it seemed inconceivable to its ruling sultan that the Dutch would appropriate not only the trade in his country's products but the land itself: 'Do you imagine', he asked as he announced his intention of defying Dutch threats, 'that God has reserved for your trade alone islands which are so distant from your homeland?' But the following year, on 12 June 1660, his capital fell after a bungled defence. Hitherto, European interlopers in the east had supplemented and confirmed existing systems of trade and added to its volume without changing its character, enriching the natives as they did so. Now a valuable slice of the gorgeous east was entirely subordinated to new masters, and the economy of part of the orient was impoverished for the benefit of shareholders in Amsterdam.

At the end of the century an Amsterdam merchant held a banquet at which he offered his guests a menu designed to celebrate the three stages of the Dutch Golden Age. The first course was of herrings and cheese, representative of an era of austerity: the time of republican revolt and of dependence

The spice islands route. The key to Dutch prosperity was an audacious new trade route, non-stop from Europe, wide of the southern tip of Africa and across the Indian Ocean, using fast southerly and westerly winds.

Merchants' houses along a canal side in seventeenth-century Amsterdam.

on regional shipping and fishing. The second was of plain puddings and roast meat, to evoke the years of peaceful accumulation of wealth from widening trade, in which there was ample provision for all of wholesome goods. The last featured French wines and delicacies: symbols of self-destructive prosperity, the luxuries which threatened to corrupt republican virtues.

In the first phase, the new republic not only fought off the armies of the old ruler, Spain, but contended mightily with an older enemy: the sea. An English visitor in the mid-seventeenth century affected contempt for this quagmire of a country but grudgingly admired the Dutch as 'gods' who 'set bounds to the Ocean and allow it to come and go as they please'. Windmills driving pumps were the new technology which made possible the spectacular progress of that era – and made Dutch hydraulic engineers sought after by drainers of lakes and fens all over the world. Two hundred thousand acres of the North Sea coast were recovered between 1590 and 1640. One man, the heroic engineer Jan Adriaenszoon Leeghwater, reclaimed 17,500 of them with a battery of forty-three windmills north of Amsterdam. As the windmills went up, canals were cut and dikes built, not only turning water into land but shaping that land with the civilising geometry of right angles and straight lines. From a distance, the landscape seems to have been branded with the

grid of the classical city. 'God made the world,' a French proverb said, 'but not Holland: the Dutch made that for themselves.'

The sovereignty of the republic was not formally enshrined by treaty until 1648, but it was effectively in place by 1609, and at this point the era of self-enrichment could begin. Its monuments were not long in appearing. The 1662 Amsterdam guidebook boasted, 'You will find no private buildings so sumptuously magnificent as a great many of the merchants' and other gentlemen's houses are in Amsterdam.' The burghers managed to give the impression of preserving the traditional citizenly virtue of parsimony by confining much of the display of wealth inside their homes. Planning regulations kept façades narrow, though the determinedly ostentatious could create double-width garden fronts or extend their frontage by collaboration with a neighbour. Exteriors could be enlivened by architectural ornament: armorial gables, richly moulded entablatures, decorative urns and busts. There are examples of such proud dwellings still standing today – buckled by age and subsidence – on the Keizersgracht and the Heerengracht. Generally, however, the houses of Amsterdam dressed modestly, with clean lines, chaste mouldings and plenty of neatly glazed windows.

The Dutch commissioned artists to furnish their homes with pictures reflecting their lives. Rich merchants wanted portraits of themselves and

TULIPOMANIA

By the beginning of the fourth decade of the seventeenth century the Dutch were experiencing an economic boom. It was during this period of prosperity that one of the most unusual of speculative ventures was born: the Dutch were gripped by a tulip craze.

Tulips had first come to Europe from Asia Minor; the word 'tulip' comes from the Turkish word meaning 'turban'. By 1623 the fabled red and white Semper Augustus was already selling for 1,000 florins a bulb (at a time when the average annual income was 150 florins). In 1624 only twelve of the bulbs were known to exist; they were valued at 1,200 florins each. By 1633 the price of a single bulb had reached 5,500 florins and in 1638, at the height of the craze, the Nederlandsch Magazijn reported the highest recorded price of 13,000 florins. Incredibly, one bulb of

Tulip *by Jan van Huysum.*

the delicate red-and-white flower was now worth more than one of the most expensive canal-side houses of central Amsterdam. An added appeal for the small-time investor in tulips was that a relatively inexpensive single-coloured variety might when flowering 'break': in other words, appear as a bi-coloured variety worth considerably more. No one knew what made some flowers break and others not – this mystery was not solved until the twentieth century.

Of course, the excessive prices and extreme market conditions could not last, and when the crash finally came in late 1638 many lost their fortunes. Inevitably a backlash against the flower followed: the Professor of Botany of Leiden University was known to thrash tulips savagely with his cane whenever he passed one.

those precious to them; humbler citizens wanted paintings of their everyday world. Simple family life was an ideal dear to Dutch hearts: a home, and a perfect homely woman, 'shapely of limb and of fleshy stock, of pleasing aspect and clean of teeth, born in the realm of our own Netherlands'.

Public building, on the other hand, could embody indulgence without restraint. For the Dutch, Atlas held the universe, and Amsterdam was its centre. The city's new town hall, built by the citizens for the citizens to celebrate their commercial success, was praised as a marvel as great as 'the human brain can conceive', with 'such treasures made by chisel and brush, under a single roof and each in its proper place' that it seemed to the Dutch poet Vondel 'the Eighth Wonder of the World'.

> *Our splendid town hall*
> *praises its citizens' power.*
> *A festive fair to which all our*
> *neighbours are invited.*
> *Its glorious banquets,*
> *and promise of joy,*

with such an abundance of treasures
as only our artists can create.

The dominant emotion of Amsterdam's citizens may have been pride; but it was tinged with an increasing unease. The last phase – at least, in the moralists' perceptions – was one of decadence bought with excessive lucre. Prostitution was the source of the images most favoured by Dutch artists and writers who wanted to display to their public warnings of corruption by wealth. An elaborate visual code was established. An open mussel or oyster, as used for example in the painting *The Stock Exchange of Women* by Jacob Cats, signified a vagina surrendered to temptation. The temptress lurked, 'eager to conquer you':

Desire is ever near.
So close your eyes –
those windows of light,
lest it invade you,
Preserve your heart,
and do not let yourself be conquered,
For desire will bring ruin,
and burning sin evermore.

The goods most coveted by the newly wealthy Dutch were the most exotic. There has probably never been a society, however poor or unacquisitive, in which this has not been true; but at its extreme the collector's obsession is an acute form of the civilising syndrome: taking objects out of their natural contexts and relocating them in sumptuous combinations that only a human imagination could contrive. Transylvanian rugs, Italian glasses, Persian silks, furs of Muscovy, Colombian emeralds, Indian sapphires, Chinese pots, Japanese lacquer and tulips acclimatised from originally Turkish specimens: these are the badges of consumption with which Dutch painters scattered the domestic genre scenes and portraits commissioned by their wealthy merchant clients. The effect of combining these outlandish elements – the further away their origins, the better, from their exhibitors' point of view – in architectural and decorative settings that were wholly Netherlandish represents the distinctive art of the peculiar culture. 'If it gives pleasure to see fruit grow in our orchards,' wrote Descartes in a letter home from the Netherlands, 'do you not think it will give us as much pleasure to see vessels arrive here bringing an abundance of all the produce of India and all that is rare in Europe? What other country could one find in which all the luxuries of life and all the rarities one could desire are so easily available?'

But beneath the opulence and celebration the unease remained. Eventually, the costs of empire proved too great for a republic corrupted by wealth. The poet's warning echoed ominously:

Where gold begins
Virtue is but wind.

WISE MEN FROM THE WEST

Outside the Americas, the rest of the civilised world still felt little threat from the west. On the contrary, it seemed obvious that the balance of the world's resources tilted eastwards; Europe was Asia's poor relation. Western trade was the barbarian 'client' of the Chinese empire, and when Europe grabbed the silver of America, the effect was to enrich China further. A western visitor of this period observed that China had more riches in a street than Flanders or Italy had in a city. When the Jesuit Matteo Ricci redrew his world map for the Chinese court, with China in the middle, he was not just flattering Chinese vanity and belief in its unique status as repository of the 'mandate of heaven', but reflecting the fact of where the world's economic centre of gravity was located.

At the first full moon of the new year which fell, by Christian reckoning, in 1682, a young official called Ts'ao Yin described the scene in Beijing:

> The out-of-towners are just like a flock of ducks, and at every crossroads the girls are bustling. They like to wander and who should stop them? The . . . festive clothes and decorated carts are numberless. Everyone is out strolling in this springtime vanity fair, with their caps awry they crowd me to a standstill; boisterously the pretty girls are playing around, reaching a turn in the road and everywhere . . . drums are beating. The full moon bursts out above the city walls, whitely translucent, perfect in shape, fresh . . . The city colours and the lantern lights compete in brilliance. Above the streets fish- and dragon-shaped

A map of China produced around 1625 by Samuel Purchas shows Matteo Ricci (above left).

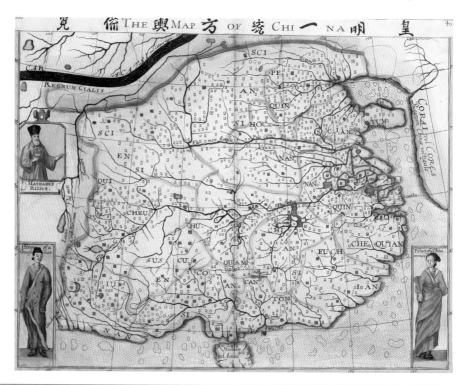

lanterns fly and dance; every single household has put them on display.
A candle gutters over scented clothes, but is not yet burned down.

That was how it looked out on the streets. But a revolution was under way on top of the palace roof, where the Chinese Board of Astronomy had its observatory. For the space had been taken over by Jesuits: representatives of a world of 'barbarism' the Chinese despised, and a religion they proscribed.

The Board existed not for the scholarly study of the heavens but for the computation and revision of a ritual calendar. The ceremonies of the court were attuned to the rhythms of the stars to ensure that earthly order reflected celestial harmony. For moveable feasts and unique occasions, benign astral influences had to be secured. The environment of a starstruck court stimulated the accumulation of scientific knowledge. Though the Board of Astronomy was young – it was created only in the early seventeenth century – the Chinese tradition in the science was ancient, and it had been practised at court for centuries. The imperial

Chinese astronomers at work with instruments provided by the Jesuits, in an eighteenth-century French tapestry.

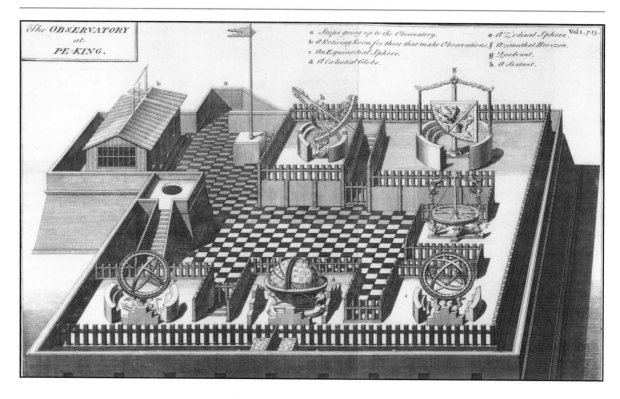

The observatory at Beijing, on the roof of the imperial palace, after reorganisation by the Jesuits.

observatory had a continuous history of some 400 years behind it, and the number and quality of recorded observations available to Chinese astronomers had been unequalled anywhere in the west until well into the sixteenth century.

Yet when the Jesuits arrived – the first being diverted from their missionary explorations to help the Chinese with calendrical problems in 1629 – their superiority over the Muslim personnel who then ran the observatory seemed so marked that the entire native tradition was abandoned and the whole practice of astronomy at court, on which the success of imperial enterprises and the life of the empire were believed to depend, was handed over to the foreigners. As one of the Jesuits argued,

> the virtue and the power of your Imperial Majesty has spread far and
> wide, so that many scores of nations are tribute-bearers and the
> nations which follow our imperial calendars extend for several myriads
> of miles. From the imperial court, authority radiates to the four
> corners of the earth. In such an immense territory, how can we endure
> an inaccurate calendar that nowhere can measure the real length of day
> and night, the correct time or the real solar periods all year round?

Calendrical inaccuracy was having grave repercussions far beyond the ritual cycles of the court. Harvesting seemed to be taking place at the wrong time. In Shan-tung in 1640,

> There was a great famine and cases of cannibalism. One day, a . . .
> palace runner . . . came across a man and a woman weeping bitterly

and asked them what the trouble was. They replied, 'We've been married over a year, but now there is no way we can both survive in this time of famine and so we weep.' A while later he saw the couple again in front of an oil seller's shop . . . and the shopkeeper explained, 'This man and his wife are dying of starvation, every day they come and beg me for a little sesame oil to keep them alive. Now the man is trying to sell me his wife. But in my house there are already more than ten women that I've bought, so what does one more matter to me? If she's cheap, I'll make a deal; if not, that's that!'

'To have the bodies of one's close relations eaten by someone else', it was commonly said at the time, 'is not as good as eating them oneself, so as to prolong one's own life for a few days.' The closest friends no longer dared walk out into the fields together.

True to the long-standing tradition of Chinese empiricism, the astronomical calculations of the westerners were tested against those of the Muslim astronomers in a series of experiments. The decisive one occurred in 1644, when Father Adam Schall von Bell presented to the emperor

the predictions of an eclipse of the sun on the first day of the eighth month of this year, calculated according to the western method, together with illustrations of the percentage of the solar eclipse, and the sun's reappearance as may be seen in the Imperial capital and in various provinces . . . Your subject humbly begs a decree . . . to test publicly the prediction at a proper time.

On 1 September, imperial officials were ordered

to bring the telescopes and other instruments to the observatory and to command the officials and students of the Bureaux of Calendar Calculation and of the Board of Astronomy to repair to the observatory to study the eclipse of the sun. Only the prediction calculated by the western method coincided exactly with the primary eclipse, the total eclipse, the passing of the eclipse, the time, the percentage, the location and other details, whereas the predictions calculated by the Chinese and Muslim methods contained errors.

The westerners' advantage derived from two inventions which the Chinese, despite their traditions of technical proficiency, had never bothered to develop. The principle of the lens was known in medieval China, as in the west, probably from Arabic scientific treatises; but no lens was ever ground and so no telescope was ever made. And while a spectacular mechanical clock had been built in China in the eleventh century, the skill was allowed to wither. One of the Jesuits' great patrons, the Emperor K'ang-Hsi, delighted in clocks and believed western learning shaped his own routine:

The skill originated in the west,
But by learning we can achieve the artifice:
Wheels move and time turns round,
Hands show the minutes as they change.
Red-capped watchmen, there's no need to announce dawn's coming.
My golden clock has warned me of the time.
By first light I am working hard
And keep on asking, 'Why are the memorials late?'

GALILEO AND THE INVENTION OF THE TELESCOPE

The invention of the telescope is generally credited to a Dutchman, Hans Lippershey. He was probably not the sole, or even first, inventor, but the telescopes he sold to the government of the Netherlands in 1608 are the first recorded. By the following year, they were appearing in Germany, France, Italy and England.

The Dutch government was interested in the military applications of the invention. Galileo Galilei, already renowned throughout Europe as Professor of Mathematics at the university of Padua, was the first man to see its possibilities for astronomy. Hearing of Lippershey's telescope, he designed his own, the first capable of astronomical observation; the largest he built had a magnifying power of 33 diameters.

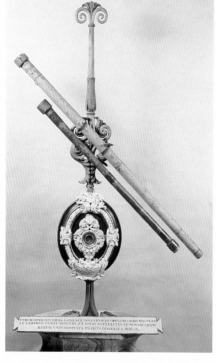

Galileo's telescopes were soon in demand all over Europe. Using his own, he concluded that the moon owed its illumination to reflection and that its surface was not smooth but was scarred with craters and valleys. He described the starry nature of the Milky Way, discovered four satellites of Jupiter and noticed spots on the sun from which he calculated its rotation. Above all, he confirmed by observation his own long-held belief that the Polish-German astronomer Copernicus had been correct in stating that the earth moved around the sun rather than sitting stationary at the centre of the universe, as Aristotle and Ptolemy, and Holy Scripture, had taught the western world to believe.

It is hard to imagine now the profoundly unsettling nature of this conclusion for the people of that time, abruptly thrown out of their home at the centre of God's created cosmos. Boldly stated, it brought Galileo into inevitable conflict with the scientific establishment of the day, and with the church, which was sincerely convinced that to persuade men of such beliefs was to condemn their souls to eternal perdition. He was summoned to Rome in 1633 and put on trial for advocating condemned doctrines. Found guilty, he was forced to recant and sentenced to imprisonment, but the sentence was commuted to lifelong house arrest at his own small estate near Florence. There, despite advancing age and failing sight, he continued his scientific work, some of which was published beyond the reach of the Inquisition in the Netherlands. His last telescopic observation, shortly before he went completely blind, was of the moon's diurnal and monthly librations – the 'wobblings' that cause its edges to come alternately in and out of view. Galileo died in 1642.

In 1669, after a brief interlude of Chinese control, the Jesuit polymath Ferdinand Verbiest took over the Board of Astronomy and completed the systematic reform of the calendar. In 1673, at the emperor's request, the observatory was re-equipped with instruments of Jesuit design, fusing western science with Chinese craftsmanship. The rooftop scene, with the instruments, decorated with mythical Chinese beasts, erected like shrines on little platforms, protected by palisades, around a tiled yard, provided eighteenth-century European engravers with one of their most popular scenes of Chinese life, enhanced and, in a sense, overawed by the apparatus of western ingenuity; today they remain, a strange symbol of the old world, among the high-rise blocks and neon of the modern city.

The reception of the 'wise men from the west' was tolerated in China because, far from subverting Chinese traditions, it confirmed the ancient scientific trend in Chinese thought: respect for observation and experiment as sources of knowledge. The triumph of the Jesuit astronomers occurred at a point of transition in the balance of advantage between cultures, paralleling the beginnings of the long process of reversal of the aeons-old balance of trade, which had enriched the east at western expense. There remained, however, a long way to go, and the ascent of the west would not continue uninterrupted. The precarious empires which Europeans had begun to found across the oceans were inherently unstable: because they were settled by malcontents, fugitives, loners and tender consciences, they were more likely to breed revolutions than the societies of home. In the next century, their fragility was to be exposed.

CHAPTER 8

Century of the
FURNACE

THE EIGHTEENTH CENTURY

I N THE EIGHTEENTH-CENTURY EAST, western science was admired as never before – and deservedly so. In the 1770s Japanese admirers of western science met six or seven times a month to study Dutch books – the only source they could get; after about a year, their spokesman said, 'We became capable of reading as much as ten or more lines of text per day if the particular passage was not too difficult.' Japanese world maps began to resemble products of European cartography. Before, they were influenced by Buddhist visions of the world, in which the continents open like lotus petals from a mystical centre. Now the image of the world was represented realistically, according to data gathered by western observation.

In the furnace of western science, potentially transforming new technologies were born, and unseen forces in nature were detected: the combustibility of oxygen and the freakish force of electricity entered the realm of human knowledge. Exploration filled in the map of the world and expanded views of humankind and civilisation. European encounters with peoples of the Pacific Ocean and the North American interior provoked questions about how society should be organised back home. A newly emerging 'Romantic' view of both humanity and landscape touched western sensibilities and – with frightening political consequences – made strength and savagery seem beautiful.

The unity of 'Atlantic civilisation' was tested in the maelstrom of intellectual and political change. The impact of revolutionary ideas in both Europe and America proved a divisive force as well as a unifying theme. In Europe, the intellectual movement known as the Enlightenment led for a time to despotism and despair; in America, towards optimism and democracy. Everywhere in the western world, 'the people' emerged as a force in politics.

The established industrial giants of world history – China and India – were challenged by adventurers and competitors from the west. But no imperial expansion could match that of China. Despite the changing world balance in resources and in scientific initiatives in favour of European powers, on most counts the west still looked backward by comparison.

Coalbrookdale at Night, *painted by Philip James de Loutherbourg, the sky lit up by furnaces, in a scene that must have been familiar in the industrialised parts of eighteenth-century England.*

SCIENCE AND THE SHAPE OF THE WORLD

In 1736 the French academic establishment sponsored the most elaborate scientific experiment ever devised. Eighteenth-century seekers after the newest developments in western science thronged to the Netherlands, where Japanese students looked for the new learning; or to Paris or London, where the scientific heroes of the day congregated; or to Madrid, where the Spanish government, by the end of the century, was spending more on science than any other in the world; or to Philadelphia, where, in the latter part of the century, private citizens clubbed together to emulate the scientific patronage of European courts. But the most spectacular and instructive experimental setting was an ice-bound river on the Arctic Circle, where a small group of Frenchmen set out to determine the shape of the world.

Was the earth a sphere, as was traditionally claimed? Or was it flattened at the poles, like an orange, according to Sir Isaac Newton's theory? Or was it shaped more like a lemon, elongated towards the ends?

'Our Academy was divided,' wrote one of the French scientists, who for the most part inclined to the latter view; 'our previous experiments had made the problem bleak and turbid, when our king decided to have this great question settled – not a vain speculation or one of those useless subtleties beloved of philosophers, but something which really mattered for astronomy and navigation.' The question could only be settled by going as far as possible towards the ends of the earth and measuring. The French Royal Academy of Sciences

The shape of the earth. By measuring a degree of latitude at the pole and at the equator, Maupertuis and Condamine could determine whether the earth was pointed at its extremities, like a lemon, or a perfect sphere, or flattened at the poles, like an orange.

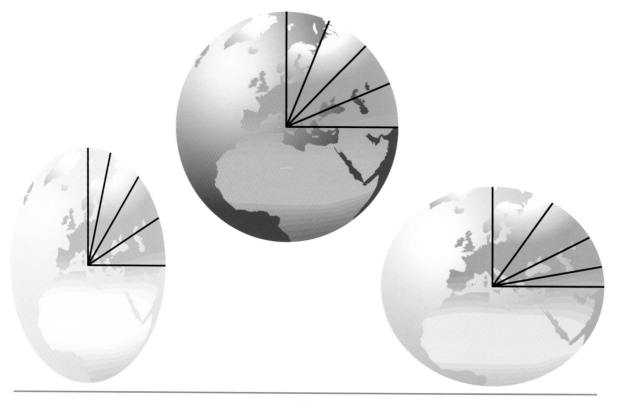

therefore resolved to finance two expeditions: one to the equator – the extreme girth of the world – and the other to the narrow north. Charles de la Condamine's mission to Quito in Ecuador was responsible for determining, as near to the equator as possible, the amount of space traced on the surface of the world by an arc of one degree of latitude. It took them ten years. The explorers coped with riots, dissension, murder, volcanoes, extremes of temperature and cripplingly rarefied air. One of the surveyors got separated from his wife by the length of the Amazon: they spent twenty years searching for each other. While this expedition bickered and suffered, the problem of the shape of the world was solved by the companion expedition, which was charged with making the corresponding measurements as near as possible to the Arctic Circle.

The leader of the northern project was Pierre Louis Moreau de Maupertuis. This poor, prickly child of decayed Breton gentry had emerged from the provinces like a hero in a romantic novel, eluding a career in the church, serving in the musketeers and acquiring an education in free-thinking in Paris taverns. His brilliance as a geometer led to a job with the Academy of Sciences at the age of twenty-five, though he made a virtue of irking the Paris establishment, where his gloomy misanthropy was almost proverbial. He claimed to think that nothing really existed except God, even advocating the 'grim idea' that perceptions are only properties of a mind.

'Science', he wrote, 'sees the world clothed with every property you can sense. It is founded on experience alone. Without science, reason goes astray, the mind of God is left alone in a universe unmeasurable.' Scepticism so intense that it verged on mysticism was typical of the age. Some eighteenth-century

Cotapaxi erupting, in an engraving based on a drawing by Jorge Juan and Antonio de Ulloa, who accompanied Condamine on his expedition to the equator to verify the shape of the world.

*The Northern Lights, in
a nineteenth-century
book illustration.*

European sceptics set such high standards of scientific verification that they did not even believe in the existence of matter.

In June 1736 Maupertuis arrived in Finland, at the Gulf of Bothnia. Here the hardships in store on the road to answering the question he had come to solve immediately became clear: 'Wherever the curvature of the earth is least a degree of latitude will be longest. But to measure one here seems impossible. We must climb hilltops and cut down forests to get clear sightings.'

Frustrated in his hopes of taking measurements by the low relief of the islands, which gave him no vantage points for observation, he followed the river Tornio northwards until he found slopes high enough. His instruments would have to be carried up a river full of cataracts or across apparently impassable forests and marshes. 'We must in these deserts', he reported to the Academy, 'put up with the most wretched diet, exposed to the flies, which in this season are so insufferable as to drive the Laplanders and their reindeer from their habitations.'

In August, after a terrible journey up the rocky river, he reached his northernmost camp. Here he stumbled into a wonderland of nature, dazzled by the effects of rockscape, ice and the Northern Lights: it seemed a place for fairies and spirits rather than bears . . . In this climate, the earth may be horrible, but heaven presents to our eyes the most enchanting spectacle. As soon as the night grows dark, fires of a thousand colours and a thousand forms illuminate the sky and seem to seek to console this land, accustomed to uninterrupted summer light, for the loss of the sun on his departure . . . It would take for ever to describe all the shapes assumed by these lights or all the motions they undergo. Even their simplest gyrations make them resemble flags flung into the air.

The most northerly work had to be done as quickly as possible as winter drew on. In a remote farmhouse Maupertuis had set up an astronomical observatory where, with the aid of the finest instruments France could provide, he could fix his latitude to a degree of accuracy normally obtainable only in a laboratory. Having established exact latitudes at both ends of the river valley, he would be able to compare the distance between these two points as calculated from the respective latitudes and as measured physically between them over the surface of the earth. If the measured distance was greater than the calculated distance, the earth would have been proven to be flattened at the poles – as in the 'orange'-shape theory espoused by Isaac Newton, among others. If it were shorter, the 'lemon'-shape theory would prevail. If the distances were the same, the earth would indeed be a sphere.

Maupertuis and his colleagues took shelter from the vicious onslaught of the Arctic climate with the native Sami people. These nomads, who lived by following the reindeer herds, took an older and more picturesque view of the earth's place in the cosmos than that of their French visitors: 'The sky is enormous – like a giant skin of leather. In the middle of the leather dome there is a star. We call it Boahi – the North Star. It is like a pole which holds up the leather dome.

Even when the two points of latitude had been established, much laborious work remained to be done. One degree of latitude represents a distance of 60 miles: far too great a span to be checked by a single measurement. So Maupertuis' team built a series of twelve signal towers on the highest points up the valley, and spent the next two months measuring the precise angles of the lines that connected each pair of towers. Only then could they make their final measurement, establishing the distance between any two of the towers, which would enable them to work out all the others.

It was December by the time Maupertuis was ready to make this measurement: of a line, some 12 miles long, near the mouth of the Tornio on the river's frozen surface – 'the longest base line that was ever used, and in the planest surface, seeing that it was upon the ice of the river that we were to measure it'. The measuring rods were made of fir wood because of all available materials it was least likely to be shrunk by cold: these had to be laid, by hand, end to end between the two fixed points.

On 21 December the survey team was ready: it was the day of the winter solstice, when the sun rose just above the horizon at noon. The surveyors suffered for science; for the conviction that the world could be understood by observation, explored by experiment, measured by men – and a vision of the whole of it deduced mathematically, from a few figures reckoned with fir poles and plumb lines on a Finnish river.

> Judge what it must be to walk in snow two foot deep, with heavy poles in our hands, which we must be continually laying on the snow and lifting again: in cold so extreme that whenever we would take a little brandy, the only thing that could be kept liquid, our tongues and lips froze to the cup and came away bloody; in a cold that congealed the . . . extremities of the body . . . while the rest, through excessive toil, was bathed in sweat.

Towers in the snow. In a filmed reconstruction, Maupertuis's men erect their signal towers.

It would have been practically impossible to achieve total accuracy under the conditions Maupertuis endured in the Arctic. But his final calculations established the truth. Here, near to the North Pole, the distance between two points was greater than expected; combined with the findings of the equatorial expedition, this proved that the earth was indeed flattened at the poles, like an orange.

Thanks to science, and to the heroic and painstaking efforts of these eighteenth-century explorers, men could envision the world in its real shape, as it looked from heaven, as if with the eyes of God. 'Let us open our eyes, explore the universe, admire it unreservedly. While we knew nothing of the wisdom of the laws which underpin it, our observations offered only muddled and obscure hints of how the cosmos is regulated. Now the truth of it is clear.'

But while subscribing to, and energetically pursuing, the quest for universal truth through observation and experiment, Maupertuis was never fully confident that science was a sufficient key to knowledge.

> The straightforward ways which the Creator followed in His work turn into labyrinths for us as soon as we try to tread them. He has given us light enough for our needs, but seems to have allowed us to see the rest of his plan only darkly . . . Who can penetrate all the marvels of the wisdom of it? Who can follow it in the span of the sky, the depths of the sea and the clefts of the earth? Perhaps it is too soon to explain the world: we can only admire the spectacle.

EXPERIMENTS IN ENLIGHTENMENT

The intellectual movement known as the Enlightenment, which spread through western Europe in the eighteenth century, favoured order, rationality, planning: a universe regulated by scientific laws, a culture bristling with scientific instruments, a world in which everything could be measured and had its place.

New spaces for the organisation of rationally planned lives opened up wherever cities were being built or rebuilt. Philadelphia, founded by a Quaker shortly before the century began, was intended to be 'a city of brotherly love'. The rectilinear grid of the founder's design is still intact, instantly visible from the air, easily perceptible on the ground at every street corner, although most of the parks and public gardens of the original plan have long since been gobbled up. This was a city where, though by the end of the century it was also home to most of the institutions of government and high finance, the biggest public building was the Free Library. Religious toleration was proclaimed in a variety of churches and temples; high-mindedness exuded from the headquarters of the American Philosophical Society. In one respect, however, Philadelphia was an unrepresentative child of the Enlightenment: for the city was inspired by a Christian vision, whereas perfect enlightenment, as the thinkers who came to dominate the movement understood it, could be achieved only by placing reason and sense-perception higher in the scale of values than revelation or mysticism or church tradition.

It was ironic, therefore, that the most dramatic opportunity to build a city in the image of the Enlightenment arose from an act of God: the great earthquake of Lisbon, which struck the Portuguese capital on 1 November 1755 – All Saints' Day.

A witness to this cataclysm described how he

was roused from my dream, being instantly stunned with a most horrid crash, as if every edifice in the city had tumbled down at once. The house I was in shook with such violence that the upper storeys immediately fell . . . The wall continued rocking to and fro in the frightfullest manner, opening in several places, large stones falling down on every side from the cracks. To add to this terrifying scene, the sky became so gloomy, it was an Egyptian darkness, owing no doubt to the prodigious clouds of dust and lime raised from so violent a concussion. As soon as the gloom began to disperse and the violence of the shock seemed pretty much abated, the first object I perceived in the room was a woman sitting on the floor with an infant in her arms, all covered with dust, pale and trembling. I asked how she had got hither, but her consternation was so great that she could give me no account of her escape. I remember that the poor creature asked me in the utmost agony if I did not think that the world was at an end.

Philosophers at Supper.
An engraving of the time shows Voltaire (with arm raised) and some of his fellow-thinkers, including Diderot and d'Alembert.

A fictional traveller – Candide, created by the sceptical writer Voltaire to be the epitome of eighteenth-century optimism – recounted the experience realistically, on the basis of a compendium of press reports and private information:

> Scarcely had they arrived in the town when they felt the earthquake underfoot. The sea was lashed to a froth, burst into the port and smashed all the vessels lying at anchor there. Whirlwinds of fire and ash swirled through the streets and public squares. Houses crumbled. Roofs came crashing down on foundations. Foundations split. Thirty thousand inhabitants of every age and either sex were crushed in the ruins. The last judgement is here!

Reactions to the earthquake reflected the contesting ideas of the time: on the one hand, the traditional belief in an unchanging hierarchical order in which God empowered the king to rule the common people, who had no prospect of betterment; on the other, the new belief – the Enlightenment belief – that the whole of society could be liberated from superstition and repression by reason. Many of those who clung to the traditional view saw the devastation wrought by the earthquake as divine retribution for the spreading tide of doubt; the new wave, by contrast, saw an opportunity to reorganise society on rational principles.

Among the latter was the Portuguese Prime Minister, the Marques de Pombal. He wanted to straighten every irrational old street, crush every antiquated institution, including the church, and remodel the world on rational and scientific principles. His reported reaction to the anguish of the king was typical of his brisk and practical approach:

'What can be done to meet the infliction of this divine justice?' the king asked him.

'Sire,' Pombal replied, 'bury the dead and feed the living.'

Pombal believed the earthquake had made the world better – smashing dark slums along with dim superstitions. The rebuilding of the capital under his supervision produced neat homes and splendid squares, laid out in an ordered geometrical pattern: all right-angles and straight lines, broad squares and bold vistas. The showpiece of the project was a great square overlooking the river and port – the commercial heart of a city dedicated to trade. Money, however, was short, and lasted only long enough to rebuild the lower part of the city, down by the port, and the resulting contrast – instantly apparent to any visitor – is eloquent: the order of the reconstructed lower town, the chaos of the higgledy-piggledy old hillside districts.

Pombal's critics were outraged by his concern for the physical renewal of the city's architecture in the face of what they judged to be an expression of divine wrath, visited on the Portuguese as a warning to others. Pombal was unmoved. The earthquake had evicted many religious orders from their property, and he made it his business to see they never came back. At the monastery of Mafra, outside Lisbon, abandoned by the Jesuits, a great library was created and stocked with over 30,000 books. Among the classics sat the works of the new Enlightenment thinkers, such as the German philosopher Immanuel Kant, whose exhortation 'Sapere aude!' – 'Dare to find out!' – resounded as the motto of the age.

The main square of Lisbon today, still showing the classical order and restraint of the parts of the city reconstructed after the earthquake of 1755.

At the most rarefied levels of the European elite, meanwhile, the cult of reason was taking on the characteristics of an alternative religion. Freemasonry emerged as the free-thinkers' alternative to Christianity. Its rites and aims – the search for enlightenment and truth – were celebrated by Mozart in his opera for the popular stage, *The Magic Flute*. 'These portals, these columns, prove that skill, industry, art reside here,' exclaims the hero, Tamino, when he finds the temple of the order of lay sages. 'Where action rules and idleness is banished, Vice cannot easily gain control. I will boldly pass through that portal. Its design is noble, straightforward and pure.' Voltaire erected his own temple to 'the architect of the universe' but regarded Christianity as 'an infamous superstition to be extirpated – I do not say among the rabble who are not worthy of being enlightened, but among the polite and those who wish to think.' Freemasons celebrated the triumph of light over darkness, reason over ignorance; but, as Voltaire's comment demonstrated, remained firmly elitist in their quest.

The text which summed up the Enlightenment was the *Encyclopedia*, a compendium of worldly knowledge compiled by leading French scholars. It was intended by its authors to stand as a beacon of the new learning against the prejudice and superstition which, they argued, disfigured traditional scholarship. Inevitably, with religious authority under threat, there was a backlash: Pope Clement XII instructed all Catholics who owned the *Encyclopedia* to have it burned by priests, or face excommunication.

But traditional authority could not be so easily reasserted: by the latter years of the eighteenth century, the genie was out of the bottle. The term 'Romanticism' is sometimes used to reflect new trends in late eighteenth-century art – a reaction against the formalities inspired by classical models and so beloved of the mid-century Enlightenment. But it was more than that. It was also a re-blending of popular feelings into the values and tastes of educated people. Its poetry was 'the language of ordinary men'; its visual aesthetics were drawn from the grandeur of rustic habitats; its religion was characterised by the 'enthusiasm' which drew thousands to Methodist meetings in the open air of rural England. Great ladies were portrayed in peasant dress and imitated bucolic idylls in drawing-room entertainments. The music of Romanticism ransacked traditional airs for its melodies; its theatre and opera borrowed from street theatre and bands of roving mummers. 'The people' had arrived in European history as a creative force.

Every day, 'when the weather was cold and wet', the most progressive intellectuals of Paris would meet to enact symbolically the power of the people. Denis Diderot – chief compiler of the *Encyclopedia* – would 'take shelter in the Café de la Regence and amuse myself watching people play chess' with Franklin, Voltaire and other radical thinkers. As their common master in the game, François-André Philidor, observed in *Chess Analysed*, published in 1748, 'pawns are the soul of chess – because they can remove the king'.

REVOLUTIONS IN THE WEST

In 1768 Thomas Jefferson began to build himself a house in his homeland, the young American state of Virginia, where he had been born twenty-five years earlier. Monticello, as he called it, was his tribute to the European Enlightenment: a classically designed building providing an agreeable, civilised environment, situated on a hill from which he could observe the thriving, prosperous land around him and within which he could indulge in his well-regulated pursuits – such as designing clocks to give order to the day.

Thomas Jefferson's house, Monticello, built by him in classical style, in tribute to the principles of the Enlightenment.

With the hardships of the initial pioneering days now some time in the past, life for the prosperous of colonial Williamsburg – Virginia's chief town – was comfortable, and its citizens confident in their status and achievements. And, as Benjamin Franklin commented, their experience was mirrored elsewhere in the new country: 'The first drudgery of settling the new colonies is now pretty well over. There are many in every province in circumstances that set them at ease and afford leisure to cultivate the finer arts and improve the common stock of knowledge.' Time to think and study along with the freedom conferred by a pioneer heritage cultivated dissent, and a respect for individual entitlements above loyalty to a far-distant authority. As the original English settlers in North America were joined by ever greater numbers of immigrants of other nationalities, with no ties to England and owing no allegiance to the British crown, dissatisfaction with colonial status – and the burden of taxation imposed thereby – began to grow, along with a sense of common identity.

The virtues of republicanism were promoted and disseminated by the press. The English radical Thomas Paine wrote in praise of the ordinary individual and against the privileges of status: 'One honest man is worth more than all the crowned ruffians that ever lived.' The implication for the restless colonies over the Atlantic was obvious to him: 'Americans should consult their independence . . . 'tis time to part.'

It was Jefferson, combining the traditions of English radicalism, the Enlightenment belief in individual rationality, a respect for popular wisdom and the ideals of the ancient republic, who drafted the American Declaration of Independence in 1776. In ringing terms it declared: 'The people are entitled to abolish those powers which deny their inalienable right to Life,

THOMAS PAINE

The publication of a forty-seven-page pamphlet entitled Common Sense in Philadelphia in 1776 was destined to establish its author among the intelligentsia of the day. Although it was originally published anonymously, it soon became known that the author was one Thomas Paine. Within three months this revolutionary pamphlet had sold over 200,000 copies, and it is said to have sold 500,000 in all. In it Paine called for an immediate declaration of independence, both as a practical measure to unite the colonies and gain Spanish and French aid, and also as the fulfilment of America's moral destiny. By freeing themselves from a vicious monarch, Paine argued, Americans would set an example for the world.

Paine was born in Thetford, England, in 1737. He pursued a number of trades and professions during his early years – including those of exciseman, schoolteacher, tobacconist and grocer – but a chance encounter with Benjamin Franklin, while he was lobbying for the rights of his fellow excisemen, was to change his destiny. Franklin was impressed by the young Paine and gave him letters of introduction to American society, describing him as an 'ingenious, worthy young man'. In October 1774 he left for Philadelphia, and it was here that he was to write his famous tract.

After the success of Common Sense Paine was appointed Secretary to the Congressional Committee for Foreign Affairs in the fledgling United States. In 1787 he left America for Europe. While there, in 1791, he published Rights of Man, once more putting forward his case for republicanism and making an explicit call to the English to overthrow their monarchy. In England he was indicted for treason and an order went out for his arrrest, but he was already en route for France. In Paris Paine adopted French citizenship and was appointed to the Convention – despite the fact that he could not speak French and had to have all his speeches read for him. With the collapse in 1793 of the Girondist party, of which Paine was a member, he was imprisoned under the regime of Robespierre for having argued against the execution of Louis XVI. Released in November 1794, he returned to America, where he lived out the last seven years of his life.

Paine was a propagandist and a populariser of contemporary thought rather than one of the great thinkers of his age. Had Common Sense never been written, there is little doubt that America would have become a free nation; but it cannot be questioned that Paine's pamphlet helped to humanise and concentrate the forces for change.

Liberty and the pursuit of Happiness.' But words alone – whether the stirring populism of the new democrats such as Paine, or the scholarly reflections of leading Enlightenment figures such as Jefferson and Franklin – could not on their own bring the American revolution to fruition. The Declaration of Independence was the outcome of a long process of self-discovery; but American freedom was secured only by seven years of war.

On 3 September 1783, two years after American troops outwitted the British at the decisive siege at Yorktown, the articles of peace were signed: 'His Britannic Majesty King George III acknowledges the said United States to be free Sovereign and independent states'. The west lay before them; but as Americans contemplated a new Eden and the enjoyment of a young society regulated on modern principles, much of western Europe was sinking into decadence. As the Americans turned their enthusiasm to new building, robust development and rational expansion, aristocratic France was occupied in designing pleasure gardens complete with purpose-built ruins – and follies. Courtiers amused themselves in the ceaseless social round of the royal circle with its banquets, operas, balls and sophisticated entertainments, unaware that the clock was ticking towards the end of their introverted idyll. Some of their compatriots, inspired alike by Enlightenment ideas close to home and by the actions of the Americans across the Atlantic – many of whom had been in close communication with them – were developing new political ideas in which the costly and corrupting lifestyle of the court would have no place. While courtiers exchanged optimistic predictions of the improvements that would flow automatically from progress in a perfectible world, reformers took a different view, claiming that 'the perfection of society can be wrought by liberty, equality and the laws of the people, which are those of nature'.

British troops surrender to General Washington at Yorktown. Two years later King George III formally recognised the United States as free, sovereign and independent states.

The French royal family were not all oblivious to the trouble in store. King Louis XV himself had an inkling of the changing times, which he expressed in terms that foreshadowed the darkest days of the revolution that was to come: 'The throne no longer possesses divine sanction as it was derived from violence, and what force had the right to establish, force has the right to topple and destroy.' His grandson, Louis XVI, was intrigued by Enlightenment ideas and could not see that they threatened him; his queen, Marie Antoinette, was enchanted by ideas of the simplicity of nature, unaware that the same Enlightenment theories that underlay her pleasure gardens declared that society should be run according to the dictates of reason, not privilege.

The French Revolution was both the creation of the Enlightenment and its destroyer. The rapidity with which the Revolution was perverted was an embittering experience for the children of the Enlightenment. It opened with noble cries – for liberty, equality and fraternity, the rights of man and of the citizen, the sovereignty of the people – but it ended with the sickening scream which forms the last line of the Marseillaise, '*Qu'un sang impur abreuve nos sillons!*' ('May impure blood run in our furrows!') Yet, for many, the French Revolution heralded the dawn of the modern age. Beyond the slaughter and tyranny, the dream of liberty for all has continued to inspire.

THE PROSPERITY OF INDIA

In the century of the furnace, revolutionary ideas and industrial initiatives together bubbled up like lava through the crust of old regimes. Volcanoes were among artists' favourite images. Industrial progress was an idea elevated by art and integrated, in educational minds, with hopes of political reform and universal improvement.

For most of the century, the world-wide balance of industry favoured India, as well as China, above Europe; and indeed, until its nineteenth-century experience of de-industrialisation, India remained the world's second industrial giant. However, the future shift in favour of the west was foreshadowed as British imperialism gained a foothold in India.

Rich in natural resources and land, at the beginning of the eighteenth century India had 20 per cent of the world's population and was the biggest exporter of manufactures. At the heart of the country's success were textile crops: cotton, silk and later jute. Silks woven with gold and silver came down the Ganges from Benares. In the south-east, Mysore had rich agriculture, silks and spices. On the Malabar coast in the west, the native traders still made more out of pepper, cardamom, perfumes, sandalwood and silk than the European interlopers who shared the trade. Production was highly specialised in some peculiarly Indian respects. In the north-eastern state of Bengal, where it seemed to a British scrutineer that 'every man, woman or child in every village was employed in making cloth', each major variety was

British expansion in India. British traders gained their first foothold in the north-east, in Bengal, then worked their way down the east coast until their progress was blocked by the proudly independent state of Mysore, ruled by Tipu Sultan.

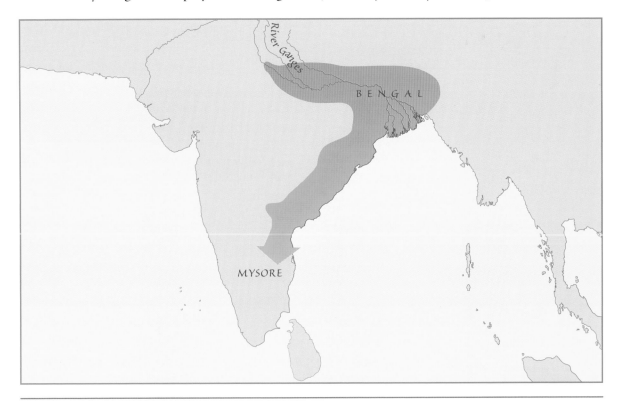

Tipu Sultan.

produced by a particular sub-caste. The scale of industrial activity dwarfed anything to be seen in Europe. In Kurnool on the Krishna river there were said to be up to 60,000 miners at work at a time. The quality of the output was correspondingly high. Until Benjamin Huntsman perfected the manufacture of cast steel in the 1760s, 'the finest steel used in this country was made by the Hindoos' and imported at £10,000 a ton.

The Moghuls made heavy, seemingly excessive tax demands on their subjects, exacting perhaps 50 per cent of the gross product of the empire. Yet this may actually have favoured enterprise by concentrating demand and creating a huge administrative class with surplus spending power. Although most Indians were, by European standards, scantily clad, sparingly shod and sketchily housed, the sheer size of the market ensured high levels of demand. In consequence, eighteenth-century India was an enormous exporter of manufactures. The Moghul state was almost certainly the world's most productive in terms of manufactures for export, despite the modest technical equipment with which its industries were generally supplied.

India's industrial collapse in the late eighteenth century is therefore astonishing. In Bengal, the long-established drain of westerners' silver into India was reversed by the 1770s. In 1807 it was a matter of complaint that 'useful trades' in Bengal had been supplanted by 'kite makers, falconers, astrologers and snake charmers'. A French missionary's analysis was candid:

> Europe no longer depends on India for anything, having learnt to beat the Hindus on their own ground, even in their most characteristic manufactures and industries, for which from time immemorial we were dependent on them. In fact, the roles have been reversed and this revolution threatens to ruin India completely.

With an exactness rare in history, India's industrial demise coincided with the establishment of British rule or hegemony over much of the subcontinent – and, in particular, over its old industrial heartlands. India's industrial strength was not matched by a corresponding political stability, and British traders were able to gain a foothold by taking advantage of the rivalry between warring states. In Bengal they acquired influence by collecting taxes for the sultan;

forming alliances with disaffected princes, they extended their reach down the east coast. Here they found their progress blocked by the prosperous and proudly independent state of Mysore: 'a garden from end to end', from the rich rice fields of Kerala to the great trading ports bustling with cargoes of bananas, oil and spices. Mysore's Muslim ruler, Tipu Sultan, was determined to hold together the Hindu princedoms he had inherited from his father and had no wish to share the benefits of trade with outsiders.

Tipu's gorgeous and defiant world comes to life in the booty of his realm, collected today in the Victoria and Albert Museum, London. He was obsessed by tigers. Of his throne, 'the proud monument of his arrogance', broken up at its capture by British conquerors, only a gold tiger's head and paws survive. He was guarded by tiger-striped guards behind fretwork shutters that imitated the scratch of a tiger's claw. Even the hammer of his blunderbuss had the form of a tiger in blue steel with gold and silver decoration. And to mock the British he designed a mechanical toy in the form of a tiger mauling a supine British officer.

Tipu recorded his own dreams. His dream-book, now in the India Office Library, includes scenes – amid emeralds, tiger-shoots and white elephants – of the expulsion of the British from India. In his portrait, his body is swathed in green and his pale, wispily moustachioed face is turbaned in the same sacred colour of Islam. His banner was a calligraphically stylised tiger's head forming the phrase, 'The lion of God is conqueror.' Yet his anti-British policy, idealised as a holy war, was underlain by political realism: by the last decade of the eighteenth century it had become obvious that the British could no longer be accommodated in the traditional Indian commercial and political frameworks. They had to be expelled or obeyed.

Tipu's cavalry repelled repeated assaults by the British and their Indian allies, inflicting a series of humiliating defeats on them; but eventually the invaders gained the advantage, and in the third Mysore war Tipu was defeated, forced to give up half his territory and a huge sum of money. When he said that he could not pay, the British demanded he hand over two sons as hostages. Eventually Tipu regenerated his economy and paid the ransom; but the British were unwilling to leave their conquest incomplete and in the summer of 1799 besieged Tipu's fortress at Siringapatam. After two weeks the food inside the capital ran out and the attackers overwhelmed the citadel.

Tipu's death in the assault marked the beginning of Britain's direct involvement in Indian affairs. The British had come not as conquerors but as barbarian suppliants, seeking commercial opportunities in competition not with indigenous traders but with European rivals. As late as 1750 the East India Company insisted that its officials were 'the factors and agents of merchants', not a military colony. Yet by 1850 Britain had established colonial rule. The Moghul empire, one of the pillars of Islamic civilisation, collapsed. India was steadily weakened, its vast wealth bled away westward.

CHINA: A VIBRANT EMPIRE

During the eighteenth century, China looked in many ways like the homeland of a more 'modern' society than any to be found in the west: a better-educated society, with over a million graduates; a more entrepreneurial society, with bigger businesses and bigger clusters of mercantile and industrial capital; a more industrial society, with higher levels of production in more mechanised and specialised concentrations; a more urbanised society, with denser distribution of population in most areas; even – for adult males – a more egalitarian society, in which the hereditary gentry shared privileges similar to those of their western counterparts, but had to defer to scholar-bureaucrats drawn from every level of society.

In the imperial arena westerners were puny newcomers by Chinese standards. Over 200,000 Chinese colonists settled in the western frontier area of Sinkiang in the eighteenth century. Other frontiers (Szechuan to the southwest, Taiwan offshore, Manchuria in the north, Dzungharia in the 'wild west') absorbed over 2 million. In 1793 the Chinese authorities sent a golden urn to Tibet with a demand that the Dalai Lama be selected from it by lot; the lamas had to convince the Chinese that they had implemented the system, while persuading their own people that they adhered to tradition. As an empire of uninterrupted growth and unloosened grip in the eighteenth-century world, China had no rival.

The frontier on China's eighteenth-century 'wild west' in Sinkiang was a huge, horizonless world. There is an adage that here even a beggar must ride a donkey: otherwise, having eaten his fill in one village, he will starve to death before he reaches the next. Colonial expansion in this direction really

took off in 1759, when the conquest of the area was completed. When the scholar Ji Yun made his journey of exile into the region in 1769, he felt the awe of entering 'another world' that Chinese commonly sensed there. From a distance, at first sight, he mistook the Turkestani Uighur merchants for women because of their long sheepskin coats of dark green and rosy purple. Yet he soon settled down on a frontier that was being civilised with remarkable rapidity. The capital Urumchi had housed bookshops, selling classical texts, for two years when he arrived. He was able to send his wife seeds from the huge chrysanthemums and marigolds he grew in his own garden. The peaches planted by a sub-prefect and the peonies of a fellow exile gave Urumchi scents and sights of home, though some of its flavours were elusive, particularly as pork – the Chinese celebratory meat – offended local Muslims. Particoloured little Nang cakes became a shared local taste. Meanwhile, about as far to the west as the empire ever reached, the poppies were famed for their size, and an emancipated convict was able to make a fortune by opening a shop selling delicacies from the eastern provinces in 1788.

Immigrants were driven to these far-flung regions by selective deportation and drawn by inducements to settle. Plenty of criminal and political undesirables were sent in by force; but for merchants the opportunities were so profitable that they were punished for wrongdoing by being sent back home. For bona fide migrants the government reimbursed travel costs and offered loans for seeds, livestock and housing. Grants of four and a half acres of land per family were available. Settlers got temporary exemption from tax.

In some respects the economy was a continuation of that of the earlier, southerly frontier of previously colonised provinces – a get-rich-quick economy based on logs floated out on the rivers and the products of mines: lead,

Kazaks present horses to the Chinese emperor Ch'en-lung. Even on its wild western frontier China's 'mandate of heaven' conveyed its authority.

copper, iron, silver, mercury and gold. But in Sinkiang settlements concentrated on arable lands north of the Tien Shan mountains, where market towns mushroomed. The lead and iron mines of Urumchi produced nothing for export: all the materials were absorbed by the frontier's own boom. Convicts worked the ores for base metals, but wage labour teased out the veins of copper and gold. Production depended on colonisation. The natives, who could not 'smell' the copper, left its exploitation to Chinese.

The swelling population of the empire, which more than doubled during the eighteenth century, helped keep up similar colonial pressure on all fronts. The Manchu conquest of Szechuan had been exceptionally savage, eliminating – so it was said – three-quarters of the people and undoing the laborious medieval colonisation of the territory. Yet between 1667 and 1707 more than 1.5 million settlers had been lured by the promise of tax immunities. Here and on the south-west frontier the pressure of intensive new settlement provoked a cycle of conflicts and solutions equally familiar to students of white colonialism: rebellious aboriginal tribes were penned in reservations; militarised agricultural colonies grew wheat, barley, peas and corn while keeping the natives subordinate; schools were erected to bring Chinese language and values to the tribes.

To the north of traditional China, in the borderlands of Mongolia and Manchuria, colonisation proceeded on a different footing. The Manchus came to power in China convinced that their own heartlands had to be preserved as a reservoir of Manchu identity, where warriors, unsullied by Christian ways, uncorrupted by Chinese contact, could continue to breed for the service of the dynasty. In the few schools in eighteenth-century Manchuria, the curriculum was limited to horsemanship, archery and the Manchu language. Chinese immigration was, at different times, actively discouraged or peremptorily banned. Yet the Manchu adopted Chinese customs, and Chinese settlers poured in, despite imperial policies. The dark, fertile soils of a land reasonably close to the competitive, thickly settled world of northern China were an irresistible incentive. Cultivable steppe could accommodate large numbers when converted from nomadic to sedentary use, especially with the efficient new crops that were introduced. Maize, potatoes and peanuts were made available through the transoceanic network of exchange that accompanied the imperialism of the age.

It was not just in size or rate of growth that the Chinese empire still outclassed all others. Although Europe was catching up and, in some respects, taking the lead in industrial production, China still had a more mature industrial economy by most standards – including size of firms, numbers employed, rates of output and degree of geographical specialisation – than any potential rival in the west. Industrial production was fed by agricultural expansion, and cottage industries multiplied all over China.

China, too, still enjoyed its centuries-old advantage over Europe in terms of trade: indeed, this remained the case until the 1860s. In the early eighteenth century, the Beneficial and Beautiful Textiles Company of Hangchow sold a million lengths of cloth a year and employed 109,000 workers under 340 contractors. In Nanking at the start of the century there were three imperial textile factories, employing 2,500 artisans and 664 looms. In Soochow in 1723 there were about 20,000 textile workers and dyers. In the 1770s and 1780s a single Chinese province imported in each year, on average, six times as much raw cotton for processing as the whole of Britain. In Szechuan there were ironworks that employed two or three thousand men. Water-driven machinery was used in many industries, including incense-pounding, rice-husking and paper-making. At the end of the century the trade of Canton was estimated to be worth £6.5 million a year.

In this vibrant economy, many people had more wealth and more leisure. Tea palaces, where sophisticated entertainments were staged to divert customers, were the most splendid buildings in many towns. As tea – said to have been discovered by the Buddha to banish sleep – became more widely consumed, so more teacups and teapots were produced; made, according to one official, by 'Year Round Thunder and Lightning'. The process of the porcelain's manufacture certainly remained mysterious to the west, where it was greatly prized and called 'China': it would take Europeans nearly 100 years to match the colours and glazes of Chinese porcelain.

PORCELAIN: A CHINESE TREASURE

In 1722, with the Qing dynasty firmly in power and a new emperor, Yung-cheng, on the throne, porcelain production in China experienced a renaissance. The industry drew on a long heritage, the translucent hard-paste porcelain having first appeared in the fourteenth century. Before that, ceramic wares were largely made from opaque stoneware or earthenware – coarser clays fired at a comparatively low temperature. It is also probably during this period that the first blue-and-white porcelain was produced, using cobalt blue painting beneath the glaze to produce the distinctive design most familiarly characterised by the 'willow pattern'. By the eighteenth century the simulation of classical wares from the Sung and Ming dynasties was popular, but this was also a time of innovation, with the development of new glazes and designs. It is also during this period that Europe made its one contribution to the art of Chinese porcelain-making, in the form of a rose-pink

Blue-and-white porcelain plate produced in China for export to Europe.

overglaze enamel devised from colloidal gold. This new style was called famille rose.

In 1729 a new superintendent of the imperial factories was appointed: T'ang Ying. He catalogued the wares requested by the court, listing sixty different types of porcelain. When he retired twenty years later there was a marked decline in the quality of the porcelain being manufactured. Blue-and-white porcelain began to go out of fashion, the bulk of it now being produced for export. None the less, the eighteenth century was a remarkable period, and the last great era, of production of Chinese porcelain. By the nineteenth century the industrial revolution in the west was beginning to have an impact in China. Europe was quickly catching up in the production of its own porcelain and this, together with the fact that shipping porcelain from China was becoming increasingly expensive, was to signal the end of Chinese domination of the porcelain market.

An eighteenth-century Chinese painting depicts the gathering and sorting of tea.

An eighteenth-century Chinese painting depicts the gathering and sorting of tea.

Inevitably, given the strict control of exports by the state, smuggling flourished. The scale of the illicit trade in China's riches was demonstrated by the discovery of a wrecked ship bound for the Netherlands, sunk in the South China Sea in 1752. Its cargo of porcelain alone would have been worth a fortune; but this had been packed not as the primary object of the voyage but merely as ballast to stabilise the real treasure: tea.

While European empires foundered and failed, the Chinese empire went on growing. A British diplomatic mission which arrived off Canton in June 1793 lacked nothing that might embellish its dignity and emphasise its prestige. King George III had elevated its leader to the peerage for the occasion and equipped him with a retinue eighty-four strong. His gifts for the Chinese court, worth over £15,000, included all the most new-fangled hardware of early British industrialisation: a planetarium, globes, mathematical instruments, chronometers of apparently magical accuracy, a telescope, instruments for chemical and electrical experiments, plate glass, Wedgwood ware, Sheffield plate, samples of textiles woven on power looms and a letter to the emperor in a box made of gold.

The Chinese were not wholly contemptuous of these efforts. Indeed, the admiration for western science established in the previous century (above, p. 194) had never waned. The imperial court was restrainedly pleased at the arrival of this 'first tributary mission' from Britain. The emperor ordered that on account of the envoys' long journey they should be accorded a better welcome than corresponding missions from Burma and Annam. He did not, however, endorse the high value the British put on themselves: the ambassador's refusal to knock his head on the ground in greeting to the emperor was indulged as a piece of barbarian bad manners, but all his diplomatic overtures were rejected. The British were told that they were incapable of 'acquiring the rudiments of our civilisation', that they possessed nothing China needed and that their representatives could not be accommodated at the imperial court. 'It is your bounden duty', the emperor concluded in his reply to George III, 'reverently to appreciate my feelings and to obey these instructions henceforth for all time.'

The Chinese attitude has generally been regarded as arrogant, unrealistic and hidebound by outmoded traditions. In fact, it reflected the world balance of power. During the eighteenth century, despite the long reach of some European empires, China's was by almost every standard still the fastest-growing in the world. European outposts of as yet unpredictable importance had been founded in Australia and the American far west; but at the same time, Britain and France had recently lost most of their American colonies, and the other European seaborne empires – those of Spain, Portugal, the Netherlands, Denmark and Sweden – all seemed to be stagnant or declining. Napoleon's opinion that 'it is in the east that great reputations are made' was based not only on his reading of the history of earlier would-be world conquerors, but also on a realistic appraisal of the opportunities of his day.

Chinese preponderance has been the normal state of this planet for almost the whole of recorded history. Now, however, at the end of the eighteenth century, signs of a challenge, which would prove irresistible, were beginning to emerge.

The reception of the British diplomatic mission, led by Lord MacCartney, at Canton in 1793. The Chinese emperor informed the British that they were incapable of 'acquiring the rudiments of our civilisation'.

CHAPTER 9

Century of the
MACHINE

THE NINETEENTH CENTURY

IN THE NINETEENTH CENTURY, the traditional global balance of economic power and
military potential was reversed as a newly dominant
west, empowered for the first time by more people
and better technology, asserted its superiority over
the hitherto ascendant east.

In these years, the populations of most European
countries roughly doubled. That of Russia
increased fourfold. There were big rises in some
parts of Asia, too; nevertheless, Europe's share of
the world's human inhabitants rose dramatically,
from around a fifth to over a quarter. So great were
the numerical increases that there was ample surplus for export to populate 'new Europes' in the
temperate parts of the Americas, Australia, New
Zealand and South Africa.

Even so, the west never had enough manpower to
dominate the world by numbers alone. The shortfall
in human resources was made up with the resources
of industrial technology. Until the nineteenth
century, the works of man had been powered by
water, wind, fire, and muscle – the openly evident
powers of nature. Now, human ingenuity found
ways to compel nature to yield up its secret
strengths and put them to work for human ends on

*The Great Exhibition held at the Crystal Palace in London
in 1851. The whole world was invited to participate in this
proud display of 'the works of Industry of all Nations'.
Britain had led the way in the triumph of industrialisation
but its commanding position as 'the workshop of the world'
would be eroded within a few decades.*

a previously unimagined scale. The power of steam made the labour of workers more effective. New guns and communications improved the precision, adaptability and reliability of European armies in hostile environments. The forces of electricity and magnetism were explored. This technology extended human capacity for good and evil beyond the limits conceived of in earlier ages. States armed with the advantages conferred by industrialisation were able to strengthen their own centralised polities and to impose imperial ambitions on most of the unindustrialised world.

The western world, after a long spell in the twilight, suddenly eclipsed the older civilisations of China, Islam and India, which had for so long shone so much more brightly in power, inventiveness and initiative. This shift in prominence was reflected in the reconstruction of the global map, as the planet's surface was re-imagined in a new form – still familiar today in old-fashioned school atlases. The mapmakers called their angle on the world 'Mercator's projection', after a long-dead cartographer; but it reflected the new realities of power. The northern hemisphere preponderated, and the new colonial powers of the west – especially Britain, the one with the biggest empire – got a disproportionate amount of space. At the centre of this vision of the world, in pride of place, stood Europe.

Isambard Kingdom Brunel stands in front of the launching chains of his steamer, the Great Eastern. *Brunel represented a new kind of hero.*

THE HEROES OF STEAM

Heroes do not make history; history makes heroes, and we learn a lot about the values and trends of an age by the heroes it chooses. In the eighteenth century, for instance, the English idolised explorers; in the nineteenth, they kept their highest accolades for engineers, entrepreneurs and inventors. Just as the writers of Renaissance Italy had produced Lives of the Artists and the scribes of medieval Europe Lives of the Saints and Kings, so the biographers of the new age celebrated its architects in Lives of the Engineers. The spirit of adulation was evident in the tone of their language. The devisers of new technology, it was said, 'approach . . . the qualities and pre-eminence of a higher order of being'. Mechanics became heroes in the 'epic of tools'. In the public arena, too, homage was paid in unashamedly extravagant terms. The band of the Royal Marines played 'See, the Conquering Hero Comes' when Isambard Kingdom Brunel stepped from the platform at the opening of the majestic iron bridge with which he spanned the river Tamar, which divided Devon from Cornwall, in 1857. William Armstrong, who designed greatly improved artillery and pioneered the use of hydro-electricity, was offered the Albanian throne. The heroes who fought merely in wars against men could hardly compete for esteem: for the engineers were conquering nature. Nor were their victories bloodless: Brunel bridged rivers and penetrated hillsides, but his victories exacted a heavy cost. One hundred workers died building a single two-mile stretch of tunnel between Bristol and London.

If there was one conqueror of nature who deserved hero status it was Richard Trevithick; but – outside a small circle of devotees – he never got it in his lifetime. Towards the end of the 1790s this Cornish mining engineer designed a machine capable of realising in practice an idea contemplated for centuries but never before translated into action. He devised a way to put steam to work under high pressure – by making it pummel a piston and then escape into the air, while the piston set other parts of the machine in motion. He began by constructing contraptions which he called 'puffers' in his kitchen. Friends came round to see them work. 'A boiler something like a strong iron kettle was placed on the fire,' guests reported. One visitor would stoke and pump the bellows. Lady de Dunstanville, wife to Trevithick's patron, 'was engine man and turned the cock for the admission of steam . . . and was charmed to see the wheels go round'.

Richard Trevithick.

Movement within an engine was impressive enough, and extremely useful. The early engines – some the size of a three-storey house – were used to pump surplus water from mines and drinking water from rivers. Trevithick, however, had his sights set on a more ambitious target: locomotion, considered the most spectacular imaginable effect of steam power – and in the long run, perhaps, the most important for world history, since railways were the fruit of it. All his earliest large-scale experiments were devoted to this aim; but he failed repeatedly. One attempt in 1801 was said to have ended when the machine expired after three or four hundred yards, whereupon 'the parties adjourned to the hotel, and consoled their hearts with a roast goose and proper drinks'. They forgot the engine, the iron became red hot, 'and nothing that was combustible remained either of the engine or the house'. In 1808, Trevithick backed his machine to outrun a racehorse. He advertised it under the slogan 'Mechanical Power Subduing Animal Speed'. It flew off its rails and wallowed embarrassingly in the mud. He rapidly lost credibility. One of the few appreciative reports appeared in a local paper in south Wales in February 1804, chronicling with uncharacteristic but prophetic accuracy the first successful experiment in steam locomotion – carrying ten tons of iron and an irrepressible crowd of joy-riders along nine miles of track:

Yesterday . . . Mr Trevithick's new-invented steam-engine . . . was found to perform, to admiration, all that was expected from it . . . It performed the journey without feeding the boiler or using any water, and will travel with ease at the rate of five miles an hour. It is not doubted but that the number of horses in the kingdom will be very considerably reduced, and the machine in the hands of the present proprietors will be made use of in a thousand instances never yet thought of for an engine.

Trevithick's engine, 'Catch me who can', demonstrated at Euston Square in 1808. It reached a speed of 10 mph.

The prophecy came true: but not soon enough for Trevithick. His engines were too heavy for the rails, and his invention 'remained buried', its inventor discouraged and impoverished. He returned to mining and took his pumps to the silver fields of Peru and the gem mines of Central America. His last scheme, for a gigantic monument to constitutional reform in London – gilded, cast-iron and raised, of course, by steam engine – was never executed. Trevithick won recognition as a hero only after he was laid in a pauper's unmarked grave in 1833. But by then his great invention was already beginning to transform the world: in 1829, George Stephenson's *Rocket* reached a speed of 35 miles per hour. A young girl – herself later to win fame as the actress Fanny Kemble – described the journey aboard the famous train: 'How strange it was to journey without any visible means of progress bar the magical machine with its flying white breath and rhythmical, unvarying pace. When I closed my eyes the sensation of flying was delightful.'

It was not long before railways were scoring the land. Initially, however, steam-powered transport worked best on water. The first commercial steamer was launched in the United States in 1807: the *Clermont* took thirty-two hours to ferry its passengers 150 miles downriver from Albany to New York. Just twelve years later, paddle steamers were crossing the Atlantic Ocean.

Richard Trevithick – temperamental, obsessive, gifted – was typical of the heralds of the new technology. Industrialisation in the early nineteenth century was not the result of an 'enterprise culture': inventors were unbusinesslike; manufacturers were often inspired by religious or philanthropic ideals. High-pressure steam was a great technical innovation; it was also a great romantic image. The engines seemed 'noble', beautiful. J. M. W. Turner painted them as if they had blended into nature; Felix Mendelssohn wrote the songs steam sang into the musical account of his steamship journey off Scotland, where he was engaged in a common hobby of the time – exploring Europe's misty, mythic past.

The technical breakthroughs that paved the way for the triumph of mechanisation were produced not by the scientific culture of Europe but, for the

The romance of steam celebrated in J. M. W. Turner's painting Rain, Steam and Speed, *depicting an engine of the Great Western Railway.*

most part, by heroes of 'self-help' – self-taught artisans and engineers with little or no scientific education. Their experiments had an air of adventure, of improvisation, and their achievements were represented as successes of perseverance, not wisdom; of action, not thought.

A similar enthusiasm for self-improvement marked the fledgling tourist industry. International travel made it essential to synchronise the world's clocks, and in 1884 the Greenwich Observatory in London was formally adopted as the zero meridian, the centre of world time, with the rest of the world divided into twenty-four time zones. Railway schedules could be drawn up with accuracy; steamships, unlike sailing ships, were not at the mercy of wind and tide. All this made possible the tourist timetables compiled by the world's first travel agent.

Thomas Cook was an itinerant evangelist who was in a better position than most to appreciate the potential of railways: in a single year, he had to walk 2,106 miles in the course of his work. From 1841 he began organising cheap

Cook's Tours. Middle-class holidaymakers visit an Italian volcano on the cover of a piece of Victorian sheet music.

rail excursions for temperance meetings, school outings and chapel groups, and pleasure trips for deserving working people. His motives were philanthropic and enthusiastic. He set about the project as an amateur; only in 1845, when the volume of travel work engaged him full time, did he attempt to operate at a profit. He remained a pastor – even while shepherding his flocks between earthly destinations – and never missed an opportunity of exhorting his clients to moral improvement. Educational sightseeing was part of every programme he drew up. In 1851, when the Great Exhibition opened in London to display to the world the wonders of industrial manufacture, Cook got the contract for arranging special excursion trains. He sold 165,000 tickets and felt enormous pride when he 'saw workpeople come out of factories in Bradford, pay five shillings and with a very few shillings in their pockets start off [for] . . . London'.

The formula Cook devised for conducting parties around the sights, whether at home or abroad, remains familiar to this day. A song entitled

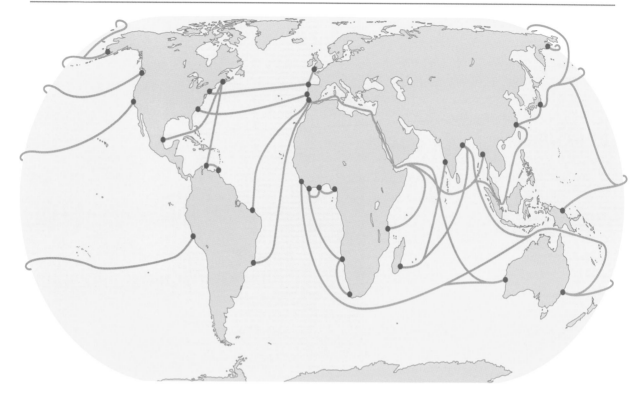

Principal oceanic routes in the mid-nineteenth century. No longer dependent on winds and ocean currents, steamship routes could encircle the world. Railways carried people rapidly across continents. Steamships and railways together made possible the movement of populations on a massive scale.

'Follow the Man from Cook's' was a standard of popular entertainers. The snobbish reaction to Cook's social mission, to bring variety and improvement to ordinary people's lives and to make travel accessible to those on modest incomes, was predictable. By 1865 Charles Lever, a British vice-consul in Italy, was looking down his nose at his fellow countrymen and women – 'tribes of unlettered British', he quipped, 'convicts refused by the Australian colonies' – who had stripped the Grand Tour of its grandeur:

> The cities of Italy [are] deluged with droves of these creatures, for they never separate, and you see them forty in number pouring along a street with a director – now in front, now at the rear, circling round them like a sheep-dog – and really the process is as much like herding as may be . . . Anything so uncouth I have never seen before: the men, mostly elderly, dreary, sad-looking; the women, somewhat younger, travel-tossed and crumpled, but intensely lively, wide-awake and facetious.

Critics of the industrial society claimed that it impoverished and exploited the masses and opened up obscene wealth gaps between classes. In a quiet way, Cook demonstrated that little by little the opposite was happening: society was becoming more egalitarian. Thanks to the 'trickle-down' of the extra wealth industry generated, ordinary people could aspire to experiences previously restricted to the most privileged.

The range of the business grew with the reach of steam technology. Cook took workers to the seaside, middle-class holidaymakers to Europe, and Britain, on the back of its empire, to the world. In 1866 he sent his first tour to America: in a land already renowned for hustle, most of the railways broke their engagements, but his son made new ones which lasted. The head of the firm took fifty clients to Rome for Holy Week and hired the Palazzo Torlonia when their hotel turned out to be double-booked. In 1868 he arranged a month in the Holy Land for £40. Cook's was the biggest operator in steam travel along the Nile – indeed, the firm was said to have assured the prosperity of Egypt. Schoolchildren in Aswan were told that Cook's son, John, was – after the ruler – 'the second greatest man in Egypt'. The travel industry had given industrialised powers a new way to expand, colonise and control the world.

Even as his portfolio of products moved upmarket, Thomas remained keen to enhance the leisure of working people at home, and in the year the Suez Canal opened he began a programme of workers' outings to the pleasure grounds of the Duke of Rutland's estate at Alton Towers: this is still one of England's most popular family days out. In the year Jules Verne published *Around the World in Eighty Days*, the company introduced round-the-world tours. In 1890 Cook's – one of the world's first multinational companies – sold over three and a quarter million tickets.

THE POND

On the morning of 3 January 1842, a small knot of travellers stared apprehensively into

a long, narrow apartment, not unlike a giant hearse with windows in the sides, having at one end a melancholy stove, at which three or four chill stewards were warming their hands; while on either side ... was a long, long table, over which a rack, fixed to the roof and stuck full of drinking-glasses and cruet stands, hinted dismally at rolling seas and heavy weather.

Charles Dickens and his fellow voyagers were contemplating in disillusionment the saloon of the Britannia, the first of the Cunard shipping line's new breed of packet steamers. The berths were bleak, the quarters cramped, the passengers bilious and the dinners of 'pig's-face-and-potatoes'. Reliability, not luxury, was the key to commercial success and the ships crossed in all weathers, 'staggering, heaving, wrestling, leaping, diving, jumping, pitching, throbbing, rolling and rocking'.

At first, they were poor performers compared with the sail packets. The first steamship to cross the Atlantic, in 1819, took twenty-seven days to get from Savannah in the southern USA to Liverpool, of which only eighty hours were spent under steam; the rest of the time, she relied on her sails. Her engine was gutted and she was sold as a sailing vessel. Gradually, however, technical progress improved the service. By the 1840s the normal duration of a crossing was ten or twelve days. Cunard commissioned a series of romantic paintings designed to advertise the superior performance of the new technology.

It was aboard a sailing packet between Le Havre and New York in 1832 that Samuel B. Morse concieved an idea for harnessing another force of nature to improve communications. Inventing the electric telegraph was his after-dinner diversion from the tedium of the voyage and from his failed vocation as a painter. At first he could transmit no further than a few yards, but collaboration with other workers in the field enabled the creation of an apparatus of intelligible communication across vast distances. The first long-range telegraph line was laid between Washington and Baltimore in 1844. A submarine telegraph cable, first laid across the bed of the Atlantic in the early 1870s, shrank the ocean to the dimensions of a pond.

GEOLOGY AND PALÆONTOLOGY.

1. SIVATHERIUM	5. PTERODACTYLUS	9. CARBONIFEROUS FERN	13. ACANTHODUS	17. ZOSTERITES
2. MASTODON LONGIROSTRIS	6. AMMONITES	10. LEPIDODENDRON	14. DIPLACANTHUS	18. AMMONITES
3. ELEPHAS PRIMIGENIUS	7. PLESIOSAURUS	11. CALAMITES	15. LEPIDOSTEUS	19. GONIATITES
4. PALÆOTHERIUM	8. ICHTHYOSAURUS	12. LABYRINTHODON	16. CLIMATIUS	20. STROPHOMENA

EVOLUTION AND THE IDEOLOGY OF EMPIRE

The most conspicuous achievement of nineteenth-century European science – the theory of evolution popularised by Charles Darwin – was thoroughly typical of its time: inspired by the idea of progress, focused on a search for a 'theory of everything' that would make the world seem simple. Most scientists already believed that life had evolved from, at most, a few primitive forms. What they did not know was how it happened. How did new species arise? They called it 'the Mystery of Mysteries'. Even assuming God to be responsible, they expected him to work through nature rather than by miracles. In the first year of the century Josef Haydn wrote his great oratorio *Die Schöpfung – The Creation* – a setting of the biblical Book of Genesis, which describes how God made the world in six days, culminating in the creation of humankind. It was an act as much of devotion as of artistic inspiration. 'I fell on my knees each day,' he said, 'to pray that God would give me strength to complete it.' In his music, the world sprang instantly into life. But the metaphor was already out of date: science had proved that it was many millions of years old, as explorers traced the fossil record back through levels of rock. There had been time for life to evolve without divine intervention.

A young naturalist intending to pursue a career in the church, Charles Darwin travelled to South America in the early 1830s as gentleman companion to the captain of HMS *Beagle*, which had voyaged to the South Atlantic on a surveying mission for the Royal Navy. Here his thoughts on the emergence of life forms were prompted to develop in new directions. He found the Galapagos islands surprisingly 'differently tenanted. These species . . . in the natural economy of the archipelago filled me with wonder.' He began to realise that species changed by adapting to local conditions; and also that man was not necessarily a creature set apart from and above all others. In a terrible and wonderful time among the natives of Tierra del Fuego, he encountered 'man in his most savage state': beastly, vile, in Darwin's perception, a 'foul, naked, snuffling thing' with no inkling of loveliness, no spark of the divine. Man was obviously an animal – a well-adapted ape.

A comprehensive theory of evolution, embracing all species, occurred to Darwin when he was back home, in the English countryside, among game birds and farm stock. He collected every known kind of domestic pigeon, to study how the breeders selected mating pairs to emphasise particular characteristics. Nature, he proposed, selected strains, as breeders do: the specimens best adapted to their environments survived to breed and pass on their characteristics. 'These facts . . . have thoroughly convinced me that species have been modified during a long course of descent. This has been effected chiefly through the natural selection of numerous,

OPPOSITE *The fossil record. An evolutionary chart of 1880 recognises the immense span of geological time and the evidence for extinct life forms.*

'Man in his most savage state'. A native of Tierra del Fuego, depicted in a book of 1839.

Three varieties of palm tree, seen by Darwin on his travels in South America, appear to illustrate the action of natural selection.

successive, slight and favourable variations.' His researches in South America had won him respect in scientific circles, but now he was racked with anxiety about the implications of his work; fearing disgrace from religious critics and professional rivals alike, he suppressed his theory for twenty years. Finally forced into print in 1859 by the news that another naturalist had come to the same conclusions, he saw his book, *On the Origin of Species*, sell out on the first day.

Darwin's interest in scientific breeding and the survival of the fittest had an obvious echo in his own personal predicament. In the tranquillity of his home in the Kent countryside, his own family – inbred and riddled with sickness – was struggling to survive. Darwin himself was tortured by ill health, often in pain and given to bouts of vomiting which lasted for weeks at a time. He had married his cousin – an act unpardonable under the laws of natural selection – and was troubled by anxiety over the weakness and vulnerability of his children. His favourite daughter's death made it 'impossible for me ever to feel joy again . . . I was no longer sure of God's existence.' He held the struggle of nature in awe, partly because his own sickly offspring were the victims of it. In formulating epitaphs for his dying children, he wrote that the survivors would be more healthy and most able to enjoy life. This was the expression of his scientific faith; his religious faith could not withstand the assaults of his personal experience and his work. He found nature 'clumsy, wasteful, blundering, low and horribly cruel'; but, 'from the war of nature, from famine and death', he wrote in *The Origin of Species*, 'the production of higher animals directly follows'. A shocking conclusion was almost inescapable: human beings, too, had been evolved by nature, not created by God. The moral implications of this claim were profound. There is no such thing as selflessness; our senses of goodness and beauty are just adaptations equipping us better to survive. Finally abandoning any thought of entering holy orders, he turned from God in hatred.

The extension of the theory of evolution beyond species to races took Darwin and his contemporaries deeper into morally murky waters. Natural selection seemed the perfect intellectual basis for the rising tide of white imperialism. The British, who succeeded in an amazing variety of environments, were clearly (it appeared) chosen by nature and proven in the struggle, as the Jews had once seemed chosen by God and tested in faith. Darwin speculated that blacks would have evolved into a separate species if imperialism had not ended their isolation: as it was, they were doomed to extinction. 'The civilised races of man', he wrote, 'will almost completely replace the savage races throughout the world.' For Darwin, this was a scientific fact; for the 'Social Darwinists' who took up his ideas, it was a political programme. His theories were appropriated by thinkers who proposed terrible refinements: if aggression is natural, war is good; society benefits from the elimination of the weak; it is right and proper that 'naturally inferior' races are subjected to more highly evolved 'master races'. Just when white power was at its most penetrative and most pervasive, scientific theory helped to ram it home. Men who called themselves 'anthropologists' worked out a ranking of human races in which whites came out on top and blacks at the bottom. The infant science of genetics offered an explanation of how one man could be, inherently and necessarily, inferior to another by virtue of race alone. The hundred years which followed the publication of Darwin's great book was – partly in consequence of its influence – an age of empires at ease with themselves, in which critics of imperialism could be made to seem sentimental or unscientific, in a world sliced by the sword and stacked in order of race.

Empires were won by technology, the uneven pace of industrialisation around the world giving a temporary but decisive advantage to conquerors borne on steamships, fortified by mass-produced quinine pills and equipped with steel guns; but they were justified by two kinds of cant. First, moral cant: imperialism was 'civilising' and its victims would be better off because of it. Secondly, scientific cant: the superiority of white men was 'natural' and proved to be so by the laws and evidence of progress. Imperialists from the white west could confront the rest of the world in confidence. They thought history was over and that their ascendancy would last for ever. Only the stirrings of revolt among their victims proved them wrong. As the unindustrialised world succumbed, there were some remarkable feats of resistance – and even of imperial competition – along the way. But most imperial stories of the nineteenth century ended in white men's victories, as the firepower and mobility of industrially equipped armies became unstoppable. It was in the nature of the industrial advantage that it was short-lived; but while it lasted, it was unbeatable. Nowhere was the West's domination more clearly seen than in Africa. At the end of the century, Africa became the victim of a wholesale colonial takeover. Here, Europe's industrialised powers played out their own battle for the survival of the fittest.

America: The Empire of the West

A fact usually forgotten or suppressed is that the most enduring white empire of the nineteenth century was founded in America. Democracy was the ideology Americans identified with; they liked to think of empires as foreign, old-fashioned things from which their own free citizens had escaped. Yet while affecting a lofty attitude towards European imperialism, US governments practised empire-building of their own, in pursuit of what they called the 'manifest destiny' of their hemisphere. And while the other great world empires of the nineteenth century have already vanished, America's is still intact. Partly, this is because the native peoples America conquered were utterly crushed, virtually exterminated. Partly, it was because the colonists' loyalty was secured by democratic government. Principally, it was because most American expansion was into areas bordering on the existing territory of the state, whereas the European powers founded far-flung maritime empires which proved, in the long run, too scattered to defend. Relentlessly, the United States swallowed up Native American, Mexican, Canadian and Spanish lands until, by the end of the century, it overspilled its home continent.

The United States relied heavily on immigrants to work in its new industries and people the expanding frontier. Steam travel shrank the Atlantic. The alliance of immigration and industry was symbolised in 1886 by the erection at the entrance to the port of New York of the Statue of Liberty, inscribed with its welcome to the 'wretched refuse' of the poor and oppressed. For the statue was a sublime industrial artefact – central iron pylon, complex flexible trusswork innards, cladding of hammered copper. She took twenty years to make, 214 crates to ship and $100,000 to erect on arrival. From her perch on Bedloe's Island, Liberty presided over a new era in American immigration. At

her feet was Ellis Island, where, from 1892, immigrants were processed, judged on their suitability as participants in the American Dream. Undesirables – mostly the carriers of disease, but also political suspects or moral rejects, such as prostitutes, polygamists and anarchists – were filtered out. By the 1880s the net gain of immigrants into the USA had reached over five and a quarter million, and ever more stringent quotas were enforced as mechanisation gathered pace and labour needs diminished correspondingly.

The alliance of industry and imperialism is nowhere better exemplified than in the story of the conquest and colonisation of the North American plain. Before industrialisation, the plains were unexploitable. You could not build, for want of wood; you could not farm, because of the unyielding sod. In 1827, when James Fenimore Cooper wrote in his novel *The Prairie* of the slow invasion of white squatters, which would eventually contribute to a new look for the plains, the territories seemed a place without a future, 'a vast country, incapable of sustaining a dense population . . . an earth of iron under a heaven of brass'. So the plains were treated as an obstacle to be crossed rather than a space to be occupied or a potential empire to be disputed with the people who already lived there.

The effects of industrialisation arrived in the region in the late 1860s. Invaders turned the ground with powerful steel ploughs and planted strains of wheat produced by scientific agronomy to flourish in the capricious climate. In the movies, cowboy towns look ramshackle and rustic, but they were products of the industrial age: machined planks and cheap nails from Chicago held them together. Construction gangs and city dwellers created demand for ranchers' beef. Wielders of repeating rifles destroyed the vital links in the earlier ecosystem: the herds of 'buffalo' (American bison) and their human hunters. There could be no more startling demonstration of the power of industrialising societies than this rapid and total transformation of one of the great features of the

Irish immigrants disembarking in New York in about 1855. The building in the left background is Castle Garden, used for the processing of immigrants before Ellis Island was opened for that purpose.

Buffalo on the American plains. Steam trains like the one whose passage they are obstructing would before long doom them to near-extinction.

earth: the subversion of the North American plains' ecology, the extermination of its people, the erection of a new economy, a new landscape and a new society, where nature – once worshipped – was now remoulded to the uses of man.

Before the European pioneers arrived, the plains were populated by tribes of Native Americans. One of the native peoples, the Sioux, had a vision of dominion stretching between mountains, desert and forest. Mounted on horses, they ranged over the prairie and imagined it united under their rule, pursuing their own imperial ambitions with guns bought from the Europeans. But there was one rival they could not match: the white invader.

The Native American tribes of the plains were sustained – in more ways than one – by the huge herds of buffalo. Their survival was directly linked with the fate of these great animals, as Dan Old Elk, speaking today for his ancestors a century ago, explains:

> The buffalo was a gift from the creator. It was given to the Native American to use, to survive, to live on this earth. We use every part of the buffalo, from the head to the hoof, for food, clothing and shelter. The spirituality of the buffalo is very important to us. It meant everything to the Native American.

The tribes hunted to meet their own needs (a favourite way of killing their quarry was to drive a group over a cliff), and never on a scale to threaten the continuance of herds adequate to meet those needs. By contrast, in the years following European settlement, the buffalo population of the plains fell from an estimated 60 million to fewer than 1,000. For the white settlers the slaughter of the buffalo became a sport, and a way of undermining the economic basis of the natives' existence.

As millions of immigrants poured into America and across the country on the new railroad tracks laid by gangs of Irish and Chinese labourers, confrontation with the Native Americans became inevitable. The attitude of the Europeans, for the most part, was unswervingly hostile. 'The more I see of these Indians,' said General William Sherman in 1867, 'the more convinced I am that they all have to be killed or be maintained as a species of pauper.' This uncompromising stance was backed up by the full power of an industrial state, with an unceasing supply of guns and ammunition. The Winchester factory alone produced two million bullets a day. The US 7th Cavalry under General Custer, employed by the Kansas Pacific railroad to defend its trains against native attack, took on a specific mission to kill the plains Indians.

Even the firepower of the US Army did not have everything its own way. On 25 June 1876 Custer's detachment of the elite 7th Cavalry was annihilated at the battle of Little Bighorn, the Native Americans' greatest victory in their long struggle to preserve their homeland and traditional way of life. But in the longer term their efforts were doomed: the victory provoked brutal reprisals, and eventually those Native Americans who survived the relentless onslaught were herded on to ever smaller reservations as their lands were taken over by the newcomers.

Not all the Europeans were blind to the plight of the Native Americans. William Cody, a young scout hired to shoot buffalo to feed the railroad workers, was renowned for his sympathy with those his compatriots had come to displace: 'I never knew a treaty with the Indians that was not first broken by the whites . . . Where is the white man that would not fight if everything was taken away from him? I'm dog-goned if I wouldn't.' Cody nurtured his own image from the start, and his exploits as 'Buffalo Bill' became the stuff of legend. Later, as the Native Americans were reduced to small subject groups living on reservations, Cody created a new theatrical role for them as participants in his Wild West Shows, which toured the world during the years from 1883 to the First World War. Giant cavalcades, resplendent with warriors in their spectacular head-dresses, travelled thousands of miles between performances on the very steamships and trains which had helped to destroy their own culture. From Venice to London, the participants in a real and tragic history replayed their bitter experience as sanitised spectacle. Buffalo Bill helped to establish the Western myth of cowboys and Indians that would soon be transmitted, through the images of the new motion-picture industry, to every corner of the globe. Industrialisation had brought the world to America. Now American culture could be taken to the world.

The Battle of Little Bighorn, as seen by the Native American painter Kicking Bear.

OPIUM AND THE DEFEAT OF CHINA

China, long confident and respected as the most powerful state of all, was the century's big loser. Since commerce across Eurasia began, China had always enjoyed a favourable balance of trade with the western 'barbarians', who had nothing to exchange for their purchases except silver: vast amounts of money flowed in to pay for the silks, porcelain and tea which the west craved. By 1800 the British demand for tea alone was worth £23 million a year. China's population numbered 400 million; its empire controlled the biggest economy in the world. All foreign business was channelled through designated national warehouses in the city of Canton, then the world's largest metropolis. The presiding genius of Canton's merchant community and one of the few officially permitted to trade with foreigners, Wu Ping-chien, known as Howqua, was the richest man in the world. Today he is an obscure and neglected figure; yet his portrait pops up in some surprising places. In the living room, above the fireplace, in one of the oldest mansions of Newport, Rhode Island, the King family – physicians, traders and mariners – accorded pride of place to an icon of this meagre, grave old man, with his wispy beard and capacious robe. The private houses and

Howqua, in a portrait of about 1840. Portraits like this could be seen all over New England.

public spaces of many New England merchant communities of his day are adorned with the same image, for Howqua was their banker, patron and protector in the richest trade in the world. Howqua's private life, however, was full of grief – resentment at the exclusiveness of China's mandarin elite and disappointment in his son, who failed his exams and was prosecuted for illicit trade in the substance which was the agent of China's fall from supremacy: opium.

At last the west had a product for which there was a demand in China. The drug came from India in British ships and was exchanged for rhubarb, silk and tea. The Chinese craved opium. It induced stupor smoothly, and foreign opium worked better than China's home-grown variety, bringing a more rapid and deeper oblivion. No one knew why: according to rumour, the foreigners mixed it with human flesh or corpses of crows. Every image associated with opium was predatory and obscene. The opium habit was blamed for the debilitation of Chinese workers and the demoralisation of the population. But the biggest menace it posed was economic.

On 14 February 1839, Commissioner Lin Tse-hsü set off down the Yangtze river to take up his new job in Canton. His orders from the emperor were peremptory, and his task was daunting: to stop the importation of opium from India. He began with an appeal to the better nature of the British, writing to the government: 'Suppose there were people from another country who carried opium for sale to England and seduced your people into buying and smoking it; certainly your honourable ruler would deeply hate it and be bitterly aroused.'

In the absence of any positive response to this approach, Lin set about trying to paralyse the trade. He confined 350 British merchants and ordered them to deposit 21,000 chests of opium near the Temple of the Three Buddhas. Thousands of balls of compressed opium were taken away, thrown into trenches, mixed with lime, and flushed into the Pearl river delta. On 19 May Lin offered 'hard bristle and soft down' – a pig and a sheep – to the sea-god; 'I advised the Spirit', he added, 'to tell the creatures of the water to move away for a time, to avoid being contaminated. After I returned to my lodgings it rained all day.' The local inhabitants were

> coming in throngs to witness the destruction of the opium. They are, of course, allowed only to look on from outside the fence and are not admitted to the actual place of destruction for fear of pilfering. The foreigners passing by in boats on their way up to Canton and down to Macao all get a distant view of the proceedings, but do not dare show any disrespect, and indeed I should judge from their attitudes that they have the decency to feel heartily ashamed.

The diary entries Lin recorded in early summer reflect his satisfaction at the progress he was making. He even convinced himself that the foreigners were losing the will to persevere in the trade. However, he grotesquely overestimated the strength of his hand. He thought Englishmen could not survive without Chinese rhubarb and that the threat of a rhubarb embargo would bring them to heel. He had no inkling of how fundamentally Britain's industrial revolution had already transformed the balance of power, nor of how vital Britain deemed the opium trade to its imperial interests; so he failed to realise that the British were willing – in some cases eager – to contemplate a military showdown with the Chinese empire. Above all, he thought the evils of opium were obvious to all well-intentioned people, British included, and that moral considerations would outweigh commercial ones.

By September, the emperor was beginning to lose confidence in his envoy. 'You speak', he wrote,

> of having stopped foreign trade, yet a moment later you admit that it is still going on. You say you have dealt with offenders against the opium laws, yet admit that they are still at large. All this is merely an attempt to put me off with meaningless words . . . The very thought of it infuriates me. I am anxious to see what you can possibly have to say for yourself.

Lin, in reply, could only admit the failure of diplomacy and advocate instead the use of force:

> Some of your advisers fear that our ships and guns will prove no match for those of the foreigners, and that some means must be found of temporising with them. Unfortunately, their appetites are insatiable; the more they get the more they demand and if we do not overcome them by force of arms there will be no end to our troubles. Moreover there is every probability that if the English are not dealt with, other foreigners will soon begin to copy and even outdo them.

In a sense, Lin was right – the British would respect nothing except force; but the logic of war against an industrialising enemy meant inevitable defeat for China.

As the Opium Wars unfolded, desperate remedies were applied to make up for China's technological deficit: ancient war-magic, biological warfare, brazen self-deceit. In February 1842, for instance, General I-ching took the omens in the temple of the war god at Hangchow on his way to the front. 'If you are not hailed by humans with the heads of tigers,' the oracle pronounced, 'I would not be prepared to vouch for your security.' Auspiciously, tribesmen from the Golden river district then reported for duty wearing tiger-skin caps. The general rewarded them handsomely. 'After this,' reported one of his most intelligent officers, Pei Ch'ing-ch'iao, 'tiger-skin caps became the rage in the general's army. There were yellow tiger-head caps, black ones, white ones, winged ones and so on. But when it came to the fighting they did not seem to help much.'

Transfixed by the omen, the general selected a 'tiger-day' (10 March) for his attempt to recapture the town of Ningpo from its British occupiers. Pei's record of the campaign is a catalogue of inefficiencies – an indictment of an unequal struggle between antiquated, ramshackle raggle-taggle and a state-of-the-art enemy. Troops suffered unendurable hunger because of the inefficiency and possibly also the corruption of the commissariat. Because insufficient suitable waterborne transport was available, guns and baggage had to be man-handled; the porters – 2,400 of them, 'half of whom were beggars of very poor physique' – deserted in droves in the appalling conditions. Fire-ships fizzled out; a plan to fling monkeys tied with fire-crackers on to English ships failed 'because no one ever dared go near enough'. An attempt to infiltrate a fifth column into the town came to nothing. A 'Rafters Militia' was supposed to crawl along roofs, drop down, seize British sleepers' weapons and cut off their heads: there is no evidence that it registered any successes. Chinese tacticians contemplated releasing smallpox-infected animals to the English, but the general thought the plan discreditable.

The distress of defeat and the humiliation of submission to the barbarians are poignantly expressed in the diary of Ts'ao Sheng. This 'old bookworm' of Shanghai helped organise a home guard as the British closed in and the opium ships sailed triumphantly up the river to ply their trade. He tried to escape from the trauma of the occupation by gazing at the Milky Way and getting drunk.

> Strictly speaking when a city falls one ought to die fighting. But to sacrifice oneself alone and unaided, to die to no purpose, is to perish like a weed. Moreover, as all the officials fled long ago, even if I were to seek death at the hands of the enemy, there would be no one to report on it. So I went on reproaching myself and finding excuses for myself, scribbling 'Oh dear! Oh dear!' in the air, hardly knowing whether I belonged to the world of the living or the realm of the dead.

He included in his account long, harrowing stories: of his attempts to elude the banditry of occupying troops and local looters; of how he smuggled his wife to safety; and of the comradeship of hunger as neighbours shared their food. At last he was reduced to begging in a city bereft of alms. The horror of his narrative mounts until the mobilisation of the garrison convinces him that a massacre is imminent. Instead, on 23 June 1842, the occupation force pulled out, content with its demonstration of superiority.

Not everyone in Britain was enthusiastic about this imperial escapade. William Gladstone, speaking in the House of Commons, was trenchant in his criticism of the government: 'A war more unjust in its origin, a war more calculated to cover this country with permanent disgrace, I do not know.'

The peace negotiations, conducted at gunpoint, were a one-sided game; every Chinese move failed. China was forced to hand over 21 million ounces of silver – in effect, to pay for the war that Britain had started – and to give up five ports to the British, including Hong Kong. Here, on China's doorstep, foreign merchants lived in buildings and boulevards modelled on those of Europe. A hundred and fifty years after the Opium Wars, these western buildings were reclaimed as Hong Kong returned to China.

China's defeat in the Opium Wars was one of the great decisive events in the history of the world. Its effects can be measured in the fortunes of the legendarily wealthy Howqua, who repaired the Pearl river dikes at his own expense, laid out vast sums for fortifications when war threatened and subscribed over a million silver dollars to the subsequent reparations. He was instrumental in negotiations with the barbarians before and after the war. 'How flaming bright are China's great laws and ordinances,' he warned them, uselessly, 'more terrible than the awful thunderbolts. Under this bright heaven none dares to disobey them . . . Tremble hereat – intensely, intensely tremble.' As his purse supported the war effort, so his prestige helped to maintain public order when things went wrong. But, having helped to negotiate the terms of China's capitulation – almost his last public act before his death in 1843 – he left a shattered world. The terms of trade which had made him rich would never be recovered. His heirs were able to carry on lucrative business in traditional products, but they would never again be able to patronise the western barbarians: the relationship of dependency had been permanently reversed. As industrialisation spread in the west, the relaxation of tariff barriers worked to China's disadvantage, favouring the more competitive western products. Further commercial concessions were the price of western help against China's rebels in the next decade. China's favourable trade balance narrowed almost to nothing and, in the 1870s, disappeared. The wonder is that it had lasted so long.

The British warship Nemesis *destroying Chinese junks during the Opium Wars.*

INDUSTRY IN THE EAST

Chinese science of the late nineteenth century was not a mere offshoot of that of the west, but a continuation, or at least a revival, of the ancient native scientific tradition. In November 1861 a Chinese bureaucrat called Wei Mu-ting wrote a memorandum pointing out that western military technology was of Chinese origin; China could use western knowledge to restore and strengthen itself. Li Shan-su, who discovered new methods of calculating logarithms, expressed the view that westerners were 'just as capable of the calculations but ignorant of the principles'. Frustrated, however, by mismanagement and traditional inhibitions – sometimes violently expressed by rebels in revulsion against 'foreign devilry' – the modernisation programme came to almost nothing. In 1894 the failure of China's industrialisation was dramatically exposed in a war with a neighbouring state where self-strengthening really had worked: Japan, the only industrial giant in the nineteenth-century orient.

The modernisation of Japan took place on the basis of Japan's own traditional culture: the modernisers' declared aim was 'not to receive instruction from the westerners, but observe them in a spirit of critical enquiry'. Industrialisation would be attuned to the Japanese national genius. The smoke from the brand-new Tomioka silk-reeling plant in 1872 seemed to a draughtsman to curl upwards in parallel with the steam from the crater of Mount Fuji. Business was perceived not only as a means of self-discipline and self-enrichment, but also as a form of service to community and state. A young man going into business in 1875 gave as his reasons 'to help promote the prosperity of our

nation'. Wealth and respect – he quoted Confucius – 'cannot be attained unless right is followed'.

In its industrialisation, Japan lagged only a little behind most of Europe. The 1880s were the decisive decade. Though figures are unreliable, output per capita seems to have more than trebled over these years – and this during the beginnings of an unprecedented population explosion which echoed those of Europe and North America. In 1881 there were only 200 miles of railways; by the end of the century over 4,000 miles were in use. The merchant fleet had 68,700 tons under steam in 1882, 102,352 tons in 1897. Over the same period, the number of telegrams sent rose from 2.7 million to 14 million

The opening of the first Japanese railway in Tokyo.

a year. Steam power had overtaken water as the main source of energy by 1887 – but it is a sign of how rapidly Japan matured as an industrial nation that electricity rapidly supplanted it. Japan hardly experienced a century of steam: it was an early participant in the century of the globe.

As in the laggard parts of industrialising Europe, the new age in Japan needed a kick-start from government investment, but most state enterprises were sold off to the private sector during the 1880s. Significantly, only the war industries were kept under government control. Like most European powers and the United States, Japan began to use its industrial might, almost as soon as it was established, to found an empire. These events were signposts to the next century and the next millennium: industrialisation was infectious. The white men's empires were not unchallengeable and western world hegemony could not be sustained indefinitely.

THE INDUSTRIAL SOCIETY

Everywhere in the industrialising world, factories renewed the state and convulsed society, drawing workers from the country to the city, uprooting people, smothering landscapes. The character of industrial society is revealed in its living and working spaces. Cast-iron arches, monumental and elegant bridges were gigantic demonstrations of the power the new technology gave to man to subdue nature. The crystal palaces of glass and steel – the covered markets, railway stations, winter gardens, shopping arcades – were the nineteenth century's equivalents of the aqueducts and marketplaces of antiquity. They were, however, lamentably fragile and some of the most magnificent examples have disappeared, among them the Crystal Palace in London, erected for the Great Exhibition of 1851 – the first large-scale display of the industrial arts of the world – and destroyed by fire; or the Mercado de la Cebada in Madrid, an irregular glass triangle erected in 1870 on columns of cast iron imported from England.

Some of the factories of the period proved more durable and still stand in witness to the attitudes of their architects and owners. Some remain in the rural settings that reflect the utopianism of early industrialists. Just outside Chipping Norton, a country town in Oxfordshire, one of the 'cathedrals of industry' – William Bliss's Tweed Mill of 1872 – was made to resemble a grand château in a parkland setting, with a balustraded parapet and corner towers crowned by urns, or an abbey with central dome and spire-like chimneystack. Templeton's carpet factory of 1889, a Venetian palazzo built in brick to be 'the finest thing outside Italy', still stands on Glasgow Green. Turquoise mosaics enrich it; it bristles with twirling pilasters, extravagant battlements and spiralling towers.

A similar blend of the fantastical and the practical shines out from a contemporary account of one of the great moments of industrial history – the discovery of the Bessemer process, which turned iron into steel. The description is typical in its suggestion of a magic trick rather than a scientific endeavour. As the great inventor, Sir Henry Bessemer, made his final adjustments,

> the primitive apparatus being ready, the engine was made to force streams of air under high pressure through the bottom of the vessel . . . the stoker in some bewilderment poured in the metal. Instantly out came a volcanic eruption of such dazzling coruscations as had never been seen before . . . as the various stages of the process were unfolded to the gaze of the wondering spectators . . . no one dared to go near it . . . and most wonderful of all, the result was steel!

With harder and cheaper steel, nations could reach further and hit harder than ever before. Armed with the guns for their armies and transport for soldiers, merchants and travellers, the first cities and states to industrialise took the advantage in economic and political competition. Japan, the first eastern state to follow the west's lead, quickly modernised to become the strongest power in the orient. In the American Civil War, the industrialised north defeated the agricultural south. Everywhere, technological initiative won power.

The most eloquent apostle of both steam and the self-help ethic was the English social and political reformer Samuel Smiles, who identified industrialisation with progress and believed that industrial work could make men good as well as rich. As Britain led the drive to mass production, growing wealthy from the exports of cotton cloth that flooded the world's markets, Smiles wrote of the 'modern inventors' who

> have availed themselves of the . . . swift and powerful, yet docile force of steam, which has now laid upon it the heaviest share of the burden of toil, and indeed become the universal drudge. Coal, water and a little oil are all that the steam-engine, with its bowels of iron and heart of fire, needs to enable it to go on working night and day, without rest or sleep. Yoked to machinery of almost infinite variety, the results of vast ingenuity and labour, the steam-engine pumps water, drives spindles, threshes corn, prints books, hammers iron, ploughs land, saws timber, drives piles, impels ships, works railways, excavates docks; and, in a word, asserts an almost unbounded supremacy over the materials which enter into the daily use of mankind, for clothing, for labour, for defence, for household purposes, for locomotion, for food, or for instruction.

Overcrowded humanity in a London riverside street, as depicted by the French artist Gustave Doré. The industrial cities were incubators of filth, violence and sickness.

And yet, for all the high ideals and ambitious projects, outside the model factories and the model towns, in the streets and slums created by the concentration of labour, the effort to erect a romantic environment for the industrial society was a horrible failure. The factories that enriched and empowered their owners created social turmoil and endangered lives among the poor. Dust and fumes choked the air and poisoned the workers. 'Whilst the engine runs the people must work – men, women, and children are yoked together with iron and steam to the machine which knows no weariness.' The French statesman and political writer Alexis de Tocqueville, travelling around England in 1835, saw the profits of industrialisation as gold issuing from a 'sewer'. 'From this foul drain', he wrote, 'the greatest stream of human industry flows over to fertilise the whole world.' As industrial revolutions migrated and spread, they left characteristic tracks: the 'bare soil' observed by the poet and priest Gerard Manley Hopkins, 'seared with trade, bleared, smeared with toil', wearing 'man's smudge'. Everywhere good intentions yielded dire effects. Steam engines now powered the leather drive-belts of new forms of industrial manufacture, and the rhythms of the human body were shattered by the relentless rhythms of the machine.

Industrialisation threw up gimcrack cities which were fearsome incubators of filth, violence and sickness. The Manchester reformer Edwin Chadwick in the 1830s and 1840s, and the Barcelona physician Jaume Salarich in the 1850s and 1860s, painted the same clinical picture of the victims of the textile mills – profuse sweat, languor, gastric trouble, respiratory difficulties, laboured movements, poor circulation, mental torpor, nervous prostration, pulmonary corrosion and poisoning from noxious machine oils and dyes. Urban reformers stressed sexual depravity as well as bad health among the effects of industrial overcrowding. Karl Marx, who slept with his housemaid, claimed that ruthless bosses threatened workers with sexual exploitation. The vanishing world of artisans and guildsmen was buried in the seismic upheavals which raised factories over old townscapes, like smoking volcanoes, and flattened the structures of traditional society. The advance of industry could be measured by counting profits and quantifying output, or by logging the diseases and disorders that germinated in overcrowded and undersanitised towns; by chanting the litany of the saints of 'the gospel of work' who created wealth through enterprise and spread it through 'enlightened self-interest', or by echoing the cries of the urban slum-dwellers, uprooted and crammed into unforgiving environments. All these voices resonate in the novels, journalism and official reports of the time.

Not surprisingly, revolution was predicted: it seemed impossible that a society so baneful could survive unpunished. Yet some at least of the victims of industrialisation also, increasingly, shared its benefits. A cycle of prosperity linked mass production, rising wages and growing demand. Manufactured goods, from sewing machines to typewriters, eased labour and changed lives. The economy of the nineteenth-century west would have been impossible without the exploitation of women and children; but it brought them long-term dividends in the form of prosperity and 'emancipation'. A new ideal of womanhood – decorative and unproductive – can be detected in a period of oppression of the sex. A similar change affected children, who became at once an exploited underclass and a source of images of angelic innocence. Eventually, they were presented with an ambivalent gift, bestowed by a boss-class in search of a useful workforce: compulsory education. The new concept of 'public health' was the goad used by reformers to get cities rebuilt. When Charles Creighton published his *History of Epidemics* in Britain in 1894, he was disinclined to share the self-congratulation of his fellow medics on the progress of their battle against disease; but he acknowledged the importance of rehousing the working class 'in regular streets opening on wide thoroughfares' and the provision of sewerage and clean water.

Life altered more in the nineteenth century alone than in the whole of the previous millennium. Now the camera had arrived to record history as it happened; and in 1898 the Lumière brothers with their first motion-picture camera filmed a steam train arriving at a station – a fitting image of a century in which the world had been transformed by the machine.

Machine-made art: a French audience watch a Lumière comedy film.

CHAPTER 10

Century of the
GLOBE

THE TWENTIETH CENTURY

B Y THE END of the twentieth century, the human species was changing the terms of its existence with bewildering speed. Some of these changes were in quantity, with the explosive spread of older inventions. These included transport, the spread of motor vehicles across the globe and the shrinking of all distances by cheap air travel. Another example was the expansion of the world's trade network into what was named 'the global economy'. Other changes were of quality. The discoveries in physics and genetics broke into quite new territory. So did the communications revolution towards the end of the century.

This was the century in which human beings first left the earth, entered space and set foot on the moon. But these technical feats, astounding as they were, mattered less than the broad change in attitudes which the space programmes helped – unintentionally – to encourage. The use of large rockets and problems like weightlessness had been discussed since the nineteenth century. What was new was the tidal ebb of human confidence about man's relation to nature which became evident at about the time of the moon landings at the end of the 1960s.

From space, the globe itself could for the first time be seen by its inhabitants. It looked fragile and lonely. The two rival 'space superpowers', the Soviet Union and the United States, loudly imi-

Man in space. In the 1960s mankind saw its own home planet for the first time.

tated Victorian nation-state triumphalism as they boasted of their scientific achievements. But the public, while proud of the ingenuity and courage which had gone into space exploration, found this boasting discordant. The sight of the earth from outside, photographed from miles out in space, suggested two obvious conclusions. First, the human race was one single family, however divided it imagined itself to be. Secondly, the resources of the planet were finite.

New perceptions and anxieties urged the need for global action, global institutions. The whole twentieth century had been marked by a crisis of faith in the inevitability of progress and improvement. Doubts about the moral benefits of science, technology and even rationality were being voiced as the century began, mostly in Europe. The period of the two world wars, surrounded by the experiences of economic depression, genocide and totalitarian dictatorship, seemed to confirm the doubters' worst predictions. In some ways, this was unfair. It was for the better, on balance, that science and technology transformed the world in the twentieth century. Nevertheless, there emerged a strengthening conviction that now was the time for the human family to combine to express its unity and to manage the planet's limited resources for the good of all its inhabitants – before it was too late. This had to be the century of the globe.

A post-war German cartoon suggests the potential for conflict as the superpowers divide the globe between them, still smiling but preparing their weapons.

THE DARKEST CONTINENT:
VOYAGES INTO SELF-DOUBT

The venture into space began in 1961 with the successful orbiting of the Soviet cosmonaut Yuri Gagarin. In one sense, the space programmes were no more than a spectacular by-product of the Cold War, of the military and political rivalry of the United States and the Soviet Union. But in a deeper way, they marked the end of a long historical episode – the age of exploration.

In practice, that age had closed several decades earlier. In the 1850s, an atlas printed in Europe or America still showed white areas in several parts of the globe. These denoted the 'unknown' – which, in a colonialist century, meant unknown to Europeans, although familiar enough to its indigenous inhabitants. By 1900, the earth's land surface had effectively been explored and much of it surveyed. Powered flight soon filled in the remaining gaps.

A limit had been reached. For centuries, 'discovery' had meant to Europeans the exploring and claiming of 'virgin' continents, the naming and settling of new Isles of the Blessed. Now there was no Terra Incognita left to find. Accordingly, the urge to explore turned in other directions – most significantly, inward: towards the unknown territories which lay within human personality and behaviour. In this century, people were to see not only their planet, but themselves as individuals, in utterly new ways.

These were not unvisited continents. Psychology was already an old study. In the eighteenth century Scots had debated the association of ideas, while nineteenth-century scholars discussed theories of brain function and the influence on thought of physical forces like magnetism. But now, in the early twentieth century, the approach to mind took a new turn. It rejected the positive physiological approach and replaced it with a metaphysical, almost religious way of talking about the psyche. This was the body of psychoanalytical theory and practice pioneered by the Viennese nerve-doctor Sigmund Freud.

Freud's ideas came to dominate not only western treatment of mental affliction but the imagination of several generations of creative artists and scholars concerned with human personality. Freud's work on repression and his use of dreams in diagnosis and in therapy were imitated everywhere; his insistence on the primacy of the sexual drive and on his concept of 'infantile sexuality' shocked and fascinated the world. But nothing he advanced was more influential than his theory of the subconscious, which seemed to end the age-old moral controversy about the existence of free will.

Sigmund Freud.

That was not Freud's own view of his work. He continued to emphasise the choice between good and evil, and resented the suggestion that he was trying to free individuals from responsibility for their actions. Indeed, although Freud

Edvard Munch's The Scream. *Although painted in 1893, it has seemed to many to symbolise the spiritual agony of the twentieth century.*

was Jewish by family origin, and was eventually driven into exile in Britain by the approach of Hitlerism, his imagination was strongly marked by Christianity. 'No one who, like me, conjures up the most evil of those half-tamed demons that inhabit the human breast and seeks to wrestle with them can expect to come through the struggle unscathed,' he wrote.

This was a traditional view of the human personality as a battleground between 'good' and 'evil'. Freud was an old-fashioned moralist when compared with many of his Modernist contemporaries in the arts. Painters, architects, composers and writers, inspired by introspection and rebellion, discarded conventional categories, whether they were the accepted rules of perspective or the idea of individual personality as something continuous throughout time. They considered all rules to be no more than social constructs, devised to repress spontaneity in art, public behaviour, personal relationships. When he treated patients for neurotic symptoms, Freud was confronting people tormented not only by half-buried childhood traumas but by the panic sense that they were adrift in a world where nothing was reliable, nothing was as it seemed. The Surrealists made clocks melt and turned heavy masses weightless. Picasso piled many perspectives into a single image, a face that was a multiple mask. Words were cleansed of meaning and reused as sounds; houses lost their thick aura of associations with hospitality, family or ancestry and became machines for living.

In science, too, universally accepted assumptions were challenged, apparently unshakeable certainties swept away, by discoveries as disturbing as anything retrieved from the unconscious mind. The century's research triumphs were both staggering in their implications and yet ambiguous in their impact. In 1905 Albert Einstein propounded his revolutionary theory of relativity, undermining the 'iron laws' of energy set down 200 years before by Isaac Newton, which had supported the technologies of the industrial revolution. The physicists who released atomic and then nuclear energy in the 1930s and 1940s, like the American scientists who devised the silicon chip in the 1960s, dealt in particles without mass or weight.

These were unsettling ideas; and, in this new and anxious age, the old eagerness for 'scientific progress' was waning. Charles Darwin's theories of evolution and natural selection had shocked his Victorian contemporaries, and yet they were absorbed by public understanding within a few decades. The work of Einstein and the generation of great physicists which followed him was found almost equally baffling, but – in contrast – proved extremely difficult to popularise. Even at the millennium, nearly a century on, relativity and quantum mechanics have not been widely understood. In the same way, ignorance and mistrust continue to hinder the technologies which developed out of some of the century's most dazzling scientific achievements.

Albert Einstein.

Nuclear power is the prime example, both in the scale of scientific ambition and achievement involved, and in the ambiguity of the human response to its implications. Tapping the elemental powers of the universe, scientists isolated the atom – the basic unit of matter – and then smashed it, setting off a chain reaction which released a colossal burst of energy. This was the first step towards the nuclear age, but its first application was a weapon. The American atom bomb was first tested in the desert south of Los Alamos in July 1945. Robert Oppenheimer, one of the US physicists who worked on the project, had no illusions about the significance of what they had brought about:

We knew the world would not be the same. Some people laughed; a few people cried. Most people were silent. I remembered the lines from the Hindu scripture, the Bhagavad Gita: 'Now I am become death, the destroyer of worlds.' I suppose we all thought that, one way or another.

In peacetime, nuclear technology seemed at first to promise a limitless source of clean energy. But problems which at first appeared marginal – the storage of radioactive waste, the danger of accidents releasing radiation (illustrated only too powerfully by the Chernobyl disaster in 1986), the costs of decommissioning a nuclear power station – have kept this resource under-used and unpopular. Much the same has been true of the great breakthroughs in genetics. The research which led to the deciphering of the DNA molecule by Crick and Watson in 1953 was met with loud applause; but consideration of its possible applications was met with equally widespread public alarm. Genetic 'engineering', whether in modified crops or in the power to clone or re-compose a human individual, is hotly contested and is still waiting for a licence to practise in the new millennium.

Other scientific advances were eagerly welcomed and by the end of the century had become familiar elements of life across much of the world. The population explosion which saw the world's inhabitants increase in number from about 1.3 billion in 1900 to 6 billion by the end of the century was brought about by applying basic nineteenth-century discoveries – immunisation, sterilisation, spraying against insects – to the public health programmes of poorer continents, almost eliminating lethal diseases like plague and smallpox. Alexander Fleming's discovery of penicillin, the first modern antibiotic, destroyed the power of bacteria, the main cause of infection and disease. X-rays enabled doctors to examine the skeleton without recourse to the scalpel. Microscopes revealed the inner structure of cells – the building blocks of living tissue.

Science could save life; it could also control its emergence. Biochemistry gave vigour to the most radical of all social movements to emerge in the course of the century. The development of a contraceptive pill, which by sheer coincidence came on sale in the 1960s, the decade that was home to so many movements of radical change, offered women a quite new degree of control over their own fertility – and over their emotional and professional lives. Curiously, perhaps, 'the pill' had no measurable effect in reducing birth rates; its real effect was on the self-confidence and independence of women. The women's movement in the west, at first concentrating on the demand for legal and political equality with men, had reached a peak by 1914. The wars and economic crises which followed seemed to push the campaign into the background, but in the 1960s the cause of women was revived with new force and depth under the banner of feminism. More than a mere call for equality, the movement was now a powerful affirmation of womanhood itself. By the 1990s male assumptions of superiority were effectively collapsing in the west and feminist self-assertion – fiercely opposed by religious fundamentalism – was slowly diffusing into traditional societies all over the world.

'MEGADEATH'

The twentieth century brought an almost unimaginable increase in human prosperity and comfort. As it closed, however, many people considered it to have been the most terrible and destructive century in the history of the species. Both statements are true, and it is the contrast between the upsurge of knowledge and the eruption of deliberate slaughter which gives these hundred years their peculiar horror.

The nineteenth century had led people to expect that a steady increase in living standards, education and enlightenment would lead naturally to a steady decline of human conflict and cruelty. It was this combination which was broadly termed 'civilisation'. But the twentieth century demonstrated that the two developments had little or no connection. Instead of the epoch of universal peace which was predicted, the years after 1914 were a time of almost continuous war – sometimes gigantic world conflicts, which cost over a hundred million lives, sometimes local or low-level wars conducted with merciless ferocity, in which the innocent civilian dead far outnumbered the armed combatants. In addition, the century witnessed the planned genocide of millions and the death of millions more who perished in the penal empires set up by totalitarian dictators. The famines which devastated tracts of Africa, Asia and western Eurasia were not only more destructive than any in the past but, for the first time, were almost all the result of human negligence or callousness.

The previous thousand years had seen nothing like this. Apart from the isolated episode of the French Revolution at the end of the eighteenth century, there had never been such a contrast between high and magnificent hopes for a new dawn of justice and equality, and brutal systems of oppression imposed by dogma and state terror. By the late 1930s the survival of liberal democracy anywhere in Europe, even outside the territories already controlled by Stalin, Hitler, Mussolini and Franco, seemed unlikely. In Africa and Asia, still mostly ruled by European imperial powers, the world slump of the early 1930s had closed down plans for economic or political development, and stagnation ruled. The United States, tormented by the Great Depression, remained isolated. World war, its approach all too visible, resumed in 1939.

And yet, as a portrait of the century, this picture is misleading. The central catastrophe took place within a space of little over thirty years – between 1914 and 1945. After that, the death toll of war and tyranny was much reduced, although it has persisted on a scale still inconceivable to the minds of our great-grandfathers. The second half of the twentieth century was, by comparison to the first, a Great Peace. The two superpowers of the Cold War agreed to coexist, and kept their respective allies on a tight leash. For almost fifty years, until the implosion of Yugoslavia in 1992, war was largely confined to the so-called 'Third World' and to the form of liberation struggles fought against individual western powers. But any hope that widespread war might

Gas-blinded French soldiers being escorted back from the Western Front in July 1918.

therefore die out as colonialism in its old form dwindled was belied by the intermittent recurrence of bitter conflict in, for example, south-east Asia and the Middle East. The Great Peace could not put back the clock. The attempt in the hopeful first years of the century to codify, regulate and 'civilise' war, by international agreement on its rules, now seemed absurdly remote. In the later twentieth century wars were not 'declared', and seldom ended in a formal peace conference. A major war between big powers was now expected to be total – fought without restraint, quite probably with the use of nuclear weapons. And the lesser forms of low-level war and ethnic conflict were no less brutal to civilians than a peasant rebellion of the sixteenth century.

The First World War was the first global conflict, but it was not quite the first total one. The American Civil War in the 1860s had already shown what 'modern war' would be like: an industrial, mass-production struggle in which hundreds of thousands of conscripted men would be brought to the front by railways. By 1914, however, new weapons – the quick-firing magazine rifle, the machine-gun, the artillery barrage with explosive shells – had enormously increased killing power, tilting the balance of strength in favour of the defender against the attacker. A single soldier, well dug in and provided with enough ammunition for his machine-gun, could kill hundreds of the enemy long before they reached his position. This was not appreciated by the military commanders of 1914, who went on the offensive in the old manner with massed infantry advances and – at first – with charging cavalry. The result was slaughter, especially on the Western Front where the war soon became an almost stationary confrontation between enormous armies facing each other in trenches.

On all the fronts, and in the naval war across the oceans, some 10 million combatants, almost all young men, lost their lives. People spoke of a 'lost generation'. The old virtues of personal courage and sacrifice seemed to count for nothing against machine-guns, howitzer batteries, tanks and poison gas. It was a nightmare in which machinery seemed to have conquered its own creators, in which war seemed to have developed its own terrible momentum which could cease only when the enemy had been utterly destroyed. The familiar political architecture of Europe, intact in 1914, collapsed as four empires – German, Austro-Hungarian, Russian and Ottoman – were overthrown by defeat and revolution.

It was not surprising that, after these shattering experiences, many Europeans turned to radical extremes. Fascism in Italy and then Germany promised to renew the nation, purifying it from the effete, degenerate elements which were supposed to have corrupted the national soul and – in Germany's case – lost the war by treachery. But the Bolshevik Revolution of 1917 in Russia seemed at first to have universal meaning for all oppressed mankind. Soviet socialism proclaimed that by liberating humanity from class exploitation and war, it could release the creative energies required to make a new and better world. This vision seized imaginations all over the globe. As late as the 1950s, millions of people (especially in Europe) still thought that the Soviet 'experiment' represented the future, even if they did not relish the prospect. 'In the twenty-first century, we'll all have some kind of communism' was a common prediction.

Fascism and communism were both central European inventions. Both ideologies were responses to typically European anxieties of the time: the appearance of a huge propertyless class (proletariat) in the cities of the industrial revolution, and the failure of traditional patriotism to save nation-states from military defeat. But their intellectual sources were very different. Communism, in Karl Marx's version, was a recasting of Enlightenment values of human freedom and self-fulfilment. Fascism, a mixture of assorted prejudices, distorted Darwinism in order to argue that human masses needed heroic leadership, and that some 'races' were destined by history to dominate others. The most striking attitude common to both ideologies was contempt for liberalism and liberal 'bourgeois' democracy. Nor, although fascism tolerated and nourished private enterprise as long as it was closely steered and regulated by the state, did either feel at ease with modern capitalism, rejected as 'alienating' and 'cosmopolitan'.

In Italy, where Benito Mussolini had taken power in 1922, the Fascist Party promoted a boastful cult of violence and death. In Germany, Adolf Hitler's followers engaged in street battles and sadistic assaults on Jews, socialists and liberals – until Hitler took control in 1933, after which he was able to thrust his racial and political enemies into concentration camps.

By then, the Soviet Union had gone far down the road to dictatorship. The Marxist vision of socialist democracy did not survive the 1917 revolution and the civil war which followed. Vladimir Lenin and Leon Trotsky, makers of the revolution, established a one-party police state which arrested and, on an enormous scale, shot 'class enemies' and political critics of Bolshevism. By 1928, with Lenin dead and Trotsky exiled, Joseph Stalin had a secure grip on power. He launched the biggest programme of forced industrialisation the world had ever seen. Then, to feed the new cities, he ordered the collectivisation of farming. Rich peasants and those who resisted were 'liquidated'. The result was the man-made famine which ravaged Ukraine and southern Russia in 1932–3.

Under Stalin, the Soviet Union was ruled by police terror on a scale which even Hitler could not match; something between 10 million and 20 million people perished in the 'Gulag Archipelago' – Alexander Solzhenitsyn's name for the empire of labour camps. But the Soviet Union also surged ahead under Stalinism to become one of the world's biggest industrial economies in less than twenty years, capable of defeating Nazi Germany by sheer weight of war production and – in Stalin's last years – to become one of the world's two global superpowers of the Cold War, equipped with nuclear weapons. Karl Marx had expected world revolution to begin in an industrialised proletarian nation. Instead, it began in backward, still largely peasant Russia. And, as the twentieth century wore on, the appeal of communism resounded most strongly in underdeveloped societies: as a pattern for breakneck modernisation and industrialisation, rather than as an ideology of liberation.

This points to an underlying theme of the whole century: uneven development. The fear of being 'left behind', the desperate determination to 'catch up', powered constant change, political upheaval and drives for industrialisation at the cost of individual freedom. Without this great grievance, nationalism in its European form might not have spread across the world to become the fundamental motive force of the whole century. European fascism appealed to nations envious of the great power status of France and Britain, with their colonial empires producing wealth for the motherlands. Communism, in Russia, China, Cuba or Vietnam, embodied the faith of peasant societies that will-power alone could hurl them in a decade or so through the modernisation process which had taken over a century in western Europe or North America. And after the end of the Cold War in 1989, the same pressures of uneven development reappeared in a new form. The economic and social gap between the richer and poorer parts of the world widened rapidly, and the violent tensions set up by these inequalities threatened to give the new millennium a turbulent beginning.

Famine in the Ukraine, 1932–3. Millions died in a human catastrophe that was the direct result of Stalin's policy of forced collectivisation.

The return of world war to Europe in 1939 came after an unhappy twenty-year interval. In the 1930s, democracy and free trade had increasingly given way to dictatorship, mass unemployment and protectionism born of economic depression. The next round of war could be clearly seen as it approached, and most people knew that it would be devastating. The Spanish Civil War of 1936–9 had already shown that warfare had become lethal in a new way with the use of bombing aircraft against civilians. The Second World War (the last to begin with old-fashioned declarations of hostilities) destroyed scores of cities by bombing and ended with a death toll of some 54 million in which, for the first time, men in uniform were a minority. Civilians perished in air raids, through murder or starvation in captivity, or as hostages in reprisal massacres. And this was truly a world war, unlike the so-called First World War which had been mainly confined to Europe and Europeans, apart from the participation of the Americans and of colonial troops, most of them from British India and the Antipodes. The Second World War became global in 1941, when the Japanese invasion of south-east Asia and its attack on the US base at Pearl Harbor opened a new theatre of war in the Pacific.

Mass killing was not caused by war alone. During the conflict, Hitler and the Nazi regime attempted a 'final solution' of the 'Jewish problem' by organising the genocide of Europe's Jews. Throughout Nazi-occupied Europe, a vast, coordinated operation rounded up Jews and gypsies and deported them to extermination camps where they were rapidly gassed and cremated in industrial

Joseph Stalin, supreme ruler of the Soviet Union from 1928 until his death in 1953.

263

'death factories'. Some 6 million Jews perished. State-sponsored genocide was not entirely new; the Turkish regime had murdered around 1.5 million Armenians during the First World War, while the exterminations of aboriginal populations by white colonists in the previous 150 years were genocidal actions. But the sheer cold-bloodedness of the Nazi crime – committed by one of the most highly developed nations in the world – profoundly undermined the cultural self-confidence of the west. So deep was the horror generated by the Jewish Holocaust that by the end of the millennium its memory had come to overshadow even the death and destruction caused directly by the war.

On and over the battlefields, killing was reaching new and repellent heights of 'productivity'. The killers incurred ever fewer casualties while the death toll among their targets multiplied. Ground combat remained costly to both sides, but in the air the Allies gained supremacy. At the German city of Dresden in February 1945, Allied bombers inflicted death on something like 50,000 people (almost all unarmed civilians and refugees) in a single night and day of bombing – at the cost of a mere handful of British and American

NAZI GENOCIDE

Josef Mengele, SS officer and 'doctor' at the Auschwitz concentration camp, was the most famous war criminal to escape arrest. His career illustrates the moral problems of science in the twentieth century in their most extreme form.

Eugenics – the vision of improving the human species by deliberate selection – was taken seriously long before Adolf Hitler came to power in 1933. The Nazis seduced Germany's doctors with the offer to transform medicine from the reactive treatment of illness to the proactive creation of a physically and racially 'healthy' human stock. The method was the suppression of 'unfit' breeders: at first by compulsory sterilisation, then by gassing of the physically and mentally handicapped and finally – during the Second World War – by the wholesale genocide of 'inferior' races, primarily Jews and gypsies.

Mengele, an ambitious medical student, volunteered for service at Auschwitz in order to

The gates of Auschwitz.

carry forward his research into 'genetic engineering'. A dapper figure, humming opera melodies, he separated incoming transports of prisoners into those who were to be gassed at once and those who were to be worked to death. Mengele also picked out subjects for his research into multiple births, with the aim of creating a fast-breeding species with 'Aryan' features. He carried out especially cruel experiments on twin children who were usually killed afterwards, their eyes being extracted for further study. Mengele, directly responsible for tens of thousands of murders, regarded himself as a 'biological soldier'.

After the war he escaped to Latin America. He was never traced, although his family regularly sent him money and he was protected only by a false name. He died in Brazil in 1979.

lives. At Tokyo a month later, Allied aircraft killed over 80,000 people, also in a single night, with hardly any casualties to the attackers.

But even these ratios of attackers to victims were utterly eclipsed in August 1945, when a single American aircraft dropped an atomic bomb on the Japanese city of Hiroshima. A few days later, another fell on the port of Nagasaki. The bombs were not dropped to defeat Japan, whose military collapse was by then plainly inevitable. Instead, their purpose was to save the American lives which would have been lost in a final invasion of the Japanese islands. Both cities were levelled by the blast. Nearly 150,000 people were killed. An uncounted number survived to die later of radiation effects.

In the Cold War decades, from about 1947 to 1989, 'a balance of terror' was slowly recognised on the basis of 'mutual assured destruction' (MAD). The United States and the Soviet Union built up enormous stocks of nuclear weaponry (Britain and France had small nuclear strike forces of their own). It was assumed that an all-out nuclear exchange would kill most of the population of the northern hemisphere and possibly, through the 'nuclear winter effect', close down organic life on the entire planet. Paradoxically, the key stabilising element in this balance was vulnerability: the expectation that the missiles would get through and that a nuclear first strike would bring an equally annihilating response. It followed that the most threatening and aggressive act short of war was to install an effective anti-missile defence system (like President Reagan's unrealised 'Star Wars' array). This expectation prevented nuclear war, sometimes narrowly, for fifty years. And a situation in which two soldiers at an underground console could, in theory, set off a process leading to the extermination of the human race brought the 'killing productivity' curve to an insane peak.

Meanwhile, outside the west, the pressures of uneven development and the hunger for modernisation set off a continuous stream of crises. Between 1947 and 1974 the British, Dutch, French and Portuguese colonial empires fell apart, in the last two cases after many years of fighting by guerrilla 'national liberation' movements. Some of these wars became proxy conflicts between the Cold War protagonists, above all in Vietnam where the United States unsuccessfully took over from France the struggle against a communist-led 'liberation army'. Their cost in human lives was enormous. But, just as in Europe, the casualty lists of war were equalled or surpassed by those inflicted by the schemes of ideological tyrants – above all in Asia.

In 1965, an abortive communist coup in Indonesia was followed by government massacres which killed hundreds of thousands of political 'suspects'. In 1975 the Khmer Rouge guerrilla movement conquered Cambodia and launched a campaign of 'class genocide' against anyone with education or an urban background, which cost between 1 million and 2 million lives. But these tragedies were overshadowed in scale by the catastrophe which overcame China as Mao Zedong, in the late 1950s, embarked on a colossal drive to overcome backwardness and catch up with the developed world.

The Great Leap Forward. Propaganda posters contrast with the reality of hunger and hardship in Mao's China.

In the space of a few months, the entire countryside was divided into vast collective farms. The 'Great Leap Forward' campaign urged the Chinese people to make steel in their own backyards. Revolutionary enthusiasm was supposed to sweep aside all problems. But the outcome, caused by the combination of bad seasonal climate and human madness, was the famine of 1959–61, the worst in recorded history. For many years the scale of the disaster remained hidden, but today it is estimated that over 20 million, possibly as many as 30 million, perished.

International communism collapsed in 1989–91, leaving ruling communist parties in only China, North Korea, Cuba and Vietnam. This was in two ways the end of an era. First, communism as the militant religion of development was dead; there was no longer an ideological challenge to liberal capitalism which threatened world war. Secondly, the fall of the Soviet Union suggested that the age of totalitarian dictatorships might be passing away. Tyranny would always recur, new tyrants periodically emerge; but dependence on the global economy, and the all-penetrating power of new communications, at least meant that future dictators would find it hard to pose as modernisers.

However, the end of the Cold War did not bring universal peace. War, like a bacillus, mutated into new strains suitable for new conditions. The last decades of the twentieth century brought a rapid spread of low-level wars, often ethnic contests for territory between communities who had managed to coexist for centuries. These were fought by local amateur militias, led by provincial warlords who sometimes had roots in organised crime. Many of these conflicts arose from the disintegration of multi-ethnic states at the end of the Cold War. The wars in Moldavia, Abkhazia and Chechnya followed the collapse of the Soviet Union; the brutal fighting in Croatia, Bosnia and Kosovo took place among the ruins of what had been Yugoslavia. Other conflicts, especially in Africa, broke out as post-colonial independent states foundered in chaos: the civil wars in Somalia, Sierra Leone and the Congo, the wars between Ethiopia and Eritrea, and above all the horrific genocide in Rwanda and Burundi which began in 1994.

Faced with this 'new world disorder', the United Nations and the west slowly embarked on a strategy of intervention. The seizure of Kuwait by Saddam Hussein's Iraq in 1990 provoked a full-dress conventional war in which an international army led by the United States expelled the Iraqi invaders. The Serbian atrocities in Bosnia and then in Kosovo were answered – reluctantly – by NATO intervention. The UN Security Council authorised these 'peacekeeping' operations, in addition to the despatch of American-led forces to Somalia in 1992 and to Haiti in 1994. By the end of the century the 'international community' (a phrase of the 1990s) was running a series of informal protectorates all over the world, including northern Iraq, Bosnia and Kosovo.

Skulls of some of the victims of Pol Pot's Khmer Rouge. The Maoist revolutionary was willing to sacrifice a large percentage of the population to his desire to destroy urban civilisation in Cambodia.

The 1999 intervention in Kosovo was especially significant. It marked the end of the old Cold War principle that interference in the internal affairs of sovereign states was the supreme crime in international relations. Kosovo was within the frontiers of the Serb-run state which still called itself Yugoslavia. But it was held in the west that the defence of human rights – in this case, against the genocidal slaughter and deportation of the Albanian majority in Kosovo – could override the rights of sovereign states. The new principle was hotly opposed by Russia and China, as well as by many states from the poorer world who suspected that this sudden concern for human rights concealed a new form of imperialism by the west.

But the Kosovo tragedy also demonstrated a change in western attitudes to war. For many decades, public acceptance of dead soldiers as the price of patriotism had been ebbing away in western Europe and North America. The televised spectacle of the Vietnam War was a turning point. In the Falklands War of 1982 between Britain and Argentina, British commanders carefully husbanded their forces against any unnecessary loss of life. The Gulf War of 1991 against Iraq, won by use of overwhelming air power, ended in an enormous slaughter of Iraqi troops with minimal losses on the western side. Fear of casualties deterred effective European and NATO intervention in Bosnia, while the withdrawal of Serbian forces from Kosovo followed several months of concentrated air offensive conceived as a substitute for committing ground forces to battle. While thousands were killed by the air attacks, the NATO side suffered no direct fatal casualties at all.

The century of 'megadeath' was ending in a paradox. In the west, a growing humane revulsion against state-sponsored bloodshed had led military planners to introduce a range of new technologies – above all, the refinement of super-accurate guidance systems for bombs and missiles. These allowed war to be conducted against less developed societies almost without danger – by aircraft from 15,000 feet up or higher. But the innovations did not noticeably reduce the total killings. They merely shifted the kill-ratio still further in favour of the side with the technology. High-tech war came to resemble a computer game, a remote business of screens, images and push-buttons. But it also recalled game theory itself: the zero-sum game in which one side wins all and the other suffers total loss.

WORLD ON THE MOVE

Looking back from the end of the millennium, the typical twentieth-century experience seemed to be uprooting. A large proportion of the globe's population had left their homes and settled elsewhere. In part, this flow was migration, the search for better lives by the inhabitants of poorer regions, countries and continents. This was not new. What was without precedent was the torrent of involuntary refugees. In this century populations were forcibly expelled from their homes, or fled abroad to escape persecution, on a scale unknown in history. The United Nations High Commission for Refugees estimated that by 1999 there were 11.5 million people currently in the refugee category, not counting almost 5 million 'internally displaced persons' driven from one part of their own country to another.

Migration in recent times has, as always, taken two forms: the move from countryside to city, and the move from one country – or continent – to another. Both went on simultaneously. In England the social and economic changes which made people emigrate to the old American colonies were also the pressures which drove people off peasant fields and into the cities. During the nineteenth century, London, Paris and Berlin were among cities whose populations multiplied again and again.

In the later twentieth century, this process of 'urbanisation' reached the cities of Asia, Africa and Latin America with even greater force. Few have kept control of their own growth or can even measure it accurately. The population

London's Chinatown. Cities around the world support thriving Chinese communities, which preserve and actively promote their customs and culture.

of Mexico City increased five times over in fifty years; the place now covers 1,800 square miles of urban sprawl. In Asia cities with over 10 million people are proliferating. Most juxtapose an impressive, Americanised 'downtown' sky-line with immense, squalid shanty-towns on the periphery. Here live the poor, most of them migrants or children of migrants from an even more poverty-stricken countryside.

At the beginning of the century, the overwhelming majority of the human race lived on the land, mostly by subsistence farming. At its close, almost half were living in towns. The historian Eric Hobsbawm called the death of peas-antry 'the most dramatic, far-reaching social change of the second half of this century, and the one which cuts us off from the past'. But why the peasants gave up their way of life is far from clear. The pull of urban possibilities – wages, excitement, choice – seems to have mattered more than the push of rural poverty. Changes in farming, bringing peasants into the cash economy and markets for the first time, were other elements of the story.

International population movements, the demand by people of one culture to be allowed to settle and make a new life in another, are more visible than silent flight from the countryside. But – contrary to popular assumptions – voluntary migration is less today than it was in the late nineteenth century. Between 1899 and 1914, something like 15 million Europeans crossed the Atlantic as emigrants to settle in North America – overwhelmingly in the United States. They came mainly from the Polish and Lithuanian

Mexico City's population increased five times over in fifty years; the vast metropolis now covers 1,800 square miles of urban sprawl.

Men and women in flight from genocide in Rwanda crowd into a refugee camp in Goma. The euphemism 'ethnic cleansing' was coined in the 1990s.

provinces of the Russian empire, from the Habsburg province of Galicia and from the older regions long known as generators of emigrants: Italy and Ireland, Scandinavia and Germany. Voluntary emigration in the twentieth century never matched this flow. In part, this was because of the virtual collapse of the world economy between the world wars: the United States and other 'host' countries, facing mass unemployment among their own citizens, closed the gates. Between 1914 and 1929, the USA admitted only 5.5 million immigrants. Population movement all over the globe dropped away. When it resumed after 1945, the situation was quite different.

The aftermath of the Second World War left Europe with something like 40 million uprooted human beings. (In comparison, the First World War had created fewer than 6 million refugees.) Some of them were survivors of Hitler's mass deportations, slave labour conscriptions and concentration camps. Many were unwilling to return to their own countries, now under Soviet occupation. Others were unable to go home. These included about 12 million ethnic Germans evicted – by the decision of the Allied war leaders – from their homes in Germany's lost eastern provinces or in east and central Europe. In the Soviet Union, whole populations – the Crimean Tatars, the Chechens and Ingush, the Volga Germans – had been expelled and exiled to central Asia.

Mass flight and expulsion went on long after the end of the Second World War. In 1947, some 15 million people became refugees when Indian independence led to partition. In the 1970s, independent Uganda expelled its Asians. In the 1990s, civil war and genocide in Rwanda and Burundi drove more millions into flight. And in the same decade 'ethnic cleansing' (what the Allies had decorously called 'population transfer' in 1945) returned to Europe with mass expulsions and deportations from Croatia, Bosnia and Kosovo.

At the same time, voluntary migration began to revive as the core economies of the west – especially in Europe – went into the spectacular boom of the 'Golden Years' between 1950 and 1974. A few years later, the long Japanese industrial boom began. But the labour shortages produced by economic expansion were met in very different ways. Japan set itself firmly against importing cheap foreign labour. Instead, Japanese industry exported investment to the countries where that cheap labour lived. Europe took the other option. The old colonial powers – Britain, the Netherlands and France especially – recruited immigrants from what had once been imperial territories in Asia or Africa. It was assumed that they would take over menial, ill-paid service jobs, freeing skilled workers to enter the expanding industrial economy. It was also assumed that they were immigrants, not visitors. West Germany, however, tried a different course. Lacking any recent colonial possessions, Germany imported millions of contract workers from southern Europe and Turkey, intending that they should return to their own countries at the end of the contract or when their labour was no longer wanted. This policy soon became unworkable as many of the so-called 'guest-workers' found ways to stay on, to bring in their families and to settle permanently.

By the end of the century, the issue of immigration and how to control it was coming to obsess the West. Ineffective American attempts to limit illegal entry over the southern border did not prevent a huge Latin American population from settling in the United States – above all in California, where Spanish is now the first language of more than a quarter of the population. Asian immigration into the United States also grew rapidly in the century's last decades: most visibly from China, but also from Korea, Vietnam and the Indian subcontinent. This marked the end of the old American 'melting-pot' ideal, the belief that all immigrants would assimilate to a single (essentially white and European) American culture. From now on, the internal unity of each of the three established zones of wealth in the world – North America, the European Union and Japan – was not so much cultural as economic.

As the pressure of would-be immigrants built up, and as the price of a down-payment on an intercontinental charter ticket began to seem a feasible goal for an African or Asian peasant, all three wealthy zones tried to raise fences around themselves. In Europe, those hoping to settle were divided into 'genuine asylum seekers' (admissible) and mere 'economic migrants' (to be expelled). But in reality no such clear distinction existed. Was it wrong to seek 'asylum' for one's family from the threat of hunger and unemployment? In any case, there was a growing feeling that, in the long run, this movement of the poor towards the lands of the rich would prove unstoppable, overflowing all quotas and regulations.

VOICES IN SPACE

At the end of the second millennium, the outlines of a single global culture uniting the entire human race were already visible. But they were merely outlines, of a process still only in its early stages. Politically, the world remained a patchwork of 192 sovereign states, ranging from huge entities like China down to micro-states of the order of Tuvalu with only 15,000 citizens. Although there was a tendency to consolidate into supranational groupings like the European Union, the total number of states was still increasing rather than diminishing. Culturally, human populations were still separated by the survival of thousands of distinct languages. English was spreading rapidly as a universal second tongue, much as Latin had served in the later classical world of Europe, but most 'mother languages' remained mutually unintelligible.

None the less, there were places – urban places, above all – where the shift towards uniformity was startling. In 1900 a traveller suddenly teleported to a foreign city would have known within seconds of looking round whether he or she was in Japan, Scotland, India or Latin America. By 2000 this identifying would take many minutes. Downtown, the world's big cities were coming to resemble one another in their identical architecture, in the vehicles on their streets, in the common imagery and music of their popular culture and advertising, and to a great extent in their marketing of globally standard clothing, household equipment and fast food.

At the root of this great convergence lay the communication revolution. In the course of the century, the globe was gradually sewn into a dense web of communication networks – terrestrial landlines, submarine cable, radio waves, satellites in orbit – which made cheap and instantaneous contact possible across every cranny of the earth's surface. At the close of the Victorian era, messages between continents had been sent by mail steamer in gaudily

Tokyo at night. Japan exported investment to countries where labour was cheap rather than importing foreign labour for its booming industrial economy.

stamped envelopes or, in case of urgency, by telegraph in Morse Code. A single long lifetime later, in 1999, 1.4 billion e-mail messages and £1 trillion in money transactions crossed national borders every day.

The United States was the main source of the new technologies which made the communication revolution possible; indeed, it is partly because of this that we can call the twentieth century 'the American century'. Where the inventions were European, as in the case of radio and television, it was often American capital which pioneered their commercial application. All these innovations, without exception, depended on electrical energy. The writer Charles Jonscher has defined them as successive imitations of human physical functions: the ear, with Alexander Graham Bell's patenting of the telephone; and the brain, with the interaction of its billions of neurones reproduced – on a tiny, relatively primitive scale – in the silicon-chip microprocessor.

Modern war was the curse of the century, but its mobilisation of scientific research gave an incomparable boost to innovation. The First World War developed fleets of large aircraft which made possible the advent of commercial airlines, while the design and efficiency of radio and telephones were drastically simplified and improved between 1914 and 1918. The British Broadcasting Company (later Corporation) was set up in 1922 as a national radio network, while the first continental telephone system spread across North America in the years after 1918. Regular TV broadcasting (to tiny audiences) began in Britain and Germany in the later 1930s, and in the United States soon afterwards.

These were all means of communication. They helped to convey not only messages but the first elements of an international culture in popular music and entertainment. Here, once again, the United States was the pioneer of global taste. Cinema had its roots in pre-1914 France, but the emergence of Hollywood flooded the world with American films and created the first truly global mass audience for entertainment, at the same time as the spread of the gramophone was bringing American jazz music to dance-halls on every continent.

A far greater impulse to communication development came with the Second World War. The teleprinter or telex, which had existed on a small scale before the war, came into general use. Radio technology grew more sophisticated and more portable. Radar evolved as a means of detecting aircraft and submarines. The Germans developed ballistic missiles which (as scientists at once saw) could be used to put satellites into orbit as well as to strike targets with warheads. The need to break German and Japanese military codes produced bulky proto-computers, constructed in Britain and America, which operated – like the radios of their time – on vacuum tubes. Once again, the return of peace brought wider civilian applications. Sputnik, the first orbiting satellite, was put into space by the Soviet Union in 1957. IBM constructed the first big computers in 1951. But computer design would soon be changed by the introduction of the semiconductor or transistor, originally devised in 1948 by William Shockley at the Bell Laboratories in New Jersey.

Marilyn Monroe, icon of Hollywood's global cinema.

TELEVISION

Television, according to popular myth, was invented by a Scot named John Logie Baird after the First World War. But the truth is more complicated. As with all the other innovations which transformed life in the twentieth century, television had no single inventor and the roots of its technology reached back to nineteenth-century research.

What Baird did, one day in London in 1926, was show that television was a practical possibility. He gave the first, very crude, demonstration of how images could be directly transmitted on to a screen without the use of any kind of film. Baird was using a mechanical system of image scanning based on a rotating disc with apertures, a device patented in Germany back in 1884 by Paul Nipkow. The trouble with the Nipkow scanner was unbearable image-flicker. But another Scotsman – A. A. Campbell Swinton – had in fact already overcome this problem in 1911, when he designed a revolutionary scanning method using cathode-ray tubes at both camera and receiver ends.

Swinton found no backers to develop his idea, but it was adopted all over the world in the 1930s and formed the basis of modern television technology. Germany was the first country to start regular television programmes, in 1935. The BBC launched a service with higher definition in 1936. Scheduled TV transmissions began in the United States in 1941. There were about 1 million TV sets in the world in 1949, 275 million by 1970, and some 1.4 billion in 1990.

An English family of viewers in the 1950s.

This was a crucial breakthrough. The new transistor batteries, tiny and robust, revolutionised electronics design. They reduced the size and cost of second-generation computers, opening the way to far wider distribution. They led to the little hand-held transistor radio, which became for a time an even more powerful instrument for spreading homogenised global entertainment than television – and the huge market for which was quickly seized and conquered by the industries of reviving Japan. Transistors, too, delivered the cheap pocket calculator, changing the whole process of accounting beyond recognition.

Television broadcasting had been suspended in most countries during the Second World War; soon thereafter, it took its place in almost every European living room. Black-and-white transmission gave way to colour; channels multiplied; the invention of videotape simplified production. Meanwhile, the 'Space Race', the Cold War competition between the United States and the Soviet Union in military and scientific rocketry and space technology, produced many spin-offs for the communications industry. The Soviet Union put the first human astronaut, Yuri Gagarin, into orbit in 1961, but the United States launched a series of communication satellites which, with the arrival of Intelsat 3 in 1968, were able to reflect signals – including television and telephone transmissions – back to earth. Suddenly it became possible for anyone anywhere in the world with access to television to watch

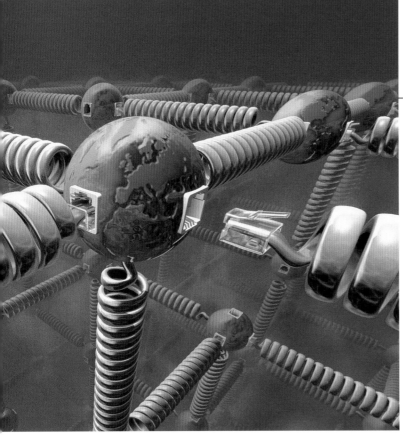

The wired world. At the end of the millennium, mankind has barely begun to grasp the social, economic and political implications of instant global communications.

an event as it took place, and the American moon landing in 1969 became the first global TV experience.

This immediacy had political consequences. It gave the news media an impact on public opinion which radio and print had lacked, a power displayed during the Vietnam War as television reporting from the battlefield poured into every American home. Global audiences and the sense of a common interest in 'big stories' multiplied. Some 200 million people across the world watched the 'fairytale wedding' of Diana Spencer to the Prince of Wales in London in 1981; sixteen years later, in 1997, no fewer than 2.5 billion viewers watched her funeral.

Up to the time of the moon landings, the communications revolution had largely been one-way, a matter of transmission to audiences. In the 1970s a radical change began as the revolution went interactive. The individual consumer of messages gained the power not only to originate and transmit material but to create his or her own custom-built memory stores. Such were the consequences of the microprocessor. By the late 1960s American researchers had discovered how to pack many transistor circuits on to a chip of silicone. But in 1974, Intel Corporation produced a microchip loaded with 4,800 transistors and able to carry out the functions of a full-sized computer. Another microchip was devised to provide the memory function. Three years later, Apple used this technology to produce the first desk-top personal computer, and the whole wealth of cybernetic discoveries now spilled out into the hands of ordinary individuals operating from their homes as effectively as from an office. Data banks sprang up, soon expanding into the uncontrolled global web of the Internet, which not only offered a quite new medium of contact through e-mail but provided access to the entire stock of recorded human knowledge and opinion.

The microchip age was not just about scientific and technical progress. It arrived in a context which meant that it also had social and political consequences. One was to thrust forward the change from large-scale commodity production to small knowledge-based industry and service employment. As the computer and software fields opened up, the early near monopoly of big electronic corporations like IBM broke up, to be replaced by a plethora of smaller firms competing in an overcrowded marketplace. Prices of the new equipment fell dramatically, and the hectic pace of innovation meant that a computer or its software could become obsolescent within a year. The microchip also coincided, especially in Europe, with the end of the long 'Golden Years' boom in the mid-1970s. The rush to computerise office work and production was also a drive to reduce costs, as entrepreneurs dismissed vast numbers of employees and replaced them with new technology.

Another consequence was to hasten the destabilisation of the communist regimes in the Soviet Union and eastern Europe. The new generation of technology was too expensive to import, but without it the communist economies began to fall rapidly behind the standards of the rest of the world, and to enter terminal economic crisis. Moreover, satellite television and then the personal computer challenged censorship in ways to which the police state had no answer. The crushing of Solidarity in Poland in 1981, when the entire national and international communications of a large nation-state were simply unplugged or switched off, soon became unrepeatable.

The communications revolution also rapidly undermined the structures on which the world relied to regulate the global economy. In the 1980s computerisation touched off an explosion in the volume of trade transactions, most spectacularly in the currency markets. Astronomical sums of money could now be bought and sold back and forth across the world at a key-stroke. This was true globalisation – but at the cost of the stability of the world's financial system, and of the authority of national governments. The speculator had become king, enthroned at his computer screen. The problem was how to limit his totally unaccountable power. Accordingly, the end of the century saw a general move to seek a new international financial mechanism which would regulate and slow down these unpredictable currency flows without compromising the free movement of investment in the global economy.

More than any other set of changes, the communications revolution had helped to create a global consciousness. This was not just a matter of swathing the world in a web of sound and vision. Even personal relationships were profoundly affected: the mobile phone, for instance, with its offer of total accessibility at all times, began to dissipate the very concept of absence – just as the coming of urban electric lighting had produced generations for whom real darkness was unfamiliar. But by the new millennium the revolution was still very incomplete. The technology had widened the gap between the more prosperous minority who had access to mobile phones and personal computers and the 'Great Unwired', the mass of the world's population. The gap widened because it was a gap of power as well as money. Membership of the wired-up world conferred almost infinite opportunities for acquiring knowledge and earning money denied to those who could not participate. In the twenty-first century, perhaps, the armoury of electronic instruments for self-advancement will become available to all. Until then, however, the fruits of the microchip seem likely to become one more prize in the struggle between the fortunate few and the globe's excluded billions.

SHRINKING PLANET, SHIFTING BALANCE

In the second half of the twentieth century, the United States came to dominate the world. This American dominion was military and political, economic and to a substantial extent cultural. The United States emerged from the Second World War as the strongest air and naval power on the globe, in possession of atomic weapons and the capacity to deliver them. The American economy, strongly stimulated by war production and then by the surge of post-war demand, had no rival. Politically, the Cold War inevitably brought the United States to the leadership of the 'free world', which broadly accepted the American emphasis on democracy and human rights. And through the diffusion of American movies, popular music, cheap clothing, soft drinks and fast food, something like a global taste in entertainment and mass culture came into being.

With hindsight, the potential for this all-encompassing power was accumulated in the nineteenth century as the United States built up a continental industrial base and colossal capital reserves. But it was the Second World War which dramatically engaged American wealth and power with the rest of the globe. The post-war Marshall Plan poured out dollars to reconstruct Europe as a zone of free international trade open to American investment. The challenge of communism in Europe and Asia ensured that the United States would remain committed to the defence of the non-communist world, that it would

Buddhist monks in Thailand. In the 1990s the United States dominated the world politically and militarily; it had long since established a dominant global position in mass popular culture and mass consumption.

finance its supporters and destabilise its unreliable clients, and that the non-communist world would absorb a continuous torrent of American capital, styles and consumer goods. But the end of the global order of the Cold War – the fall of the rival superpower in Moscow – posed unexpected problems. The Soviet collapse should have left the United States triumphant, enjoying a monopoly of world leadership. Instead, as the disciplining pressures of the Cold War fell away, American influence over world affairs actually declined.

An obvious question arises. If the twentieth century belonged to America, to whom will the twenty-first century belong? But the question could well be the wrong one. The circumstances which made American supremacy possible – a deeply divided world of sovereign states, the immense economic opportunities offered by reconstruction after world wars – may not recur. And while the world continued to unify politically as it approached the twenty-first century, it was no longer ready to unify under the authority of a single nation-state.

Europe – the vigorous old Europe of empires – is plainly in relative decline. Global industrial exports and military power have passed away. The unprecedented surge of prosperity during Western Europe's 'Golden Years', between the 1950s and the 1970s, was mostly an internal affair: an upwards spiral of rising wages, rising consumption and economic growth. At the end of the century, the European Union seems to be developing into a loose, introverted association of states with a unified but rather stagnant economy, more anxious to preserve its own living standards against immigration and external competition than to be active on any global scale.

It may be too early to speak of American decline. Its enormous internal market survives, and demand thrives. At the same time, America – like Europe – is rapidly losing its old industrial strength and moving towards a society in which wealth and employment are concentrated mainly in the service sector. The inventive brilliance of its electronics is as strong as ever, and software from American laboratories continues to lead the rest of the world. But there is a sense that this pre-eminence will not last, and that the steady invasion of American markets by producers from other regions of the globe is passing a point of no return.

Will Asia succeed America as the earth's dominant power? The most spectacular change in the world's economic balance over the past twenty years has been the emergence of powerful, aggressive capitalist economies in eastern Asia. These 'tiger economies' have provided a torrent of industrial goods for the world market, in the 1970s almost taking over the manufacture of transistor radios, television sets and other consumer electronic items. In recent years, they have increasingly exported capital as well, not only into the less developed parts of the world but into the old fortresses of the industrial revolution – the Japanese and South Korean car firms in Europe and America, for example. By about 1990 Japan and South Korea between them accounted for 15 per cent of the world's income, while Japan had the highest per capita income of any country.

But the productivity of the 'Pacific Rim' countries is only half of the Asian picture – at most. Japan, South Korea, Taiwan, Malaysia, Singapore and Hong Kong are exporting economies. Beyond them lies the potential market of the millennium: China. A communist state committed to internal free entrepreneurship, China already has a population of a billion. Chinese exports, produced on low wages in almost unregulated factories, are already making rapid inroads into the low-quality end of the world market. But it is the domestic market – when and if it is thrown open to the outside world, when and if the purchasing power of individual Chinese workers and peasants becomes sufficient to carry a consumption boom – that fascinates the business world outside.

The Pacific Rim is in any case unlikely to inherit the sort of ascendancy enjoyed by the United States. The 'tiger economies' fell sick in the later 1990s, a severe reaction to wildly overstretched lending and overvalued currencies. While they may recover, they have never made up anything like an international political bloc. Increasingly, the ultimate influence over the rise or fall of these economies will lie in China, whose own political future is uncertain as the communist regime falls into corruption and decay.

Whatever happens around the Pacific Rim, the tide of globalism is running too strongly to be turned back. Uniformity is taking hold. While peasant societies are still coloured by a variety of cultural traditions, urban life is becoming standardised. Seen from an approaching aircraft, the new Shanghai might be San Francisco, Buenos Aires or Frankfurt. The evening crowds promenading through downtown Tokyo, London or Paris chatter in different languages, but they are wearing the same T-shirts, eating the same hamburgers, blinking under

Downtown Shanghai. Although still part of communist China, the city epitomises the international character of the great commercial centres of the late twentieth century.

the neon logos of the same multinational corporations selling soft drinks, hatchback cars or sports footwear. As the sunset sweeps westwards across the planet, they will watch television from the other side of the world, play a computer game against somebody in another continent, gossip by phone or e-mail to distant relations.

And yet this steady erosion of differences creates its own counter-movement. For one thing, the difference that really matters – between the poor and the rich of the world – is not eroding at all but growing. In Europe at the last turn of the century intellectuals wrestled with what was then called 'the problem of poverty' – the phenomenon of deepening social misery in a period when national prosperity and middle-class wealth were so evidently increasing. A hundred years later, the same enigma has recurred. The global free-market economy is not only widening the gap between rich and poor countries but is creating new inequalities even in the most advanced societies. Between 1979 and 1990 the average hourly earnings of a tenth of the American population actually fell by nearly 10 per cent.

The Festival of the Burning Man, Nevada. A giant neon figure is destroyed amidst fireworks and jubilation, symbolising the rejection of materialism and a return to nature and eternal values.

It became fashionable to predict the imminent death of the nation-state. Its old authority and sovereignty were not compatible with the free play of market forces in the new global economy. But the nation-state, for all its faults, had become in the twentieth century the most effective engine for the redistribution of wealth ever devised. It was not surprising that the social damage wrought by globalisation provoked a revival of nationalism throughout the world. With this revival went a new cult of collective identity. As old customs and traditions were washed away, people searched nostalgically for a sense of community and solidarity in the past and its heritage. Submerged historical nations 'reinvented' themselves (another key vogue-word of the 1990s), and sought to regain control of their destinies as self-governing regions or as states.

This was at once the most dazzling and the most terrible century in human records. For most of the world's population, the improvements in health, comfort, knowledge and prosperity were so steep and rapid that the very sense of continuity with the past of the human race grew weak. And yet this social transformation did not prevent organised and deliberate slaughter on a scale once unimaginable.

The globe grew smaller as human beings all over the world became able to see each other, to talk to each other and to find a common concern for the sustainable management of their planet. Somewhere ahead lay the hope of world government. But the rush towards uniformity set up new anxieties, fear of a new and artificial environment which would eventually atomise the human population and cut it off from its roots. People wanted to become global in their awareness. But they also wanted to stay close to the earth, air, water and fire which had formed the world of their ancestors.

INDEX